Behavioral
Coaching

Behavioral
Coaching

How to build
sustainable personal
and organizational
strength

Suzanne Skiffington & Perry Zeus

The **McGraw·Hill** Companies

Sydney New York San Francisco Auckland
Bangkok Bogotá Caracas Hong Kong
Kuala Lumpur Lisbon London Madrid
Mexico City Milan New Delhi San Juan
Seoul Singapore Taipei Toronto

National Library of Australia Cataloguing-in-Publication data:

Skiffington, Suzanne
Behavioral coaching: how to build sustainable personal and organizational strength.
Includes index.
ISBN 0 074 71328 0.

Employees—Training of. 2. Organizational change. 3. Self-actualization (Psychology).
I. Zeus, Perry. II. Title.

658.312404

Published in Australia by
McGraw-Hill Australia Pty Ltd
Level 2, 82 Waterloo Road, North Ryde NSW 2113
Acquisitions Editor: Javier Dopico
Production Editor: Rosemary McDonald
Editor: Bronwyn Collie
Proofreader: Tim Learner
Indexer: Diane Harriman
Designer (cover and interior): Jan Schmoeger/Designpoint
Illustrator: Alan Laver, Shelly Communications
Typeset in 10/12 pt Trump Mediaeval by Jan Schmoeger/Designpoint
Printed on 80 gsm woodfree by Pantech Limited, Hong Kong.

The **McGraw·Hill** Companies

Contents

About the Authors

Perry Zeus B.A., Fellow VAAR

In the 1980s Perry Zeus worked as a project and business development management consultant in the United States, Australia and Asia. In the early 1990s, as an executive coach and management mentor, he conducted various specialist coaching clinics with a wide variety of professional groups. In 1995 he teamed up with Dr. Skiffington to establish a coaching practice that spanned six countries. He and Dr. Skiffington then went on to establish specialist coach training workshops. Perry is also the founder of the 1 to 1 Coaching School (which provides courses for qualified professionals looking to establish an external or internal coaching practice) and the Behavioral Coaching Institute (which instructs organizations on how to design, build and manage internal coaching programs). As well as being the course registrar, he is a sought after consultant, facilitator and lecturer. He has written numerous articles on organizational coaching, co-authored *The Complete Guide to Coaching at Work*, *The Coaching at Work Toolkit* and *Behavioral Coaching* and now devotes much of his time to coaching research and development. His varied formal training includes financial accountancy, business management, workplace counseling and fine art.

Dr. S. M. Skiffington B.A., MCP, PhD, MAPS, MISH

Dr. Suzanne Skiffington has a doctorate in clinical psychology. In the early 1990s she delivered coaching seminars and workshops to hundreds of organizations and professionals. An authority on organization behavior and development, Dr. Skiffington has been at the forefront of integrating behavioral science with principles of leadership, management and organizational development. In 1995 she teamed up with Perry Zeus to establish a coaching practice that spanned six countries. She is one of the world's leading educators in psychology-based professional coaching. Over the past decade, working with Perry Zeus as an educator, she has provided specialist coaching services to clients around the world. As the Head of Education at the Behavioral Coaching Institute, she personally facilitates a coach training course with a global delivery program from Australia to the United Kingdom, from Canada to Asia and the United States. She has accredited several hundred professionals in validated, successful personal change coaching methodologies and coaching business practice management. Her respect for the values of education, personal responsibility and accountability to clients is embedded in the philosophy of the school whose world-class standards attract the best students from around the world and celebrates a growing list of successful and influential alumni.

Industry-recognized coaching certification lends credibility

The demand for credentialing in coaching has gathered momentum in light of the increasing numbers of coaches and the proliferation of coach training schools. Furthermore, internationally, there is growing user demand for accountability from organizations and professionals that provide coaching services. Clients, coachees and the general business world have the right to know what they can expect from coaches in terms of their credentials and expertise.

Contrary to popular belief, there is as yet no "international" association that has been accredited by any government body and certainly none that is truly representative of full-time, professional, practicing coaches in the workplace. Through our coach training and certification school (Behavioral Coaching Institute), course applicants seek to distinguish themselves from the many ill-trained coaches using outdated and/or mislabeled coaching practices. Our graduates are also able to achieve distinction as Registered Behavioral Coaches through personal certification and training by Dr. Skiffington.

Our books are popular course reference texts in many universities, colleges and coaching schools and for numerous Fortune 500 companies' internal training/coaching programs. Nevertheless, becoming a competent, successful coach demands more than reading textbooks. A professional coach will welcome the opportunity to explain his or her specialist training.

A professional coach is a highly trained specialist in the use of validated, psychology-based change and learning tools. Reputable coaches are trained by faculty members of an accredited coaching school with university-trained educators who have firsthand knowledge of "world best skill practice standards," who practice what they teach as experienced, organizational and/or business coaches and who are trained in the behavioral sciences.

Behavioral Coaching Institute
Coach training courses available worldwide

For the past decade our coach training schools have endeavored to establish "world-best practice" standards for training professional coaches working in an organizational setting. The key to sustainable, measurable coaching outcomes is a sound psychological base that sits at the intersection of counseling, clinical and organizational psychology. Our course participants are trained in the use of behavioral science practitioner models and management practices that are being successfully applied in executive, business and personal coaching.

The 1 to 1 Coaching School provides a rigorous, personalized educational experience for busy professionals with demanding schedules by offering a focused, short-course structure. The "how to" courses are not academic or generic, but are industry focused and tailored to participants' specific needs. The school's coaching education is unique in the world because there are no large classes, only one-to-one, personalized dialogue between Dr. Skiffington and the participant, and, as a consequence, a genuinely customized course format. Certification by Dr. Skiffington assures quality and excellence in the educational level achieved by her graduates.

The Behavioral Coaching Institute incorporates proven industry expertise, research facilities (a behavioral research laboratory) and academic and management resources in coach education and the development of validated coaching systems, curricula tools and techniques. These world-class coaching processes are taught and practiced globally with our organizational clients.

The 1 to 1 Coaching School specializes in coach certification courses for persons looking to establish a world-class coaching practice. The school has a close working relationship with some of the world's leading educational institutions and various professional coaching bodies, and its programs are tailored to meet the specific practice, business and cultural needs of each participant and the market in which she or he operates.

Through two decades of research and practice, Perry Zeus and Dr. Skiffington have created a unique coaching methodology, as well as the tools and standards of business practice for coaches. This ongoing, intensive research, development and testing program allows our school and institute to significantly update its renowned Registered Behavioral Coach® Certification Program every three months, thus insuring that graduates receive the best of the best in world-standard professional coach education, follow-up support and resources.

Course types

The following highly interactive, "how to" one-to-one (Dr. Skiffington and the participant only) or small group (four to six persons) courses are delivered on site in Australia, Asia, Canada, Europe, the United Kingdom and the United States.

- *4 Day Registered Behavioral Coach Course with follow-up one-to-one mentoring.* A unique, one-to-one professional development program with Dr. Skiffington for: (1) professionals wishing to learn how to plan, establish, market and manage a successful coaching practice and receive personal instruction in the use of essential psychology-based behavioral change tools; (2) established internal/external coaches working in organizational settings who wish to learn how to use proven industry processes/behavioral change tools and business management practices that relate to their specific working environment.

    With the course material resources and the guidance of Dr. Skiffington, participants learn how to build their own coaching practice and develop programs that relate to their workplace situation. Customized, personal-ized exercises and role-play situations are tailor-made to simulate participants' workplace needs. Coaching resource manuals, including a toolkit (on disk) containing free coaching forms, reports, assessment instruments and other coaching materials and resources that the graduate coach can re-brand and personalize are also provided.

- *4 Day Certificate of Applied Coaching Management Course—one-to-one or group.* Coaching is change and change is a psychological process. Coaches and coaching program managers have to understand and be confident and competent in the behavioral science aspects of coaching. This requires specialist training. If coach program managers are to successfully manage coaching initiatives and the coaches who conduct them, they in turn require specialist training and resources.

  Nominated, qualified participants acquire market intelligence, professional analysis and insight, data, business models, tools and resources for organizations that want to better understand coaching and the benefits of establishing a behavioral coaching program. Alternatively, participants want to insure they are effectively managing existing coaching programs and obtaining the best results. This course includes customized, personalized exercises and role-play situations and instruction on how to design a coaching program and establish a coaching culture.

- *Mentoring Program (client management and business practice support).* This important follow-up support service is personally provided by Dr. Skiffington upon completion of any of the above courses. The one-to-one telephone support can involve multiple levels of agreed-upon assistance and guidance. This invaluable support provides foundational strength and resilience in the execution and mastery of the coaching skills that have been learned and in the application of successful practice management protocols and procedures.

- *Specialty Coaching Workshops* are interactive, small group workshops for practicing coaches to further develop their coaching skills and techniques.

- *Accreditation Program.* This is for existing coaching practices (external or organizations' in-house coaching programs), where one or more members undertake a five-day program (conducted on site) of coach development and assessment and evaluation of existing practices/ coaching programs. An accreditation rating is awarded to the coaching provider (see web sites below).

Regional partner program

- *Strategic Partnership License.* A specialist five-day, one-to-one course during which qualified individuals, an educational institution, business or organization are trained and licensed to supply Dr. Skiffington's introductory level A+ Certified Coach Training Course in their organization or particular country and region. It includes backup and support from Dr. Skiffington and Perry Zeus.

For further information on any of the above, we encourage readers to visit: http://www.behavioral-coaching-institute.com or http://www.1to1coachingschool.com.

Preface

Since the publication of our first two books, *The Complete Guide to Coaching at Work* and *The Coaching at Work Toolkit*, there has been growing demand from coaches and their clients for a coaching model based on scientifically validated methodologies. It is in response to this demand that the behavioral coaching model was developed and is now presented in this book.

In the past two decades the applied behavioral sciences, including psychology, sociology and anthropology, have yielded significant benefits in education, industry, the military and health services. Behavioral coaching is also founded on the behavioral sciences.

Behavioral coaching was first employed in sports, work safety, the military, health and education. Because it has developed separately within these areas, there are different meanings attached to the term. Nevertheless, common to all these areas is a coaching methodology based on the behavioral sciences that provides a body of evidence attesting to its validity and effectiveness. The common purpose in using a behavioral coaching model is to achieve genuine, lasting change, while acknowledging that it is difficult to break habits.

The term behavioral coaching has also been applied loosely and used inappropriately by practitioners engaged in professional or personal development conducting traditional coaching and training programs. In this book, we present a standardized model of behavioral coaching as used by the growing number of trained and credentialed professional behavioral coaches around the world.

Behavioral coaching integrates research from many disciplines. It incorporates knowledge from psychology (behavioral, clinical, social, developmental, industrial and organizational), systems theories, existential philosophy, education and the management and leadership literature. Although behavioral coaching is grounded in the scientific method, which demands empirical verification, it also adopts a phenomenological approach to the study of the individual. The individual's experiences and perceptions of events are considered as important as the events themselves. Behavioral coaching is a scientific approach to coaching that results in validated, measurable, sustained learning acquisition and change in individuals and organizations.

The overall goal of behavioral coaching is to help individuals increase their effectiveness and happiness at work, in education, in health-care settings and in the larger community. Behavioral coaching seeks to enhance the individual's life and work performance. It emphasizes the coachee's relationship with all aspects of his or her self—the cognitive, emotional, physical and behavioral selves. Behavioral coaching strives to engender self-knowledge and self-regulation of thinking, feelings and actions.

Behavioral coaching is not simply about repairing deficits. It involves assessing and appreciating individuals as decision makers with choices and the potential for self-mastery. In recent years, psychology has highlighted the importance of the scientific study of human strengths and potential. Such an approach is very much in line with some of the basic tenets of behavioral coaching. For example, both emphasize understanding and building on an individual's positive qualities, such as optimism, courage, interpersonal skills, self-awareness and the capacity for pleasure. Both also examine core values, as well as limiting beliefs and automatic behavior.

In a period of rapid social change, a loss of shared values and uncertain career prospects, many individuals experience stress in various aspects of their lives. In order to address these concerns, behavioral coaching has adopted a holistic approach, in that any aspect of the individual's life can be relevant to the coaching agenda, even though the focus may be related to work. The individual's life goals, meaning and purpose, values, health and support networks are all valid areas of inquiry in behavioral coaching.

As many coaches confirm, even when individuals recognize that their beliefs and behaviors are ineffective and unhelpful, they often revert to these, particularly when under stress. Behavioral coaching attempts to address the issue of slippage or reversal. It does not make simplistic assumptions that people are always rational and predictable, and it recognizes the time lag between our new and changed thoughts and behaviors and our new or changed emotions. Behavioral coaching highlights the fact that the difficulties an individual may be experiencing are evidence that she or he is learning new ways of thinking, feeling and behaving. The role of the coach is to support and guide the coachee through what may be a difficult transition period and put in place processes to prevent slippage or regression to earlier, unhelpful ways of behaving.

Behavioral coaching can be defined as the science and art of facilitating the performance, learning and development of the individual or team, which in turn assists the growth of the organization. While science forms the basis of the behavioral model, the art of coaching lies in the personal input of practitioners and their unique interpretation and use of methodologies. Behavioral coaching, a fusion of many disciplines, can also be seen as a montage, or a synthesis of different forms into a new shape.

As we are all aware, continuous learning and growth are now accepted as cultural norms for successful firms and organizations. Increasingly, such organizations recognize that to survive, thrive and maintain a competitive edge in the global economy requires rapid change at all levels, and that producing such change is difficult and time-consuming. For example, senior managers are required to provide leadership in increasingly diverse and dynamic environments. They are under tremendous pressure to generate results and develop their overworked, and sometimes under-resourced, staff. Indeed, some research indicates that workloads and stress levels are increasing by 7–15 per cent each year.

Furthermore, there is a general consensus that career development entails lifelong learning. Learning and change, therefore, are permanent features of contemporary work life. Importantly, studies show that individuals and groups who have been trained to manage personal and professional change make better leaders, perform better, exhibit greater morale and enjoy better health.

Today, leaders and managers in organizations face more demands to create, implement and manage change. Recent research suggests that of the four principal levels of change in individuals (knowledge, attitudinal, behavioral and group or organizational), effecting changes in behavior is significantly more difficult and time-consuming. Frequently, organizational change initiatives are instituted with complex models and processes, but little attention is paid to actual behavioral change. As a result, many such programs fail or peter out long before there is any evidence of real, sustainable change. Behavioral coaching capitalizes on "strategy and processes" by focusing on the behavioral component of the change program, that is, on the behaviors of the individuals involved.

Many organizations and coaches claim to use behavioral coaching simply because they are dealing with behavior. On closer scrutiny, however, they are merely attaching a new name to the old workplace counseling model; that is, the "coaching" is remedial, occurs on an as-needs rather than an ongoing basis, involves little monitoring or evaluation and does not attend to preventing slippage. Furthermore, some professionals claim to practice behavioral coaching simply because they employ personality profiling.

The Behavioral Coaching Institute (a global information and coach training and certification course provider) arose from this perceived gap in formal definitions and models of behavioral coaching, as well as in response to increasing demand from professionals to be trained in this field. This book is derived from several years of research and work in this area.

Behavioral coaching is based on the following scientific assumptions:

- All behaviors result in positive or negative consequences for the individual and those around him or her.
- Behaviors that have positive consequences tend to be repeated.
- Exploring and changing core values, motivation, beliefs and emotions can result in significant behavioral change.
- By carefully assessing the target behaviors, learning and reinforcing new behaviors, conducting ongoing monitoring and evaluation, and maintaining behavioral change, sustained personal and organizational growth can be achieved.
- Change involves learning and there are established laws of learning and methods whereby learning can be transferred from one situation to another.
- Individuals are systems within systems, and each individual affects and is affected by these systems and the constant changes they are undergoing.
- Understanding behavior and how to change it involves exploring the dynamics of human interaction and the personal and organizational variables at play.

The critical importance of developing reliable and valid measures of behavior underpins behavioral coaching. Coaches are encouraged to use outcome measures that are sensitive to a broad range of cognitive, emotional and behavioral change. This book is about a scientific approach to intentional change. It presents a structured methodology for coaching, which includes assessment, "operationalizing" the variables to be measured, monitoring, reinforcement, evaluation and validation.

Behavioral coaching, however, does not focus only on collecting and analyzing data, identifying problems, designing change programs and measuring and evaluating outcomes. It also allows for investigation of the complexities of the individual, as well as the organization's dynamics and response to change. Organizations are not machines, but rather a collection of individuals with aspirations and expectations.

Behavioral coaching results in sustainable change and sustainable learning acquisition. Throughout this book, the themes of critical, intentional change and the components of learning are addressed. Behavioral coaching emphasizes the role of overlearning, learning by increments, practice and postlearning follow-through. It also highlights the importance of management commitment, systems to track follow-through and the need for clearly stated rewards for behavioral change.

Our first book, *The Complete Guide to Coaching at Work*, was a general introduction to definitions and applications of coaching. In our second book, *The Coaching at Work Toolkit*, we provided behavioral tools and techniques for coaches in various specialty areas. The basic definitions and principles of behavioral coaching, however, have evolved rapidly in the past few years. This book, then, is the first to present a coherent definition and model of behavioral coaching based on validated behavioral principles, theories and strategies that aim to bring about lasting change.

The book is intended for coaches, consultants, trainers and individuals in the business and corporate sectors, and for executives, managers and those involved in personal coaching, health, education, sports and the public sector. It is written for people who are leading, managing and relating to others. Everyone involved in personal and professional development needs to understand and appreciate basic behavioral processes, including cognition, motivation, emotion, learning, human development and social interaction and how these relate to individual functioning and organizational performance. Behavioral coaching addresses these factors.

It should be noted that coaching education today is experiencing new and exciting growth. Already coaching courses have reached academia. Coaching departments and coaching courses at the masters level are not uncommon; frequently, business degrees include a coaching component. Research into the outcomes of coaching programs is growing and the need for a more scientifically rigorous approach to the discipline is being met. Behavioral coaching is part of this impetus.

In conclusion, the aim of this present book is to provide a scientific, structured model of behavioral coaching. It clearly describes the principles, mechanics and benefits of behavioral coaching in relation to individuals and organizations. The book offers guiding principles, models and validated strategies for individuals engaged in effecting durable personal and organizational change on the cognitive, emotional and behavioral level.

1

An Introduction to Behavioral Coaching

Coaching in organizations today

Executive coaching, as we now know it, dates back to the late 1980s, although many professionals claim to have been coaching before this. Since its inception, coaching has, on the one hand, become more specialized, while on the other there has been a blurring of the distinctions between various types of coaching and related disciplines. Coaching has become more scientific, with an emphasis on targeting measurable behaviors rather than relying solely on personality profiling. Coaches now employ an increasing array of validated behavioral change techniques, rather than simply motivating, championing and challenging coachees.

While the impact of psychologists (organizational and clinical) on executive coaching has been fairly well documented, the contribution of sports psychology is underappreciated. It was in the 1980s that the influence of sports psychology was felt in the business world. Issues such as trust, personal best and the idea of coaching top performers derive from sports psychology. Today, a considerable amount of research from the field informs executive and business coaching. Some areas include goal setting, motivation, focus, accelerated learning techniques, planning and assessing a coachee's preferred style of learning.

It is generally agreed that we live in a world of rapid change, even of chaos and turmoil. People in corporations, organizations and small businesses are under constant pressure to change. These demands may manifest within the personal behavioral realm or be imposed by external market forces. Leadership derailment figures have reached alarming levels and major corporate initiatives such as mergers and acquisitions are subject to high rates of failure. Recognition of the need for excellent leaders in this changing and chaotic world continues to grow, and greater emphasis is placed on encouraging senior managers and leaders to think more creatively in order to guide and inspire their staff. Furthermore, economic borders are collapsing while cultural barriers remain, which presents increasing challenges for both individuals and businesses. Job security is a thing of the past, and individuals are largely responsible for their own learning and development.

All these factors have contributed significantly to the rise and popularity of coaching, and, as a result, the coaching profession has evolved considerably in the past decade. The marketplace is now more sophisticated and requires greater content and experience from coaches. Increasingly, clients are demanding that coaching proves "value-added." Coaching has also evolved because of the growing number of coaches. Not all of them are trained. The blurring between related disciplines such as training and consulting has provided added impetus to coaching.

As we will discuss later in this chapter, executive coaching is blending with strategic planning consulting, leadership development, change management consulting, project management, human resources (HR) services and outplacement and recruitment coaching. Consultants, with their established client bases and extensive resources, are strongly positioned to play a significant role in the continual development and growth of coaching.

While executive coaching initially involved only senior executives and senior managers, middle managers are now also candidates for coaching. More than a decade ago, large management consulting groups were forging new ground in the area of executive coaching at both the senior and middle levels. As a result, there is now a huge number of companies (e.g., Fortune 500 companies) working with management consulting firms on executive coaching. Most of this work is private and the results of the coaching programs are not published.

Coaching practices have also changed. Today there are fewer generalist coaches. Increasingly, coaches are specializing, in one-to-one executive coaching (for leadership and development), team coaching, life coaching or business coaching. Even within these categories, there are many subspecialties. In order to meet the demand for specialty or niche coaching, many coaches form partnerships or develop strategic alliances with other professional coaches rather than function as sole practitioners.

Finally, it is worth noting that the coaching movement, which began with life coaching, was initially driven by females who encouraged a more participatory, nurturing style. With the emphasis on coaching shifting toward business, more males are joining the coaching profession. As a result, coaching seems to be adopting a more task-oriented, "hard skills" approach to learning and change.

Coach training

Coach training began with an emphasis on training for life coaching. Training courses were directed toward the mass market and offered mostly a "cookie cutter" approach to coaching. The GROW model, developed by Graham Alexander in 1984, was the most common, if not the only, model for coaches. Virtually anyone was eligible for such training.

Today, the market is more sophisticated, both in terms of clients and providers, and there is a proliferation of all types of training courses. The quality of such courses is variable, with many lacking solid theoretical and practical foundations and rigorous methodologies. Some courses have extremely low entry requirements and students learn basic coaching skills far removed from the exigencies of daily work life.

Courses at our Behavioral Coaching Institute differ from those of other providers in that they offer short-term, highly focused, customized training and certification for busy professionals who wish to work or are already practicing as internal and external coaches. The "hands-on" courses, conducted globally, explore the practical aspects of behavioral coaching as they relate to the individual's own workplace, as well as the business requirements for establishing a successful coaching practice.

In order to meet the requirements for behavioral and business expertise, a coach training school's faculty members should be university-trained educators, licensed psychologists and experienced, practicing business and executive coaches. The Behavioral Coaching Institute meets these requirements for training, and also provides a vital follow-up, post-training mentoring program.

Each year, a growing number of higher learning institutions offer coaching components in courses ranging from undergraduate to MBAs. Psychology departments also offer PhDs in executive and life coaching. Nevertheless, coach education remains a contentious issue within the coaching world because of low entry standards, and the fact that coaches working in organizational environments come from diverse backgrounds (such as business, psychology, HR and consulting) makes it difficult for any one body or discipline to nominate national, least of all international, standards. Increasingly, academia is producing coaches with postgraduate qualifications.

As yet, however, there is little research to determine which qualifications correlate with successful coaching outcomes. Although there is broad consensus on the requisite knowledge, skills and abilities, especially in executive coaching, there is as yet no agreement on how these are best obtained. Likewise, any post-training professional development remains largely up to the individual.

Coaching across cultures

Over time, coaching has become an international practice, partly due to globalization and the presence of multinationals. For instance, at the Behavioral Coaching Institute we train and certify coaches from Australia, the United States, Canada, India, South-East Asia, China, the United Kingdom, Europe and Scandinavia.

The international expansion of coaching raises interesting and challenging questions for behavioral coaches working in cross-cultural environments. Understanding verbal and non-verbals signals, recognizing what is not said and appreciating preferred individual and cultural methods of learning are critical if coaching is to be successfully adapted or "transplanted."

Furthermore, different cultures adopt various management and leadership styles. Collectivism can be more important than individualism, and the leader's role can be more autocratic than that typically espoused by coaching. Understanding "respect" and the position of the coach in relation to the coachee is critical. Some cultures, for instance, adopt an "apprentice/master" approach to learning. In this case, the coach is seen as an expert who not only offers solutions and advice but is not to be challenged. Obviously, this type of relationship is far removed from the "democratic" paradigm that coaching typically embraces.

The experience and display of emotion in the workplace also varies remarkably across cultures. Behavioral coaches appreciate the importance of understanding these factors when coaching in culturally diverse situations or working with a coachee who is transferring to a different culture. For instance, in Western cultures, individual displays of emotion are encouraged, whereas in Korean workplaces group displays of emotion are more common. A further difference is seen in the high level of aggression in conflict situations in American workplaces, which contrasts strikingly with the Chinese avoidance of confrontation in the interests of preserving group harmony and saving face. In Chapter 7 we discuss coaching in a cross-cultural context and how behavioral coaches can manage the inherent challenges.

Coaching and research

Both quantitative and qualitative research is increasingly being undertaken on the effectiveness of coaching in the corporate, business and public arenas. For example, the Manchester Consulting Inc. study, conducted between 1996 and 2000, showed a return on investment (ROI) of almost six times the cost of an executive coaching program. An evaluation study, conducted by MetrixGlobal LLC, a Fortune 500 company, reported an ROI of 529 per cent from a coaching program for leadership development, in addition to significant intangible benefits.

One-to-one career coaching has been shown to significantly enhance staff retention, with an ROI of 100 per cent. In a public sector municipal agency, training compared with training with follow-up coaching yielded productivity gains of 22 per cent and 88 per cent, respectively. In another public sector company, improvements were seen in communication, teamwork, leadership, innovation, customer service, productivity, goal setting and effectiveness as a result of a six-month executive coaching program.

Training for emotional skills with follow-up coaching in a telecommunications company resulted in productivity improvements of 19 per cent and 28 per cent for directors and managers, respectively, and 38 per cent and 48 per cent for engineers and support personnel, respectively. Another study showed eye movement desensitization and reprocessing to be an effective method of desensitizing executives to distressing workplace situations, developing more positive beliefs about these experiences and enhancing workplace performance.

A cross-sectional field study showed that, as a result of coaching, executives became more aware of themselves and others and took more responsibility for their actions. A person-to-person career coaching program at Sun Microsystems resulted in an estimated ROI of more than 100 per cent through enhanced retention. The career coaching program resulted in improved workforce flexibility and reaction time to changing customer needs and helped strengthen the connection between individuals and the organization.

Finally, research shows that executives associate "good coaching" with honesty, challenging, feedback and helpful solutions. Unhelpful coaching practices included coaches pushing their own agendas, trying to sell more consulting time and providing only negative feedback or that based on subjective reports rather than data and results.

Qualitative surveys across various industries have demonstrated that coaching yields the following benefits: improvement in individual work performance, growth and self-actualization of the individual, increased job satisfaction, increased openness to learning and development, ability to use talent and potential more effectively, improved morale and higher staff retention.

Although research is needed to support these claims, it is generally agreed that coaching is neither appropriate nor likely to be effective under certain conditions. Unless the individual being coached appreciates the potential benefits of coaching and is willing to make a genuine effort to change, the results will be negligible. Additionally, experience shows that more companies are using coaching as a final "performance management" exercise in order to "let go" of employees.

While research in coaching is still in its infancy, it is growing and the empirical foundations of the profession are strengthening. There is still an obvious need for further, methodologically sound studies that not only evaluate the effectiveness of coaching but examine which elements of the coaching process are critical for a successful outcome. The question of which coaching strategies are most effective for dealing with particular coaching issues also needs to be addressed. We discuss these challenges in more detail in Chapter 8.

A definition of behavioral coaching

Definitions of coaching abound. While individual coaches are entitled to define their role and services as they wish, the coaching profession would benefit from a standardized definition of coaching. Research (Lyle 2002) suggests that a comprehensive definition should:

- differentiate coaching from other professions
- identify critical features or criteria that must be present to meet the definition
- list the key elements of the coaching process
- be applicable to professional and expert coaches' practice
- be able to be used in the practice of coaching.

In view of these criteria, we define behavioral coaching as a structured, process-driven relationship between a trained professional coach and an individual or team, which includes: assessment, examining values and motivation, setting measurable goals, defining focused action plans, and using validated tools and techniques to help coachees develop competencies and remove blocks to achieve valuable and sustainable changes in their professional and personal lives. Organizational behavioral coaching is defined as the science of facilitating the performance, learning and development of the individual or team, which, in turn, will assist the growth of the organization. Increasingly, coaches are adopting a behavioral model. There is growing recognition of the need to assess, strengthen and change behaviors and to evaluate these changes within a scientific framework.

Forms of coaching

In this section, we discuss a typology of five forms of coaching within the coaching process: coaching education, skills coaching, rehearsal coaching, performance coaching and self-coaching. Whether coaches are working within traditional coaching models (as discussed later in this chapter) or a behavioral coaching framework, these five forms span the entire coaching process. Each of these forms of coaching demands varying degrees of knowledge, expertise and ability.

Coaching education

As discussed in detail in Chapter 6, clients/sponsors frequently require education about coaching. The coach acts as a teacher and educator, informing the client and other stakeholders about the following aspects of the coaching program: the definition of coaching, the coach's role, the coaching process, the benefits of coaching and the varying time frames necessary to effect the desired changes. In addition, the coach informs the client of the organization's role in promoting the coaching program and providing a supportive environment in which coaching gains can be reinforced and sustained.

Behavioral coaches also function in a teacher and trainer role when delivering seminars and workshops on such topics as leadership, team building, dealing with the stress and chaos of change, the manager as coach and life balance. There is no conflict between the coaching and training/ teaching roles, provided the coach has adequate knowledge and experience in these areas and possesses the requisite training or teaching skills. Importantly, these roles come under the rubric of coaching only if there is a follow-up process to insure that participants have the opportunity to practice, transfer and evaluate what they have learned in the seminars and workshops.

Within individual and group coaching sessions, coaches assume the roles of teacher and trainer. For example, coachees frequently participate in training in areas such as presentation, negotiation and assertiveness. Others are instructed in the use of certain techniques such as problem solving, strategic planning, relaxation, self-monitoring, goal setting and effective

Table 1.1 Forms of coaching and the coach's role

Form of coaching	The coach's role
Coaching education	providing information: • to marketplace about coaching • to prospective clients about the program and benefits to their organization • information to coachees about the process of coaching, mutual roles and responsibilities in the coaching partnership • to coachees about behavioral change methods, monitoring and measurement techniques.
Skills coaching	• teaching coachees the requisite skills to meet objectives and goals (e.g., planning skills, assertiveness, interpersonal and communication skills, presentation skills, self-regulation skills).
Rehearsal coaching	• supervising practice, role-playing, video taping of new skills • monitoring the practice of elements of the new skills in the workplace.
Performance coaching	• supporting and providing feedback on coachees' performance of skills in the workplace • ongoing monitoring and measurement of performance.
Self-coaching	• insuring coachees' autonomy, confidence and competence in self-generating and self-regulating skills • putting maintenance and follow-through strategies in place.

problem solving. Coachees learn methods to challenge limiting beliefs and to better manage their emotions. All these coaching interventions include a greater or lesser degree of instruction.

Skills coaching

In the literature, skills coaching is frequently referred to as a specific type of coaching, compared with performance coaching or development coaching, for example. In the behavioral coaching model, skills coaching refers to coaching that occurs as an essential part of any coaching program. The coach collects data, conducts assessments, targets behaviors to change, and with the coachee sets goals and develops an action plan. The coach then begins to teach the coachee the identified skills.

In order to change behaviors, all coachees require new skills. Some of these will enable a completely different way of behaving, others will simply enhance current skills. Either way, skills coaching is involved. For example, a coachee may acquire effective planning skills, team development skills, presentation skills, assertiveness skills, communication skills, methods to manage difficult colleagues, assertiveness skills, networking skills and sales skills. A coachee may also become skilled in behavioral change techniques that facilitate the acquisition and maintenance of new behaviors.

Rehearsal coaching

Once coachees have learned new skills, they rehearse them before taking them back to the workplace. Rehearsal coaching occurs within coaching sessions and involves video rehearsal, role plays and analogue situations. Rehearsals are monitored and measured. It is at this stage that practice and "drilling" are most critical.

Rehearsal also takes place within the work environment. A coachee whose ultimate objective is to make excellent presentations to prospective clients, for example, may initially practice the learned skills in a non-threatening, less demanding environment, such as before a small, select group of existing clients.

Performance coaching

At this stage, a coachee is fully applying the learned skills in the workplace. During this phase, the coach supports the coachee, as do the aligned manager and coaching program manager. The new behaviors are measured by the coachee and peers, and the coach also shadows or observes the coachee executing the new skills.

Performance coaching entails a considerable degree of measurement, for it is now that the new behaviors can be compared with the coachee's precoaching performance. The coach employs 360-degree or other multirater assessments and the coachee self-monitors to obtain comparative data. Such data plays a significant role in the final evaluation of the coaching program.

Performance coaching demands that the coach has the skills to manage fluctuations in the coachee's performance and is able to deal effectively with blocks or resistances within the coachee or the work environment. Importantly, the coach provides ongoing, effective and constructive feedback on the coachee's execution of the learned skills.

Self-coaching

The emphasis during self-coaching is on maintaining the gains made during coaching sessions. During coaching education, skills coaching, rehearsal coaching and performance coaching, the coach is the key driver. Nevertheless, each form of coaching aims to make knowledge and skills accessible to coachees so that, ultimately, they can develop autonomy and independence from the coach. The coach's ultimate goal is to insure that coachees can effectively self-coach.

While maintenance is built into the entire coaching program, once a coachee is performing the new skills, the coach will take specific steps to insure that what has been learned will be practiced and retained. One method behavioral coaches employ to do this is to carefully measure the coachee's progress and identify any factors that require immediate attention and adjustment. Ongoing self-monitoring, as well as observation and feedback from others, therefore begins as soon as the coachee starts applying the skills in the workplace. During this period, the coachee learns to recognize triggers for both desired and undesired behaviors and ways to self-correct and self-regulate. As well as establishing the coachee's self-efficacy or confidence in these areas, the coach conducts a preliminary exploration of what might present obstacles to the coachee once the coaching relationship has ended. Together the partners identify potential barriers and develop strategies to avoid or overcome these. The coach also establishes ongoing support mechanisms for the coachee.

Areas of coaching

In this section we will examine three major areas of coaching today. These are:

1 Coaching in organizations
2 Business coaching
3 Life or personal coaching.

Coaching in organizations

Management or executive development

Sometimes referred to as "agenda coaching" or "coaching for leadership," coaching senior managers, executives and leaders for development is driven more by the needs and aspirations of individual coachees than those of the organization. Individuals, usually senior executives, at times employ and pay for the coach's services from their own budget.

Coachees sometimes define their own objectives and strategies, as well as their notion of success and what constitutes a positive coaching outcome. The coach's role is generally non-directive. The coaching relationship can last for up to five years, with some executives taking their coach with them as they move along or up the corporate ladder.

Executives typically seek a coach to work on their personal and business strategies, as well as life balance, goal setting, career planning and developmental needs. Behavioral coaches also work with leaders to develop research-based executive competencies such as cognitive capacities (planning, analytical skills, metacognitive skills, creativity); social capacities (behavioral flexibility, negotiation skills, persuasion skills); personality (openness, flexibility, adaptability, risk propensity, locus of control and self-discipline); motivation (need for achievement, self-efficacy, socialized power); and knowledge and expertise (functional and social expertise, knowledge of environmental elements). In some organizations, senior managers are trained to coach and mentor junior staff, especially regarding career development and career transition.

Enhancing performance

While executive coaching has been accepted and practiced for more than a decade, it is not always affordable for middle managers and lower ranking personnel. Coaching around performance needs rather than development issues is an effective and cost-efficient way of meeting these people's coaching needs. Coaching for sales performance, for example, focuses on more than a single skill or even several skills. Sales performance requires that the organization identifies and links the behaviors that will define high performance. There must be well-defined, critical technical and performance skills requirements for individual coachees. The training is generally provided by an internal coach with the necessary product and technical knowledge or by external trainers.

External behavioral coaches, then, unless they have experience in the specific industry arena, do not provide the training component. Rather, they work with managers, individuals and teams on the "psychological readiness" aspects of performance to insure that product and technical knowledge are used effectively and on a sustained basis.

Coaching addresses both short-term (e.g., sales targets) and long-term specific goals (e.g., becoming a member of the top-performing team). Coaching to enhance performance usually occurs over three to six months and includes both individual and team coaching sessions. The organization's agenda drives the coaching initiative, and the coach must balance coachees' values and needs with those of the organization.

Coaching to enhance performance was initially viewed from a deficit model whereby the individual was seen as underperforming, and, therefore, in need of coaching. This perspective has changed over time, however, with even top performers now recognizing the value of coaching. Indeed, coaching is viewed by some recipients as a status symbol and evidence of the company's belief in and willingness to invest in their development.

Coaching for sales, particularly, is an excellent means of introducing behavioral coaching to both small businesses and large organizations. The psychological aspects of selling are well established, and the results are tangible and measurable. Sales coaching therefore provides a unique opportunity for behavioral coaches to pilot a coaching program, measure its results and validate it before it is rolled out in the larger business or corporation. We discuss how behavioral coaching is being used in sales coaching in more detail in Chapter 7.

The following model for sales coaching differentiates those aspects of performance that require training and those that lend themselves to coaching.

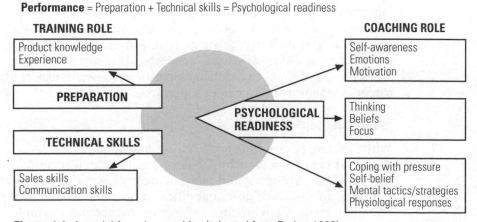

Performance = Preparation + Technical skills = Psychological readiness

Figure 1.1 A model for sales coaching (adapted from Butler, 1996)

Personal and professional skills development

As discussed above, skills coaching is a core component of the overall coaching process. Some individuals, however, seek out coaching or are referred for the specific purpose of enhancing their personal or professional skills. In this case, behavioral coaches work with individuals to enhance their skills capabilities, which include planning skills, delegation, time management, negotiation, dealing with difficult colleagues and enhancing individual interpersonal skills. Line managers or supervisors in organizations are sometimes trained to adopt a coaching style to enhance the skills of their staff. When coachees are referred by the organization, the organization's agenda takes precedence. Coaches, however, are careful to balance individuals' personal needs and goals with those of the organization.

Team or group coaching

Team or group coaching is an increasingly popular form of delivery. It is more cost-effective for the client and time-efficient for the coach. Coachees also benefit from the exchange of knowledge and ongoing support and feedback from colleagues. Team coaching often involves team building, developing a newly established team and working with top-performing teams to meet demands for higher productivity.

Several theoretically driven team training strategies are adopted by behavioral coaches. These include cross-training, team-coordination training and team leadership training. Team coaching is informed by research showing that team training is most effective when it is theoretically driven, focused on required competencies, provides realistic opportunities for practice and provides ongoing feedback to team members.

The objectives of team coaching are specific and are generally set at the beginning of the coaching program. A program typically involves several (four or five) two-hour team sessions on a weekly or second-weekly basis over a three- to six-month period, depending on the degree of urgency and the team's objectives. Best practice suggests that team meetings are enhanced by at least three concurrent individual coaching sessions, during which members work on their action plans as they relate to the team's objectives.

Team members are often encouraged to develop a "peer coaching" relationship with another team member. This usually takes the form of regular meetings, discussions about roles and responsibilities and mutual, ongoing support and feedback. This coaching process is typically less structured and more informal than that between a professional coach and coachee.

Team coaching requires considerable competence in core facilitation processes. These include analyzing information about the purpose, desired outcomes and expectations of all stakeholders to determine the best approach; designing the structure of the meetings; establishing the group climate, roles and norms; creating structures and processes to solve problems, make decisions and achieve goals; manage group dynamics; institute behavioral change techniques; and insure follow-up action.

Business coaching

The term business coaching is used interchangeably with executive coaching. For the purpose of clarity we will discuss business coaching in the context of a coach working with small-to-medium enterprises, entrepreneurs, start-ups and businesses other than large organizations. Interestingly, although business coaching has grown considerably in the past decade, most of the literature focuses on executive coaching. Yet working with businesses other than large organizations is an attractive proposition for many coaches, particularly sole practitioners who have limited resources and are not well networked in the corporate world.

Business coaches are generally employed on six month to one year contracts and rather than charging an hourly rate, work on a retainer basis or for a daily or monthly fee. Coaching usually centers on areas related to growing and developing the business. This can include business planning, marketing strategies, management competencies and dealing more effectively with customers and staff or developing a business for sale. Other areas of business coaching include increasing sales and profitability, improving leadership skills, managing transitions, establishing vision and mission, reducing workplace stress, developing and motivating staff and strengthening management systems.

Business coaches generally come from a business background and many have owned and operated their own businesses. Their role is one of advisor, strategist and sounding board. While coaching is typically on a one-to-one basis, the business model of coaching small groups of business owners is gaining popularity. The group coaching format usually involves the coach facilitating a group of six or so business owners who meet weekly or every second week over three to six months to discuss relevant business topics. There may be a set agenda that was agreed on at the commencement of the program. For example, for one session, the group will discuss and set individual goals and action plans around planning strategies. The next session will focus on marketing, followed by enhancing customer satisfaction or whatever the agenda dictates. Alternatively, each of the participants will bring a specific issue to the table for one session, and for a nominated period (e.g., fifteen minutes) discuss the matter, seek advice and input from the group and set up an action plan. Regardless of the format of group meetings, participants also receive several individual coaching sessions centered on their action plans. These are usually conducted by telephone.

Life or personal coaching

Life or personal coaching is a structured process of examining values and setting goals and action plans to help individuals remove blocks and achieve measurable and sustainable benefits in all aspects of their lives. Life coaching, to some degree, remains the most controversial of the coaching specialties. Perhaps this is because it addresses issues that can cross over into the therapy arena. Many therapists, in fact, are moving into life coaching and claiming it as their domain.

Life skills coaching began as an educational service for underprivileged adults in the United States. Interestingly, there are now also group coaching programs in the United States designed to prepare disadvantaged individuals for the workforce. In addition, there is growing interest from life coaches to work with adolescents and young people to help prepare them for life and career challenges. Life coaches also work in specific health areas, such as coaching individuals with attention deficit and disruptive behavior disorders.

Generally, though, life coaching addresses an individual's need for a more harmonious, balanced and successful life. Coaches work with individuals to enhance their relationships with their family, community and peers and to establish and develop more satisfying personal relationships. Areas such as health, fitness and lifestyle are increasingly popular niches for life coaches and many personal trainers are adding tailored coaching programs to their training services.

Life balance remains a central concern for many individuals. Coaches work with coachees on time management, prioritizing and making choices to achieve greater harmony and fulfillment in their lives. Managing chaos and stress is another related area that life coaches address, both with individuals and within the corporate arena.

Life coaches also work with individuals during transition periods, such as career preparation, career change, pre-retirement, retirement and after the children have left home. Coaching for cross-cultural issues is rapidly gaining prominence in both life and executive coaching and we discuss these developments in Chapter 7. Finally, emotional growth, spiritual development and increased wealth are other goals addressed in life coaching.

Major influences on the behavioral coaching model

There are numerous laws, principles, philosophies, theories and techniques that contribute to the behavioral coaching model we practice and present in this book. Here, we provide a summary and brief discussion of these influences, which are examined in greater depth throughout the remainder of the book.

Psychology

Psychology is clearly a major influence on behavioral coaching that is based on psychological principles. As noted in the Preface, behavioral coaching adopts a scientific approach to coaching to bring about measurable, sustained learning acquisition and change in individuals and organizations. Antecedents, behavior and consequences of behavior can be managed effectively within the scientific framework of behaviorism. We learn and unlearn according to established laws, and validated behavioral change techniques can alter the way we behave. Behavioral coaching also incorporates social learning theory, which builds on behavioral principles and integrates reciprocal interactions among cognitive factors, environmental factors, and the behavior itself.

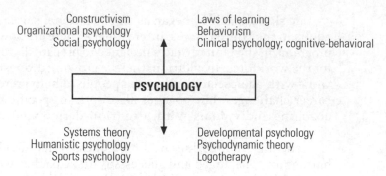

Figure 1.2 Psychology and coaching

As Figure 1.2 shows, behavioral coaching is also underpinned by constructivist thought, which posits that individuals construct their own meaning of life and the world.

In addition to behavioral psychological principles and techniques, behavioral coaching is informed by organizational and social psychology, which explain individual and group behaviors, organizational culture, attribution theory, cognitive dissonance, self-efficacy and the relationship between thoughts and effect. Clinical psychology offers validated and replicable methods of assessment and ways of managing thoughts, feelings and actions more effectively. For instance, disputing self-limiting beliefs, self-regulation of emotions, assertiveness training, dealing with resistance and relaxation methods are some of the clinical techniques employed by behavioral coaches.

Behavioral coaching assumes a systems approach when working with an individual or group. Organizational forces are considered in the light of supporting or sabotaging the gains made during coaching. Individual coachees are also situated within their "stages of development" and the "tasks" or challenges that arise at various life phases. The importance of exploring individual growth and personal development is in line with humanistic psychology, while questions of meaning and authenticity echo the central concerns of logotherapy, as discussed in Chapter 2.

Psychodynamic theory, particularly the constructs of self-awareness/ insight and defense mechanisms, provides coaches with valuable information, especially when working with resistance. Finally, as previously mentioned, sports psychology has generated a significant body of research that affects executive and business coaching. The body of knowledge of particular relevance to behavioral coaching includes research findings on goal setting, focus, being in "the flow," motivation and commitment.

Education

As Figure 1.3 demonstrates, the principles and practices of education play a significant role in behavioral coaching.

A coach's understanding of how individuals learn and their preferred learning style facilitates knowledge acquisition. Coaches also must be

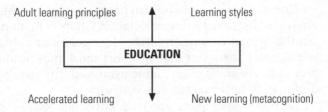

Figure 1.3 Education and coaching

familiar with the guiding principles of adult education in order to tailor the delivery of their coaching programs. Finally, accelerated learning techniques are particularly effective when a coachee is acquiring new skills. We discuss these matters in detail in Chapter 3.

Furthermore, as noted previously, the education of clients/sponsors, as well as individual coachees and teams, is one of the core roles of a behavioral coach. For example, coaches are in an excellent position to educate clients about current research relating to learning acquisition, coaching and change, as well as the relationship between managing human capital and profitability.

Consulting, mentoring, training and facilitation

As noted, there is a blurring of distinctions between coaching and related disciplines. Figure 1.4 sets out the major contributions that consulting, mentoring, training and facilitation have made to the theory and practice of behavioral coaching.

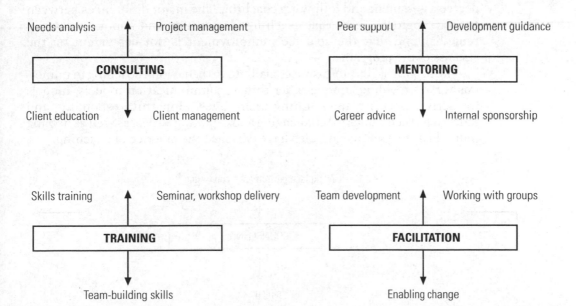

Figure 1.4 Consulting, mentoring, training, facilitation and coaching

Consulting practices inform many coaching techniques. Coaching needs analyses (discussed in more detail in Chapter 6), in many respects, follow a similar format to that employed by consultants. Many coaches also work with clients on project management and supervise and manage the coaching program. As well, client education and client management in coaching derive from best practices in consulting.

Mentoring practices are frequently adopted by coaches working with senior executives or business owners. The coach as mentor usually has expertise and experience in the specific coaching arena. For example, the coach may have functioned as a CEO or a small business owner and therefore offers peer support as well as developmental guidance on both business issues and career moves.

Training theory and practice inform behavioral coaching in several critical areas. Coaching for skills, methods of seminar and workshop delivery and team-building strategies are founded on established training methodologies.

Facilitation is sometimes used synonymously with coaching. While there are significant differences, facilitation skills that enable growth and change are essential in team-development coaching, working with groups and coaching for change, both on an organizational and on an individual basis.

Counseling

Counseling, as we discuss it here and as shown in Figure 1.5, refers chiefly to the HR or manager's role of counseling for performance and to the practices of the counseling or helping profession.

Workplace performance counseling, especially when it is related to performance appraisal systems, influenced the coaching practices of 360-degree assessment and follow-up coaching. The major differences between the two approaches are that coaching is voluntary and is not necessarily remedial, and that the coachee's employment is not dependent on the success of the program.

The helping skills profession contributes to behavioral coaching in numerous ways, providing, among other things, communication models, models for active listening, questioning techniques, empathic responding and reflection. Techniques for challenging and exploring issues, as well as helping individuals to gain insight, also have enriched the practice of coaching.

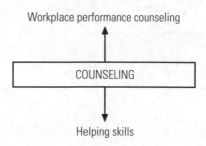

Figure 1.5 Counseling and coaching

Philosophy

Philosophy influences the behavioral coaching model in that coaching inevitably addresses a coachee's view of the world and her or his guiding philosophical or moral principles. Usually, these issues surface when meaning, values and vision are explored. On occasion, these issues come to light in the context of self-limiting beliefs or blocks to progress.

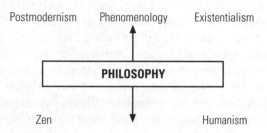

Figure 1.6 Philosophy and coaching

Behavioral coaching is postmodern in that it does not place the coach in the role of an expert. Rather, knowledge is constructed through dialogue and social discourse and acknowledges a multiplicity of truths. Phenomenology, or arriving at the truth through subjectivity, underpins behavioral coaching's exploration of the individual's subjective experiences in addition to objective behavioral measurement. Existentialist thought informs behavioral coaching through its emphasis on meaning, choice and self-responsibility.

The influence of Zen philosophy can be seen in the importance coaching places on living in the present, letting go of the past, being mindful and not being attached to outcomes. Finally, as noted above, coaching is humanistic in that it views the human being as the ultimate measure of all things and recognizes that every individual has a capacity, even yearning, for growth and fulfillment.

Leadership development

Leadership development evolved on an almost parallel course with executive coaching. As shown in Figure 1.7, leadership development has had an impact on behavioral coaching in four major areas.

Figure 1.7 Leadership development and coaching

The leadership literature is prolific, nominating essential executive or leader competencies and models of leadership that incorporate these. Executive and business coaches work with these competencies to enhance leaders' existing skills and to develop future leaders. Coaching for career transition at senior leader levels is also a growing specialty for experienced coaches.

Behavioral coaches also work with leaders on cross-cultural opportunities and challenges. Although we discuss this coaching niche in detail in Chapter 7, it is relevant to mention here the extraordinary recent growth in cross-cultural coaching. Behavioral coaches partner with leaders to understand and manage cultural variables that research has shown to be critical to any successful personal or business enterprise. These include how cultures accept an unequal distribution of power, how they try to avoid uncertainty, to what degree a culture values collectivism over individualism and to what extent it values material goods over quality of life.

Organizational development

As Figure 1.8 shows, organizational development research, theory and practice offer coaching a broad, in-depth understanding of how individuals behave and how groups function within organizational cultures. Research on team building, change models and how to effectively build skills and alter behavior provides a cornerstone for coaches working in organizations. We discuss behavioral coaching within the context of organizational development in detail in Chapters 3 and 4.

Current influences

Having discussed the impact of various disciplines on behavioral coaching, we will now briefly examine some individual contributions to the field.

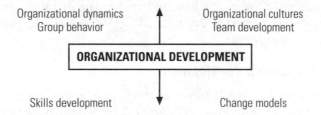

Figure 1.8 Organizational development and coaching

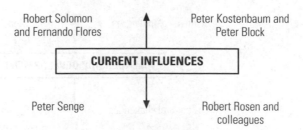

Figure 1.9 Current influences on behavioral coaching

The work of Robert Solomon and Fernando Flores on developing trust alongside honest confrontation between colleagues provides a blueprint for ideal relations within the coaching framework. These include interactions between the coach and coachees, the coach and the organization and coachees and their coworkers.

Kostenbaum and Block apply existentialist principles to the workplace. The authors view workers as "units of freedom" who can employ philosophical enquiry, choice and free will to enhance their lives and work. Importantly, Kostenbaum and Block show how modern organizations mitigate against genuine freedom and that true leadership is an exercise of freedom that includes confronting others with their own freedom. Behavioral coaching incorporates existentialist tenets when exploring an individual's personal meaning and world view. This paradigm, however, also presents valuable guidelines for coaches on extending and exploring these principles within the workplace.

Peter Senge's work on change offers valuable insights for behavioral coaches involved in change management or initiating coaching programs. His exposition of the resistance and limiting processes faced by change agents, the challenges facing a true learning organization and guidelines for establishing pilot projects have enriched the knowledge and procedural expertise of coaches working in both small businesses and large corporations.

Robert Rosen and his colleagues have made a significant contribution to the literature on cross-cultural diversity, especially in relation to their construct of "global literacies." Coaches working with leaders and individuals on cross-cultural issues assess and develop competencies within this framework of "global literacies." These include personal literacy, social literacy, business literacy and cultural literacy.

Coaching boundaries

One of the critical issues facing any emerging or newly established discipline is that of boundaries. Initially, there were clearer demarcations between coaching and related disciplines such as training, consulting, mentoring and HR services. Over time, these distinctions have become increasingly blurred, although the differences between coaching and therapy remain relatively clear. Here, we will discuss each of these professions as they relate to coaching.

Training and coaching

In the coaching literature, training was initially discussed in terms of its ineffectiveness due to a lack of follow-through and provisions for the transfer of learning. While this remains true in many instances, recent research suggests that training can be effective. The science of training has made considerable advances in developing training theory, understanding training needs analyses and exploring antecedent training conditions, methods and strategies, as well as post-training conditions. Many trainers therefore are more aware of the need to employ coaching techniques such as individual action plans, follow-up coaching sessions and insuring that the organizational environment supports the acquisition of new learning.

As mentioned earlier in this chapter, behavioral coaches often perform the role of trainer or teacher. However, the single critical differentiator between training and coaching is that the former is more information-based. In addition, training is more circumscribed and assumes that participants will learn and use the information to a similar degree. The objectives and goals are predetermined and because of the amount of information imparted, there is generally little room for deviation from the prescribed agenda. In contrast, coaching is tailor-made, allowing individuals to learn in various ways and at different rates. It caters more to the individual's agenda, even when the objectives and goals are organization-based.

Consulting and coaching

Internationally, many consultants and large consulting firms are adding coaching to their services, whether or not consultants have coach training. Initially, consulting was viewed more as a directive, advisory role, with the consultant dealing mainly with changes in systems and processes. Increasingly, however, consultants are also working within the personal and behavioral realm as it affects business change and growth. Indeed, consultants who are trained as coaches are in a unique position to work with clients on both the hard and soft skills necessary for businesses and organizations to compete successfully in the marketplace. These skills include strategic planning, establishing and communicating vision, use of information technologies, change initiatives and project management.

Coaches, too, provide consultancy services. For example, one of the roles of the Behavioral Coaching Institute is to work with businesses and organizations to establish a coaching program or to evaluate an existing program. We train internal coaches, then act as consultants to the key players and stakeholders. Internal coaches also frequently act as consultants on learning and development programs that include training and coaching.

Mentoring and coaching

Behavioral coaches working at senior levels, for example with CEOs or owners of small- to-medium businesses, frequently function in a mentoring capacity. Typically, they themselves have performed successfully in similar roles, so as well as acting as sounding boards, they offer advice and solutions. Strategic planning and business expansion are often on the agenda. Such mentor coaches are skilled at political maneuvering and are rich resource providers not only in terms of experience but in networking and general business savvy.

HR and coaching

The role of HR personnel has changed dramatically in the past decade or so. For example, hiring, which was once a function of HR, is now often handed over to recruitment agencies. Many former HR tasks are outsourced. At the same time, increasing numbers of HR personnel are adopting an internal coaching role. Coaching for leadership at the senior and middle management levels frequently comes under the mantle of HR. HR personnel also work with managers to develop a coaching style and are involved in team coaching and coaching to enhance skills and performance. In general, however, the role of HR personnel remains diffuse, so that it is sometimes difficult to clearly delineate their coaching role from their other responsibilities.

Therapy and coaching

As mentioned, there has been less blurring of the boundaries between therapy and coaching than between coaching and other disciplines, although the demarcation remains a concern to many coaches, especially those without a psychology background.

The differences between therapy and coaching have been widely discussed in the literature. Focusing on the present rather than the past, actively rather than passively listening and dealing with everyday emotional difficulties rather than pathology are some of the main differentiators of coaching. While these are clear enough in one sense, the differences are often a question of degree. Rather than discuss these differences in detail, we believe it is more helpful to answer some of the questions about therapy and coaching that our students frequently ask.

Question: When a coachee continues to talk about past experiences, what does the coach do?

Answer: It is critical to allow a coachee to talk about matters and issues that are of concern, and not to minimize or discount these. Nevertheless, as coaching is situated in the present it is important to encourage, even direct, the coachee to what is happening in his or her life and work now. Useful interjections include: "How is this past experience affecting what is happening in your life and work now?" and "Clearly, we can't change the past, but we can change the present or at least change our attitude to what is happening now. What do you think needs to change now? How do you think we can best go about making these changes?"

Question: How long should the coach allow a coachee to talk about or "ventilate" negative emotions?

Answer: Depending on the coachee's level of distress or anger, it may be necessary for that person to spend virtually the entire session pouring out her or his feelings. However, toward the end of the session, the coach has to bring some closure to the episode and alert the coachee to the fact that there is work to be done if there is to be any progress. It can be helpful to say: "You've talked today about how distressed (or angry) you are about (the particular situation). It's obviously a very difficult situation for you. It might be helpful if for our next session you could write down at least three aspects of your current circumstances that you can change.

In our next session, we can begin to look at these and discuss some objectives and strategies so you can start moving forward."

Question: How does the coach know when a coachee should be referred for therapy?

Answer: Two of the most common problems people face in everyday life and which therefore are more likely to surface in a coaching relationship are anxiety and depression. These can cause the individual to lose focus or simply give up on the coaching tasks or decision-making processes. The coach can employ techniques such as challenging the thoughts that may be generating these unwanted emotional states in the coachee. However, if the emotional interference is so strong or frequent that it negatively affects the coaching relationship and goals, then the individual should be referred to a clinician. It is important that coaches be aware of the signs and symptoms of anxiety and depression so they are not interpreted as resistance or lack of commitment.

Anxiety can range from mild to moderate or severe. Some of the most common research-based signs and symptoms of anxiety are listed in Appendix 1. If the coach believes that anxiety may be significantly affecting the coachee's ability to function at work and/or at home, he or she can use this list as a discussion point to determine the frequency and intensity of the anxiety and whether or not it can be addressed in the coaching sessions.

For instance, if the coachee experiences mild anxiety in certain situations, such as making presentations or dealing with superiors, then relaxation techniques and cognitive strategies to challenge self-defeating beliefs may be adequate. If, on the other hand, the coachee's anxiety resembles panic or is more pervasive or generalized, then referral to a clinical psychologist is advised. As we have stated throughout our work, we consider it imperative that coaches form a working alliance with a clinician to discuss whether a coachee requires and would benefit from therapy.

Depression, like anxiety, can range from mild to severe. The signs and symptoms of depression, which are based on extensive research, are listed in Appendix 2. Again, the coach can use these as discussion points in order to ascertain the severity of the problem. Of course, regardless of how subjectively depressed the individual may report to be, if there is any mention of suicide, the coachee should immediately be referred to a clinician.

The anxiety and depression scales are not intended as diagnostic instruments for the coach. Rather, they offer the coach and coachee an opportunity to explore whether there is an existing problem and how to best manage it.

Finally, rather than list the differences between coaching, training, consulting, mentoring, therapy and HR, it is helpful to establish the degree to which identified elements of coaching occur in each of these disciplines.

Table 1.2 Coaching compared to training, consulting, mentoring, therapy and HR services

Core elements of coaching	Coaching	Training	Consulting	Mentoring	Therapy	HR
Problem solving	high	high	high	moderate	high	high
Examining values	high	low	moderate	moderate	high	low
Behavioral change	high	moderate	moderate	moderate	high	moderate
Politics	high	low	moderate	high	low	high
Resistance	high	low	moderate	low	high	high
Giving information	high	high	high	high	moderate	moderate
Support	high	low	moderate	high	high	moderate
Reinforcement	high	low	low	moderate	high	low
Personal growth	high	low	low	moderate	high	low
Goal setting	high	low	high	moderate	high	high
Action planning	high	low	high	moderate	moderate	high
Transfer of learning	high	low	low	moderate	high	moderate
Providing resources	moderate	high	high	high	high	moderate
"Expert" role	low	high	high	high	high	high
Teaching	moderate	high	high	moderate	moderate	moderate
Challenging	high	low	low	moderate	moderate	high
Strategic planning	moderate	low	high	moderate	low	low
Exploring beliefs	high	low	low	moderate	high	low
Evaluation	moderate	low	moderate	low	low	moderate
Confidentiality	high	low	moderate	moderate	high	moderate
Data collection	moderate	low	high	low	moderate	high
Individually tailored	high	low	moderate	high	high	low
Research based	moderate	moderate	moderate	low	high	moderate
Giving solutions	low	high	high	high	low	high
Advising	low	high	high	high	low	high
Transformational possibilities	high	low	low	moderate	high	low

Theoretical models in coaching today

The purpose of this section is to review several of the most common approaches to coaching that also have a basis in the behavioral sciences. These are appreciative coaching, reflective coaching and cognitive coaching. We will also discuss several other, more recent and popular types of coaching, including observational coaching and peer coaching.

Appreciative coaching

Appreciative coaching derives many of its fundamental premises from the work of David Cooperrider and his colleagues. Through the use of appreciative language, the coach and coachee move away from the traditional coaching paradigm of feedback and confrontation directed at performance deficits. Appreciative coaches emphasize that individuals, executives and organizations do not need to be "fixed," but rather require constant affirmation. Coaching, therefore, does not involve dialogue around looking for weaknesses or problems, but focuses on existing strengths and distinctive competencies. It assumes that executives, managers and entrepreneurs have already achieved a significant degree of success because of their distinctive and unique strengths; that is, something already works well and coaching serves to access this and bring more of it into play.

A fundamental assumption of appreciative coaching is that the solutions we seek and the resources we need are already within us. It is a question of accessing, amplifying and integrating these to move coachees forward to reach their objectives. Compassion and concern for the coachee are central to this style of coaching, which attempts to move the individual toward self-reflection and self-responsibility through appreciating their values, goals and intentions.

Similarly, behavioral coaching underscores the importance of highlighting the strengths and accomplishments of the individual and the organization. Although based on sound, validated psychological practices, it does not subscribe to a pathology or deficit language model. Individuals and organizations do have expressed needs, issues and concerns that have to be addressed. Nevertheless, they also have considerable strengths to leverage in producing results and bringing about shifts in paradigms and visions of future achievements. Importantly, behavioral coaching highlights the role of affirmation or praise as a major source of reinforcement of behavioral change, both at the individual and at the organizational level.

Reflective coaching

Reflective coaching is grounded in philosophies and theories relating to how we interpret and make meaning of our experiences, how these can change and what this change means. The basic idea is that the way we see the world at any particular time, or our "structure of interpretation," determines how we act. The coach's role is to help coachees become aware of their own unique structures of interpretation, which are shaped by personal experiences, beliefs and intentions.

Language plays a critical role in reflective coaching. How the coachee speaks, what she or he says and how it is said are evidence of the coachee's structure of interpretation. According to this model, it is through language that people make meaning out of their experiences and generate new distinctions, and therefore new meanings. Once the individual can see what was previously not seen, new actions are possible. Change, therefore, does not occur by directly influencing behavior, but rather through working on the coachee's structure of interpretation. Nevertheless, the coachee must take action for learning and change to occur. Ultimately, the coachee becomes self-correcting and self-generating.

Similarly, behavioral coaching considers reflection to be a critical ingredient of every meaningful encounter between a coach and a coachee.

Although the aim of behavioral coaching is not specifically to alter the individual's structure of interpretation, it emphasizes the importance of understanding the coachee's world view. This is discussed in detail in Chapter 2.

The coachee's language is of paramount importance in behavioral coaching. Coaches explore not only how language reflects the coachee's world and relationships, but how it creates the individual's reality. In particular, behavioral coaching encourages, even demands, that the coachee reflect on his or her language, beliefs and assumptions, especially within the context of values, self-limiting beliefs and resistance to changing.

In behavioral coaching, coachees are encouraged to look at situations from alternative viewpoints and to look for different ways of behaving. Finally, the goal of reflective coaching is similar to that of behavioral coaching, in that coachees learn strategies to challenge and correct their own behaviors and to generate new behaviors after the coaching sessions have ended.

Cognitive coaching

Cognitive coaching is based on the notion that metacognition, or being aware of one's thinking processes, facilitates learning and change. The objectives of this style of coaching are to enhance and build confidence in the coachee's thinking skills and to improve conceptual thinking and decision making. The model is frequently employed in educational settings, with both teachers and students. For example, a coach instructs and facilitates teachers to use questioning to ask students about their own thinking and to guide them through a structured process of decision making and action. According to the behavioral coaching model, metacognition, or "thinking through" before trying a new behavior, can be a powerful means of new learning. As well as improving thinking skills, it is a particularly useful tool for dealing with old, learned behaviors that do not serve the individual well.

As we discuss in Chapter 3, behavioral coaching uses accelerated metacognitive techniques such as having the coachee perform both the old and the new, desired behaviors, comparing the two and describing the differences. Only when the coachee has understood the differences is the new skill or behavior practiced in a systematic fashion.

Observational coaching

Observational coaching, sometimes referred to as "live coaching," is employed in small business settings, with executives and in large organizations. Essentially, it is conducted in three phases. The first of these is data collection. Data is often obtained by direct observation or shadowing individuals as they go about their daily business routine or carry out nominated executive or organizational tasks. In the second phase, the data is analyzed in a detailed, systematic manner and feedback is provided. The third phase involves developing various strategies and action plans to enhance personal and professional development and business growth.

Observing behavior is a core component of the behavioral coaching model. For instance, coachees observe their own behavior in order to enhance self-awareness, as well as to monitor changes in their responses. Coaches also observe coachees in action and provide feedback on specific skills and behaviors. The coaching program manager or colleagues are sometimes enlisted to observe and provide feedback on specific aspects of a coachee's performance.

Furthermore, as described in Chapter 5, data collection and analysis are central to any behavioral intervention planning within the behavioral coaching framework. Developing goals, action plans and business objectives are also core elements the coach addresses when designing a coaching program.

Peer coaching

Peer coaching describes situations where colleagues interact with each other in a non-threatening, supportive environment to achieve mutual growth and development. It allows individuals to gather observation and feedback data from their colleagues and to co-create development plans that will ultimately improve their work performance. Peer coaching, which is frequently employed in educational settings, differs from mentoring in that there is no "expert" on the coaching issues.

As discussed in Chapter 7, behavioral coaching initiates and supports peer coaching relationships and networks in both organizational and educational settings. For example, teachers coach their colleagues and students and students are trained to coach each other. Behavioral coaching emphasizes the importance of peers collecting feedback and data from each other that is measurable, rather than anecdotal or subjective. For example, teachers have peers rate them on specific behaviors, such as the number of times they went "off task" in response to a disruptive student or how many times in a lesson they successfully dealt with disruptions.

The coach's role today

As mentioned, coaches today assume the roles of trainer, mentor and consultant. Some HR personnel also adopt an internal coaching role. Although each coaching specialty (e.g., executive, business and personal) demands specific abilities and knowledge, coaches generally perform the following generic roles.

- *Increasing the individual's self-awareness* Regardless of whether the coaching relationship is focused on personal or professional matters, the coach typically strives to enhance coachees' awareness of their strengths, weaknesses, cognitive style, ways of relating to others, motivational factors, values and long-term objectives. Engendering self-awareness demands that the coach be cognizant of how much self-knowledge and awareness an individual is capable of, how relevant it is to the coaching task, and the most effective means to explore the subject. For instance, some coachees already have some understanding of how others react to them. While they may learn more effective ways to manage their thoughts and feelings, there is no fundamental shift in how they view themselves or the world. In contrast, other coachees actually undergo what is known as transformational learning, and the coaching relationship results in their viewing themselves and their place in the world from a different, enriched perspective.

- *Modeling desired behaviors* Excellent communication skills are a requisite for all coaches. Clear thinking and speaking, and active listening and empathic responding, are central to the coach's role. How the coach deals with conflict, either through avoiding it, maximizing it or dealing with it openly and effectively, sets a standard for coachees. The degree of openness, assertiveness, sincerity and humor the coach brings to the coaching dialogue establishes the basis for ongoing communication between the two parties. Similarly, the degree of trust, collaboration and commitment exhibited by the coach establishes a blueprint for relations not only with coachees but also between coachees and their organization or business. Finally, how the coach values and models cross-cultural issues and diversity can have an impact well beyond the coaching relationship.

- *Getting to the core of the issue* Many of the coaches we train express concern about their ability to diagnose or get to the core of an issue quickly and effectively. There is no easy answer here. Knowledge and experience play key roles because they inform our hypotheses and questioning. As we gain and learn from experience, we should also be prepared to make mistakes. We have to test our hypotheses and be open to coachees' responses. Coaching is a partnership and if the coach is unsure of the core issue, the coachee's assistance can be invoked. Together, in a spirit of openness and flexibility, the partners can then generate a list of possible explanations or "root causes" and systematically explore these, dismissing those that don't fit. Often, what initially seems to be the core of the matter is in fact a side issue. Nevertheless, learning is still taking place, and provided the coach does not succumb to anxiety or time pressure from self, coachees or the organization, the central issue or issues will surface.

- *Giving instructions* Because of the emphasis on coachees finding the answers "within," some coaches are reluctant to give instructions or teach even though this may be appropriate. Coachees learn new techniques taught by the coach. These include methods of problem solving and models for challenging self-limiting beliefs and regulating negative emotions, as well as more effective methods of planning and goal setting. Some coachees become frustrated when the coach continually deflects questions. It appears that the coach either does not have the knowledge or is withholding it as a power play. It is true that the coach has to first exhaust the coachees' knowledge and suggestions, but having established the need for information, it should be given without restraint.

- *Targeting behaviors to be changed* One of the core principles of behavioral coaching is that specific behaviors have to be targeted and evaluated if they are to be either increased or decreased. We discuss this matter in detail in Chapter 3. Here, it is sufficient to underscore the importance of choosing a behavior or behaviors that yield a baseline measure and are able to be changed, and that this change is measurable.

- *Giving feedback* Giving feedback can be subject to difficulty. Most people do not like to receive "negative" feedback, regardless of what they might say to the contrary or how euphemistically the suggestion of providing such feedback is presented. Yet, giving both positive and negative feedback is a central role of coaches across all specialties. How they do this models how coachees will give feedback in their workplace and life. It is important to prepare coachees for feedback and to allow for an initial defensiveness. The information can be presented as another perspective, rather than reality. Finally, acknowledging and leveraging a coachee's strengths to work on the revealed "gaps" contributes to delivering feedback constructively and with minimal harm to the receiver.

- *Insuring practice and rehearsal* New skills and ways of behaving are not learned overnight. They require rehearsal and ongoing practice until they become automatic. The coach sometimes functions as "a drill master," insuring that coachees practice new skills or behaviors over and over until they are solidly entrenched.

- *Keeping the coachee focused and on track* Some simplistic coaching models suggest that coaches work with coachees to set goals and action plans and then follow through with motivational "speeches" and confrontation if coachees fail to live up to their commitments. Yet being focused and on track is part of every coaching session. It means that whatever the coach and coachees are discussing and planning, it has relevance to the coaching objectives and goals. While this appears straightforward, both parties can get sidetracked and distracted. Moreover, it is easy to slide over genuine blocks and resistances that coachees are experiencing by dismissing these as "a lack of commitment." Being persuasive is part of the coach's role, but it should occur in the context of focused conversations that explore what coachees really want and what is getting in the way of moving forward.

How coaching is conducted today

Face-to-face coaching

Typically, high level senior executives prefer face-to-face coaching on their own territory. This appears to be a function of logistics rather than control issues. Behavioral coaches working at these levels invariably conduct initial sessions in person in order to establish rapport, complete an assessment and clarify objectives and goals. Once the coachee has action plans and strategies in place, the remaining coaching sessions are sometimes conducted by telephone.

As yet, there doesn't appear to be any research to suggest whether face-to-face or telephone coaching is more effective, although, intuitively, some coaching topics lend themselves to a particular form of delivery. For example, business coaches working with start-ups, entrepreneurs and business owners wishing to grow and sell their business are usually required to be on the premises. They need firsthand experience of systems, processes, customer contact and quality control.

Telephone coaching

Coaching by telephone has some obvious benefits over face-to-face meetings. It can be conducted from the coach's office, home or current location and both the coach and the coachee are saved the time and cost of travel. Telephone coaching is frequently used in conjunction with email contact, with the coachee notifying the coach of her or his agenda for upcoming sessions.

Telephone coaching is also used for follow-up or booster sessions after a face-to-face coaching program, either of an individual or a team. Conference calling is employed by team coaches who facilitate discussion of strategies and current issues. These calls are particularly effective for virtual teams or team members who are geographically isolated.

Life coaching sessions are more often than not conducted by telephone, although some coachees and coaches prefer face-to-face interaction. Although telephone coaching is particularly effective for follow-up and "crisis coaching," it is not useful for assessments, teaching behavioral change techniques, role plays, practice or rehearsal.

Some individuals are uncomfortable using the telephone. They prefer email with its facility for thinking through issues before committing to an idea or action. It is true that email sidesteps any opportunity to explore and discuss non-verbal signals, but this varies in relevance, depending on the coaching topic. Email allows a coachee to receive feedback from the coach when the need arises and he or she is therefore prepared to take immediate action. Coachees can also use a computer to monitor their behavior and feelings, which are easily collated and forwarded to the coach for feedback and discussion. Email is also used by coaches to provide information or resources and to remind coachees of agreed-upon goals or tasks. In general, coaching programs are not conducted solely by email. Electronic sessions are usually held in conjunction with face-to-face or telephone coaching.

Video coaching

Video conference calling and video via the Internet allow the coach and coachee face-to-face contact regardless of their location. Depending on how sophisticated the technology is, it can be used effectively for skills rehearsal, reviewing and feedback.

A conceptual framework for behavioral coaching

Coaching, as with any discipline, demands a conceptual framework that will provide a common language and a basis for research and create a blueprint for coaching practice and education. Of course, this is not to say that behavioral coaching is the only conceptual framework for coaches to work within. Nevertheless, such a framework does allow coaches a structure in which to operate and discuss and debate issues such as best practices, the most effective tools and techniques, the most efficacious forms of delivery and the competencies and training necessary for successful coaching outcomes.

Table 1.3 illustrates a conceptual framework for behavioral coaching. It nominates key concepts in coaching, the purpose or reason for including these in the model and typical questions surrounding these concepts.

The behavioral coaching model

Table 1.4 on page 32 presents an overview of the behavioral coaching model and the interrelationship of the four stages of change, the five forms of coaching and the seven-step coaching process. We refer to each of these elements throughout the reminder of the book, and examine the model in detail in Chapter 5.

Behavioral coaching compared with traditional coaching

The following brief discussion establishes the major differences between behavioral coaching and what we term "traditional coaching." By traditional coaching we refer to simplistic models of coaching and to those counseling or training models that are mislabeled and presented as coaching.

It is important that the ideas, processes and techniques presented in behavioral coaching are not distorted. It is necessary to guard against individuals without training or a true understanding of the model, labeling what they are doing as behavioral coaching to unknowing clients. The following points, therefore, clearly distinguish behavioral coaching from traditional coaching. We elaborate on each of these points throughout the remainder of the book.

- Behavioral coaching is an integrated model informed by the behavioral sciences as described above. Because of the breadth of these influences, it adopts a holistic, multifaceted approach to learning and change. Research and best practices from allied disciplines are adapted and incorporated into the model.
- Learning is at the heart of coaching. Behavioral coaching is based on established, scientific, psychological laws of learning.
- Change is central to most coaching models. Behavioral coaching, however, employs a validated stage model of change (Prochaska's methodology), which provides proven methods of instituting change and insuring that these changes are maintained.
- Unlike many traditional coaching models, behavioral coaching does not explain an individual's behavior purely in relation to her or his

Table 1.3 Elements of a conceptual framework for behavioral coaching (adapted from Lyle, 2002)

Concept	Purpose	Typical questions
Language/terminology	Communication Professional development Areas of expertise Comparative outcome studies	What do we mean by coaching education; skills coaching; rehearsal coaching; performance coaching; self-coaching; the coaching process; coaching interventions? (Chapters 1, 5)
Purpose and nature	Defining roles and boundaries	What are the differences between coaching and mentoring, consulting, training, HR and therapy? (Chapter 1) What are the coach's responsibilities and limitations and how are these addressed? What are coachees' responsibilities? (Chapters 1, 2, 5, 6)
Critical elements	Coaching programs Coaching tools and techniques	What are the critical factors in a successful coaching outcome? Which tools and techniques are most effective for which coaching issues? (Chapter 3)
	The coaching process	Which elements of the process are necessary and sufficient? Does coaching lend itself to a linear process? (Chapters 3, 5)
	Personal development	Which aspects of personal development play a central role in coaching? How does personal development affect coaching for work issues? How does the coach assess and explore these aspects? (Chapter 2)
	Blocks to growth	What factors mitigate against change and growth? How can these be dealt with? When won't coaching work? (Chapters 3, 4)
Expertise	Coach education and training Knowledge, skills and abilities; professional development	What are the necessary knowledge, skills and abilities for a behavioral coach? Do these differ significantly depending on the coaching specialty or niche? What are the coach's specific functions in the various coaching roles? (Chapters 1, 5, 7)
Values	Understand motivation; set appropriate goals and action plans	How can an individual's and organization's values be best addressed—stated and in-use values? What is the coach's role when there is a clash between individual and organizational values? (Chapters 2, 4)
Roles	Role conflicts; responsibilities	How do organizational factors affect the coach's role? What resistances do internal and external coaches face? What are the role differences between individual and team coaching? (Chapters 1, 4)
Measurement and evaluation	To evaluate and compare coaching outcomes; to prove value; to foster research	How can coaching programs be designed to be measurable and replicable? How does the coach manage discrepancies between the coachee's and the organization's measures of success? (Chapters 4, 5)

Table 1.4 An overview of the behavioral coaching model as developed by Zeus (2000)

Stages of change	Five forms of coaching	Seven-step coaching process
Reflective	Coaching education	EDUCATION
Preparation		DATA COLLECTION
		PLANNING (target; goals; action plans)
	Skills coaching	BEHAVIORAL CHANGE
	Rehearsal coaching	
Action	Performance coaching	MEASUREMENT
		EVALUATION
Maintenance	Self-coaching	MAINTENANCE

personality profile. Instead, it recognizes and assesses environmental factors such as culture, values and organizational and team dynamics. Behavioral coaching acknowledges that organizations are socially constructed and it provides guidelines for coaches to explore culture and to recognize and manage forces of resistance.

- Critically, on a micro level, behavioral coaching assesses behavior in relation to environmental antecedents, consequences and the factors that are maintaining the behaviors.
- Assessment in behavioral coaching is specific and related to individuals' required competencies and areas of development. Rather than administering broad batteries of assessments that may or may not be relevant to the coaching focus, behavioral coaching identifies the requisite positional knowledge, skills and abilities and targets specific behaviors within these.
- Behavioral coaching recommends a variety of assessment tools and behavioral change techniques to meet the unique needs of the individual and organization.
- Behavioral coaching does not rely solely on anecdotal, subjective reports by the coachee. It conducts stringent, objective, multiobserver, ongoing measurements of the coachee's performance.
- Unlike many coaching approaches, behavioral coaching emphasizes the importance of self-understanding on the part of coachees in order to achieve profound changes and to generalize learning and skills to other situations.
- Behavioral coaching also explores the individual's life stage development and the tasks associated with it. Self-concept, self-efficacy and self-esteem are explored within validated frameworks.
- Traditional coaching models pay little attention to unconscious forces within the individual and the organization. Behavioral coaching highlights the importance of unconscious elements and offers guidelines

for coaches to explore and work with resistance and psychological defense mechanisms.

- Behavioral coaching goes well beyond the "accountability" model, which basically involves goal setting, action planning and relying on coachees' commitment and motivation to move forward. Instead, it employs validated behavioral change techniques to insure that goals are achieved and changes sustained. These include strategies to assess and manage thoughts, feelings and behaviors.

- Behavioral coaching uses an established behavioral model that includes a structured process of data collection and assessment, targeting behaviors for change, baseline and postcoaching measurement and evaluation.

- Behavioral coaching clearly differs from outdated, deficit-based models of coaching that situate coaching in a performance counseling paradigm. It is not a manipulative technique to increase performance and productivity.

- Behavioral coaching identifies broad coaching competencies, as well as specific knowledge and skills required at each stage of the coaching process. It emphasizes the importance of ongoing professional development by coaches.

- Behavioral coaching clearly differentiates coaching and therapy and provides guidelines for coaches to recognize the differences.

- Behavioral coaching is not a "quick fix" and does not offer any magical solutions to individuals or organizations. Rather, it underscores the necessity of effort, practice and rehearsal to obtain lasting behavioral changes.

- Traditional coaching models typically focus on extrinsic motivational factors, such as the demands of the workplace and performance rewards. Behavioral coaching explores the individual's values and works on the premise that real motivation and change are situated in the individual's intrinsic motivation.

In summary, behavioral coaching is a model of theory and practice that, through the use of validated behavioral change techniques, enhances learning, performance and development. The model differs significantly from traditional coaching approaches and is increasingly identified by coaches, individuals, businesses and organizations as a proven vehicle for change and growth.

2

Coaching as Personal Development

Coaching and personal development

A history of personal development

Behavioral coaching, whether it is to enhance work performance or achieve greater satisfaction in one's personal life, involves personal development and growth. Such development typically occurs within the context of self-knowledge and self-awareness. The notion of the value of personal education and self-knowledge is not new. After all, Socrates exhorted us to "know thyself." Socrates and his pupil Plato engaged in a dialogue method of education, whereby the student was led to question his or her understanding of truth and beauty. Behavioral coaching, although it does not necessarily employ "Socratic dialogue," does, through questioning and challenging by the coach, attempt to lead coachees to a deeper and rational understanding of their own personal truths and values.

Historically, the human race has not valued or pursued the study of self. Perhaps psychological or scientific enquiry into the nature of human beings threatens our egocentric view of our place in nature. As we all know, Copernicus suffered dire consequences for suggesting that the sun, not the earth and the human race, was at the center of the universe. Likewise, Darwin was reviled for claiming that humans evolved along with all other living things. Even today, his theory of evolution is refuted by some religions. Nietzsche claimed that the trend of the mind was toward illusion, and Francis Bacon stated that we tend to believe what we prefer to be true. It is hardly surprising, then, that Freud's view of humans as being subject to unconscious forces was met with resistance and outrage by some sectors of society. Today many people continue to reject the existence of the unconscious and its role in our behavior.

While this is clearly not the place for a detailed discussion of our place in the universe, the question has significant bearing on coaching.

After all, as coaches, we promote the notion of authenticity and fulfillment. We discuss values and purpose with coachees and attempt to arrive at some understanding of the individual's existential position or place in the world. Coaching recognizes the uniqueness of the individual and her or his contributions, but does not attempt to downplay or deny our insignificance.

Freud underscored the importance of self-knowledge. He claimed that the aim of psychoanalysis was to make the unconscious conscious. By doing this, we obtain greater self-understanding about how we think, feel and act. We become freer to make choices that are in synchrony with our values and goals. Exploring our thoughts, feelings and fantasies is a pathway to a more truthful and enriched idea of who we are and what we want.

Although Freud's theories had a great impact and continue to be associated with literature and the arts, his emphasis on personal self-knowledge and growth was eclipsed in mainstream psychology by behaviorist theory. In the second decade of the twentieth century, behaviorism, which is associated primarily with Pavlov, Watson and Skinner, proposed that we study only overt behaviors and the way in which they are controlled, or conditioned, by external stimuli.

It wasn't until the 1950s, when the humanist movement arose, that notions of the individual self and growth reclaimed attention. The humanist tradition, associated chiefly with Carl Rogers and Abraham Maslow, has its roots in ancient philosophy and the theories espoused during the Enlightenment. Although they didn't dismiss psychoanalytic thinking entirely, the humanists believed that the analytic approach to life was too pessimistic because it had grown out of work with sick people.

The proponents of the so-called "Third Force" (against psychoanalysis and behaviorism) believed that people were free, creative individuals with an enormous capacity for growth and self-realization. Maslow and Rogers looked at a broader range of human experience. However, while Maslow's work has influenced education, business management and coaching, he did not develop any specific methods of self-help to enhance or expedite the process of self-actualization, which he proposed took thirty or forty years to achieve.

The quest for personal authenticity as proposed by Maslow was grounded in the belief that we all have a natural drive to healthiness and self-fulfillment. Like Kierkegaarde, Nietzsche and Sartre, the humanists believed that certain human needs, such as the search for meaning, authenticity and transcendence are universal, and part of the human condition. These existential issues are particularly relevant to personal development and growth. The existential approach to life underpins many of the theories of humanism, and, indeed, coaching. For instance, Sartre talks of the individual's "responsibility," by which he means that we are the author of our own lives.

Existential therapy, embodied in the 1960s by the much maligned R. D. Laing, claimed that the basic determinants of human behavior reside not in the past but in the present, in the kinds of choices we make to shape our future. The importance of choice, of understanding what we can change and what we cannot, and assuming responsibility for our choices, play a central role in any successful coaching outcome.

The humanist movement was also influenced by Zen Buddhist teachings. The 1950s in the West saw a wave of interest in eastern philosophy and religion. In 1957, Jack Kerouac published *On the Road*, which became a blueprint for 1960s counterculture. It embodied a search for existential freedom, spiritual growth and an escape from materialism. Individual, subjective experience was promoted. Around the same time, Allan Watts published a well-received book on Zen and the beat movement and D. T. Suzuki was translating Japanese Zen for the West. Behavioral coaching also derives some of its tenets from these teachings, which include being in the present, being mindful, transcending the self, remaining unattached to outcomes and enjoying the process as much as the outcome. As we noted in our first book, *The Complete Guide to Coaching at Work*, the first wave of coaches hailed from the generation that was exposed to these influences.

Personal growth and development, particularly for the middle class, was given impetus by Gestalt therapy, led by Fritz Perls in the 1950s and 1960s. Gestalt emphasized "being in the here and now" and taking responsibility for our choices. Perls developed experiential methods of observing consciousness whereby individuals gained powerful insights into their emotions and behavior. The Esalen Institute, T-groups and various other workshops developed mechanisms for public self-disclosure, discussion and feedback about others, as well as mutual honesty and truthfulness. Although in a modified, perhaps more conservative form, these elements remain critical to successful team coaching today.

The growth of the personal development movement, sometimes referred to as "the new consciousness," was a product of the 1960s. After an era of political turmoil, there was a growing awareness that radical politics had not addressed personal or existential issues. Individuals turned inward in a search of meaning and truth. It was, therefore, during the 1970s that the personal growth movement reached its zenith. It included transactional analysis (TA), primal therapy and est. Neurolinguistic programming (NLP), allegedly based on Gestalt and TA principles, also emerged around this time.

The 1970s, labeled by journalist Tom Wolfe as "the me generation," have been the subject of harsh criticism. The therapies spawned by the human potential movement emphasized the importance of the individual's will and the search for personal well-being, health and psychic security. Several observers claimed that this excessive preoccupation with the self led to social isolation and little concern for community. Indeed, Christopher Lasch talks of the period in the context of a culture of narcissism. It is true that whereas Freud dealt with neurosis and repression, therapists during and after the 1970s were seeing more and more individuals diagnosed with narcissistic personality disorder, which includes issues around self-esteem, grandiosity and feelings of emptiness.

Since the 1970s, contemporary mainstream psychology has moved into studying cognitive processes, and recently attempts have been made to reconstruct Maslow's theory within a cognitive–systemic framework.

Although it does not focus on personal growth and development with the intensity of humanistic theory, contemporary psychology does provide tools and techniques for growth and change. For example, the notion of challenging and disputing self-defeating beliefs to bring about change in one's emotional state and behavior is typified by rational emotive therapy, which is associated with Albert Ellis and the work of Aaron Beck. Working with self-limiting beliefs is a core aspect of behavioral coaching.

Self-help literature and personal development

Today, Gestalt, TA and NLP still exist, although in modified forms. Nevertheless, they all still emphasize the importance of self-awareness and self-accountability in the pursuit of personal growth and development. These movements all contributed to the development of the burgeoning self-help industry, although the first self-help book was written in 1859. Today, as we are all aware, there is an ever increasing array of self-help and self-improvement books and a multibillion dollar self-help industry. Estimates suggest that some 2000 self-help books are published each year. Many of these make unsubstantiated claims based on untested theories about change. Frequently, they lack any practical application. Furthermore, many do not teach individuals how to obtain greater self-knowledge and become more self-correcting and able to generate their own solutions for growth.

Nevertheless, a significant body of research suggests that, for specific problems such as depression and panic, certain self-help books or methods can be as useful as treatment administered by a therapist. Only a limited number of self-help techniques, however, have been proven to be effective. Behavioral coaching employs many of these specific techniques, which include challenging negative beliefs, regulating emotions and working through the stages of change. Behavioral coaching aims to provide the user with a general understanding of the principles of behavioral change. It also aims to disseminate useful and reliable information about how we learn and how we can modify our behavior and enhance our performance.

In addition to the self-help literature, self-help and support groups have emerged as a vehicle for personal development. Alcoholics Anonymous (AA) set up support groups as early as 1935, but it wasn't until after World War II that their benefits were widely recognized. Research suggests that the self-help movement was fueled by the 1960s civil rights movement in the United States, through which people recognized the impact of collective power. Life skills coaching in New York City in the 1960s could be defined as professionally led self-help groups characterized by experiential knowledge, support, information, education and social advocacy. More recently, a study in the United States revealed that more Americans are trying to change their health behaviors through self-help than through all other forms of professionally designed programs. On-line self-help groups continue to flourish. Clearly, coaching belongs in the contemporary landscape of personal development methodologies. Its aim is for the individual to become more self-aware, to assume greater responsibility for his or her life design and to grow and develop as a person.

Self-help: How behavioral coaching differs from traditional approaches

What we can and cannot change

Although, as we have suggested, coaching can be classified under the umbrella term of personal development, behavioral coaching answers some of the questions that remain unasked or unanswered in the typical self-help literature. For instance, many self-improvement books and courses suggest that we can change any aspect of our personality. Personal development is presented as something that can be attained relatively easily, as long as we have the will to change. It may be that we have misinterpreted the notion of "free will" and exaggerate our power over what we can change. Some research does suggest that, typically, humans overestimate their sense of control and underestimate their vulnerability to control by others or force of circumstances.

Longitudinal research on development through the life span suggests that our behavior is both stable and subject to change. As coaches, we need to recognize those behaviors that can be modified through coaching and those that are immutable. Fortunately, there is now a growing body of research into models of personal change and the various stages of change people go through. Behavioral coaching goes beyond false promises about change and examines what we can and cannot change. It presents research-based and scientifically validated means of instilling new optimism about achievable change. We discuss these methods in Chapters 4 and 5.

The notion of the self

The notion of "the self" is not clearly defined in much of the self-help literature. Often, terms such as self, self-concept, self-esteem, self-efficacy and ego are used interchangeably. Again, if we are to evaluate and measure changes in any of these areas, clear working definitions are needed. Behavioral coaching provides these definitions, as well as frameworks for coaches to work within, both inside and outside organizations. In particular, in Chapter 5 we examine the construct of self-concept within an organizational setting.

Self-knowledge

Self-knowledge is a core feature of personal development in behavioral coaching. Historically, the concept of self and identity was grounded in the socioeconomic position of our parents, in geography and in gender. A lot about who we were was fixed. These days, the individual has to forge her or his own identity and seek personal growth and development as she or he defines it. Some research suggests that developing a modern self, discovering its nature and maintaining a high degree of self-knowledge, self-esteem and personal growth can be burdensome. Increased self-knowledge, such as we pursue in coaching, can come at a price.

Baumeister and Boden (1994) suggest that what might be necessary is "a shrinking of the self" through a process of "mental narrowing" or "cognitive deconstruction." This thinking is in fact in line with Maslow's notion of "peak" or transcendental experiences, which involves self-forgetting or self-transcendence. Similarly, Csikzentmihalyi's concept of the "flow experience" suggests that individuals feel happiest when they are completely absorbed in a task and lose their sense of self, time and other people. Behavioral coaching views self-transcendence as an important element of personal development, and later in this chapter we discuss methods coaches can use to help coachees access such states.

Traditional coaching typically employs a battery of extensive tests that focus on areas of self-exploration and self-knowledge that are irrelevant to the issue or issues a coachee wishes to explore. Behavioral coaching, on the other hand, addresses the notion of "shrinking" the self by focusing on self-awareness or self-knowledge in relation to the targeted coaching issue. The behavioral coach, then, must determine just how much self-knowledge is necessary for the individual in his or her pursuit of personal development. Self-knowledge is critical and cannot be dismissed or overly embraced. Perhaps we should note Nietzsche's remark that "insight for its own sake is the ultimate snare that morality sets for us. We shall be completely ensnared in it one day."

Self-responsibility

The self-help literature typically does not address the critical issue of self-responsibility in life. It has been suggested that in modern society we consider the idea that we can responsibly guide and control our own behavior to be an illusion. General self-help knowledge and classes are not big business and we tend to resort to self-knowledge and development only when we are in crisis. Often, we wish to improve our circumstances but are reluctant to change and improve ourselves.

The notion of self-responsibility as assessed and explored in behavioral coaching owes much to the works of Nathaniel Branden, reality therapy and existentialist thought. According to Branden, for example, self-responsibility is one of the pillars of self-esteem. It includes being responsible for the achievement of one's desires, for one's choices and actions, for the quality of one's communications and for one's own personal happiness. These aspects of behavior as addressed in behavioral coaching are discussed later in this chapter.

Behavioral coaching does not highlight morality or ethics to the same extent as Glasser and Branden. Nevertheless, like both these authors, it does place importance on how the present is not meeting the individual's needs. It works with the coachee to develop more satisfactory methods of meeting these needs without negatively affecting the rights of others. Behavioral coaching adopts a systemic approach that situates the coachee in the realms of the individual or personal, the team and the organization. Ultimately the coachee is responsible for the way in which her or his behavior affects these three areas.

Control

Behavioral coaching, unlike much of the self-help literature, explores the construct of control and investigates various styles of gaining control. When discussing control we take into account research that raises questions about the nature of self-control. This includes questions about whether self-control is merely a belief or whether it is actual control, whether it is simply self-mastery or whether it also involves yielding and accommodating to circumstances. We suggest techniques coachees can employ to gain control, and how these can also be used to assess individuals and to open up avenues for developing alternative or more appropriate styles of behavior.

Self-regulation of emotions

Dealing with emotions is an increasingly popular topic of self-help books. Again, though, many of the suggested techniques are simplistic and not backed up by research. Indeed, there is often little attempt to differentiate emotions and mood, and terms such as anxiety, fear and phobias are used interchangeably. Behavioral coaching explores the self-regulation of emotions within a scientific framework, using research-based, validated techniques.

Motivation

Finally, although the self-help literature frequently discusses motivation, this is often in the context of some driving force or forces that propel us in a certain direction regardless of what stage we are at in our life development. Behavioral coaching emphasizes the fact that coaching is a developmental process and that we are faced with different "tasks" or "goals" at the various stages of development. It underscores the importance of the coach understanding and appreciating the coachee's developmental stage in order to assess and explore the issues that are relevant and critical to the individual. Later in this chapter, we discuss the various stages of adult development and show how behavioral coaches are working effectively within these frameworks.

In summary, coaching has evolved from a long tradition of personal education, self-awareness and self-knowledge. It derives many of its principles and emphases from the human potential movement and the cultural emphasis on the self of the 1970s. Workshops in the 1980s and later became more focused and goal-oriented than previously, and personal development was pursued not so much for its own sake but frequently in the context of work and work relations. Behavioral coaching has taken this further, with an emphasis on the individual and working with his or her specific goals in the context of work and life. Behavioral coaching is the current evolution in personal development. It is a scientific model that can be used across a variety of situations for individuals seeking permanent growth and personal and professional development.

Behavioral coaching and personal development

As Figure 2.1 illustrates, behavioral coaching is underpinned by the construct of personal development discussed earlier in this chapter. Behavioral

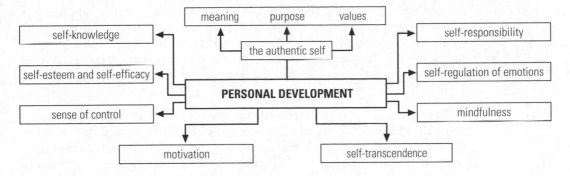

Figure 2.1 Elements of personal development in behavioral coaching

coaching is a vehicle whereby critical components of personal development can be assessed, explored and worked with to build a solid foundation for lasting behavioral change, both at the individual and at the organizational level. We consider behavioral coaching to belong to a tradition that represents a collective and universal desire for meaning, fulfillment and growth.

Personal development within the behavioral coaching framework encompasses the notions of self-leadership and "kaizan," the Japanese term for continuous improvement. Behavioral coaching promotes authenticity, self-responsibility and self-efficacy. It helps individuals to better recognize and regulate their emotions and behavior and thereby gain a greater sense of control over their lives. It also underscores the importance of motivation and how this affects growth and development. Finally, in line with many of the personal growth "movements" discussed above, behavioral coaching encourages mindfulness and self-transcendence as pathways to connectedness and well-being.

Although behavioral coaching can be placed within the tradition of self-help and the human potential movement, it is important to define some of its specific guiding or working principles. These include the following:

Principles of personal development in behavioral coaching

1   There is no single source of knowledge about what it means to be an authentic, fulfilled or "self-actualized" individual or how to engender growth and develop human potential. Personal development within behavioral coaching incorporates research and strategies from psychology, philosophy and sociology. As we know, each of these disciplines uses different standards of measurement to judge the validity and usefulness of their principles and concepts.

2   Personal development in behavioral coaching is not prescriptive. It is not another "sermon on the mount" exhorting coachees to act in ways that are tantamount to sainthood, or at least beyond the capacity of most of us. It does, however, assume that most individuals, unless severely damaged or traumatized, do have a natural tendency to develop,

grow and change. At the same time, behavioral coaching appreciates that growth and change may be difficult and that many of us resist the processes and work involved. In the model of behavioral coaching we describe in this book, we emphasize research-based methods and techniques for assessing and dealing with blockages or resistance to growth.

3   Personal development does not occur in a social vacuum. Behavioral coaching adopts a systems perspective whereby change within the individual affects and is affected by her or his environment, be it family, organizational or cultural. We subscribe to Albert Bandura's notion of "reciprocal determinism," whereby the individual acts on and is acted upon by the environment in a bidirectional manner.

4   Although personal development is situated loosely within the framework of Maslow's "self-actualization" model, behavioral coaching recognizes self-actualization or self-fulfillment as a fluid state that cannot be truly finalized or achieved. It is constantly being redefined and restructured according to the individual's ongoing and changing circumstances. Growth and fulfillment constitute a journey or path, rather than a final state.

5   Behavioral coaching emphasizes self-responsibility and self-regulation. Although we discuss these aspects of personal development in more detail later in the book, we would like to emphasize the morally neutral approach we adopt to these concepts. It may be important that we live according to principles and that we are responsible for how these play out in our lives. However, coaches could benefit from exploring at a deeper level a coachee's stated principles because, as Nietzsche remarked: "One uses one's principles to tyrannize or justify or honor or affront or conceal one's habits. Two men with similar principles may easily want totally different things with them." *(Beyond Good and Evil)*

6   Personal development in behavioral coaching incorporates the notion of "peak experiences," as discussed above in relation to Maslow and others in the human potential movement. We believe that individuals are capable of experiencing transpersonal or mystical states. Rather than focusing on experiences involving a "loss of self" or "altered states," however, behavioral coaching emphasizes the well-documented benefits of experiencing "flow states" associated with the work of Csikzentmihalyi and discussed later in this chapter.

The "self" in behavioral coaching

Behavioral coaching clearly emphasizes the self and the individual's potential for growth and development. When as coaches we talk about developing the self, however, it is imperative that we have a working definition of what the self is. Along with many of our fellow coaches, we find the following definitions to be useful. Later in the book we discuss the self in both personal and organizational settings and suggest methods of assessment and strategies to explore and work with various aspects of the self.

In line with Hamachek, we define the self in the following ways:

- *Self* is a sense of personal existence.
- A *self-concept* is our idea of personal identity and what we think about ourselves.
- *Ego* is a barometer of our emotional strength.

Research by Nancy Leonard and her colleagues has established four aspects of self-concept that have particular relevance to behavioral coaching.

- The *perceived self* refers to the traits, competencies and values we have.
- The *ideal self* refers to the traits, competencies and values we would like to have.
- *Social identity* is how we identify the self and locate and define it in the various social categories to which we belong.
- *Self-esteem* includes the evaluative component of the self, which is a function of the distance between the ideal self and the perceived self.

In Chapter 5 we examine the application of this model of self-concept to coaching individuals and organizations. We outline a framework used by behavioral coaches to assess self-concept in relation to coachees' motivation.

Elements of personal development in behavioral coaching

As illustrated in Figure 2.1, the following nine areas of personal development are integral to the behavioral coaching model:

- the authentic self and its relation to meaning, purpose and values
- self-knowledge
- self-responsibility
- self-esteem and self-efficacy
- self-regulation of emotions
- a sense of control
- mindfulness
- self-transcendence
- motivation and life stages.

We will discuss each of these domains of personal development and the role of coaching within them.

The authentic self

Behavioral coaching aims to develop and enhance those aspects of the self that constitute authenticity or what a person truly is. Individuals who live an authentic life strive to determine life's meaning, seek their purpose in life and ascribe to and live by values that are truly theirs, rather than those imposed by organizations or culture. They are motivated to seek self-improvement for the sake of authenticity. They are not, in Erich Fromm's terminology, "marketized individuals" who seek growth and development purely for higher status. Authenticity in behavioral coaching also implies a genuine encounter between two human beings.

Meaning and purpose

Virtually all personal growth movements and various types of therapy have highlighted the importance of meaning and purpose in the individual's life. In our previous books (*The Complete Guide to Coaching at Work* and *The Coaching at Work Toolkit*) we discussed meaning, purpose and values chiefly in relation to goals. We emphasized how goals had to be in synchrony with these aspects of the individual's life if they were to be achieved. In this chapter, we focus on meaning and purpose more as they relate to behavioral coaching as a vehicle for personal development and growth.

The meaning of life continues to occupy philosophers, artists, therapists, writers, poets, film-makers, cynics and cartoonists. Even if we do not belong to any of these categories, most of us have asked ourselves about the meaning of life at some time. Behavioral coaching asserts that such a question is critical to development and change. When discussing meaning, purpose and values in coaching, we integrate and draw from Maslow's work, the school of logotherapy, Adlerian psychology, Freudian psychology, rational emotive therapy (RET), cognitive–behavioral therapy, Gestalt therapy and existential philosophy.

Behavioral coaching is based on the following premises:

- Humans are meaning-making and meaning-seeking.
- Authentic living means being true to one's values and ideals.
- Although genetic and environmental factors affect our makeup, we have the capacity to choose and be the authors of our own lives.
- Our beliefs determine, to a great extent, our emotions and behavior.
- It is possible to find meaning in suffering.
- Personal development and growth can occur through learning.
- Finding meaning demands a certain self-detachment so that we can see the intrinsic value in the world. Meaning can be found *in* the world and not without reference to the world.

Victor Frankl and logotherapy practitioners claim that one should not seek an abstract meaning to life because meaning is subject to change. It is not the meaning of life in general that one should question, but rather the specific meaning of an individual's life at a given moment. Furthermore, rather than ask what is the meaning of life, the individual should ask what life asks of him or her. Each of us is questioned by life and we can answer only for our own life and be responsible only for our own life. Similarly, the philosopher Martin Buber claims that a person's foremost task is the actualization of her or his own unique, unprecedented and never-recurring possibilities. Yet what is unique and precious about us is revealed only when we know our *central wish* or purpose.

According to Frankl, the modern individual has almost too much freedom to choose. No longer guided by instinct or tradition, many of us fall into "an existential vacuum" where our will to meaning is frustrated. The existential vacuum manifests chiefly as boredom, but can also reveal itself as a will to power in the form of a will to money or a will to pleasure. Frankl suggests that we can discover meaning by:

- creating a work or performing a deed
- experiencing something such as beauty or truth, or truly encountering and loving another
- our attitude to life in the face of unavoidable suffering.

Existential–analytical understanding (which includes Frankl, logotherapy and writers such as Buber) suggests that we are only truly free to find the meaning of a given situation if four fundamental conditions of existence are fulfilled. These are:

- acceptance of a situation
- being "touched by" something
- understanding our behavior as truly our own
- the ability to recognize the demands of a situation.

Implications for behavioral coaching

The above brief discussion about meaning and purpose raises the question of how to deal with these critical issues in coaching. In our experience and that of fellow behavioral coaches, the following list of questions serves to increase self-awareness in coachees and provides fertile ground for exploration, growth and development. Typically, coaches report that coachees find it difficult to answer the questions on the spot. It is more effective, once rapport has been established and coachees have been given a rationale for exploring these areas, to give the questions as a homework task. Coachees' responses can then be discussed in the following coaching session.

- What is currently meaningful to you in your life?
- What do you think life "asks" or demands of you?
- What is unique about you and your current life situation?
- What is the core or central purpose of your life?
- What work or deeds are most meaningful to you? Why?
- What is it about your current life situation that you readily accept?
- What is it about your current life situation you find difficult to accept?
- What elements of your current behavior do you not "own" or might be carrying out in relation to the demands or needs of others, rather than yourself? What, if any, of these would you like to change?

Closely related to meaning and purpose in life is the notion of happiness. Several philosophers suggest it is an error to expect to be happy and that all happiness is transitory. Furthermore, some research suggests that pleasures wear off, that they are always contingent upon change and that they disappear with repeated satisfaction.

As coaches we have our own version of happiness—what it means, what induces it, what destroys it and how central it is to our existence. We, too, may have difficulty describing what happiness really means to us. Because of the difficulty in operationalizing the term, it is helpful for coaches to focus on the construct of "subjective well-being" (SWB). The construct of SWB, associated with Diener and his colleagues, explores areas such as happiness, life satisfaction and morale. Individuals are evaluated in terms of their satisfaction with their life or job, as well as the presence of joy in their lives.

Although several valid and reliable instruments are available to measure SWB, these typically involve only self-reports. It is important that coaches are aware of some of the limitations of self-reports and heed recommendations to use various methods to assess coachees. For example, it has been suggested that peer reports and coding of non-verbal behaviors can lead to a broader and more valid assessment of an individual's level of SWB.

COACHING AND MEANING

C. W. is a chief financial officer for a multinational corporation. He is in his late forties and is extremely competent and successful. Despite this, however, he experiences periods of feeling unmotivated and vaguely dissatisfied. A friend recommended an executive coach. As part of the assessment, the coach gave the above questions on "meaning" to C. W. As a result of the ensuing exploration and discussions, C. W. realized that his work no longer represented what he believed was central to his life; that is, developing and teaching others. Furthermore, he recognized that his behavior was sometimes dictated more by the needs of the board and shareholders than by his own needs and ethics. The coach determined that this was a central issue that could be addressed. Because of the wealth of corporate experience and knowledge he had accumulated, C. W. did not wish to leave the corporate arena. In addition, one of his strengths was public speaking. After careful consideration, including a detailed costs–benefits analysis, C. W. and the coach agreed on a plan for C. W. to develop and offer a series of seminars and workshops to other CFOs around issues such as meaning and ethics in the corporate world. The initial goal was for C. W. to research the topic over a period of two weeks. The second step was for C. W. to develop an outline of topics for a seminar. It was agreed that as well as ongoing monitoring and evaluation of each specific goal, C. W. would complete the questions on "meaning" at a three-month and a six-month interval.

Values

Definitions of values abound. Behavioral coaching subscribes to the definition of a value as a reason to prefer one action, thing or behavior over another. Three categories of values have been identified by Frankl:

- *Experiential values* When we experience something good, pleasant or true, such as music or a landscape, we absorb something valuable and in doing so realize meaning.

- *Creative values* By making something valuable, such as work or building a home, we bring value into the world and experience ourselves as valuable.
- *Attitudinal values*   In suffering, we can resort to one final value and that is to maintain the attitude we have toward life.

Implications for behavioral coaching

Each of these three values refers to the fundamental value or the often profound feeling a person has about his or her existence. In many coaching situations, the coach provides the coachee with a checklist of values. While this can certainly help to elucidate what is important to the coachee, simply ticking or naming certain values can side-step what might be a core or critical issue that needs to be addressed. For instance, research by Argyris (1982) shows that we may be able to nominate our beliefs and values quite clearly and believe that we apply these. In practice, however, we often unconsciously apply a different set of beliefs and values. It is therefore important to establish whether there is a gap between a coachee's stated values and in-use values. One way to do this is to ask certain questions. For example:

- Are there times when you don't act in accordance with your values?
- How do you behave in these situations?
- How do you feel about these situations?
- Are you experiencing a conflict of values? Describe these situation(s).
- Is there a conflict between your values and those of the organization?
- Is there a difference between the organization's stated and in-use values?
- Is there a conflict of values between you and the coach?

We are not encouraging coaches to interrogate coachees, and, once again, our position is morally neutral. A wealth of experience, however, indicates that it is in a coachee's best interests and in the interest of a successful coaching outcome if potential values conflicts can be unearthed and explored. Obtaining behavioral evidence, for example through 360-degree feedback, can corroborate or contradict what the coachee or organization is saying. We have found that adapting the distance model developed by Dr. David Upton is useful when investigating values, especially within organizations. At its simplest level, this model, as applied to coaching, views the coach's, the coachee's and the organization's values on three points of a triangle. Ideally, the three should be equidistant, as shown in Figure 2.2.

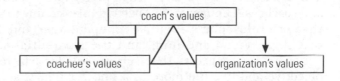

Figure 2.2 The distance model of values (adapted from Upton, 1995)

However, as Upton notes and our experience confirms:

- If the values of the coach are closer to those of the coachee than to those of the organization, the coach could collude with the coachee against the organization.
- If the values of the coach are closer to those of the organization than to those of the coachee, the coach may collude with the organization against the coachee.
- If the values of the coachee and the organization are closer to each other than to the coach's values, the organization and the coachee may collude against the coach.

Clearly, as this model implies and many coaches report, the question of values can be complex and can derail a coaching initiative. It is the coach's responsibility to try to establish his or her own stated and in-use values, as well as those of the coachee and those of the organization. Self-reflection and self-knowledge on the coach's part is imperative. The coach is not an expert on values and does not have a mandate to convert others to his or her values, principles or beliefs. Yet neither should the coach collude or surrender to the values, either stated or in-use, of the coachee or the organization.

COACHING AND VALUES

P. K., a behavioral coach, has been hired by the learning and development manager of a large manufacturing company to work with a senior colleague (M. H.) on interpersonal skills in the workplace. During two meetings with the learning and development manager, P. K. found herself feeling somewhat antagonistic toward him. All that seemed to matter was productivity; the "human element" was simply a background issue. He appeared totally lacking in empathy for M. H.'s position and focused only on the negative aspects of the coachee's performance. These values were antithetical to those of P. K. As a result, in the coaching sessions she found herself accepting M. H.'s interpretation of events without seeking any corroborative evidence. Furthermore, her final report on M. H. was biased in that she slightly exaggerated his achievements and underemphasized areas of his behavior that clearly demanded further attention. She, in fact, had colluded with M. H. against the organization. Interestingly, it was only in case discussions with other coaches that P. K. realized how her values had affected her professional conduct.

Self-knowledge

The discussion on self-knowledge that follows applies equally to coaches and coachees. The approach of behavioral coaching to self-knowledge echoes that of philosophers such as Schopenhauer and Nietzsche, Buddhist teachings, Freud and Jung, and the existential school. For instance, Schopenhauer suggests that self-knowledge can help us become more objective and live life more as a knower than a sufferer. Similarly, Jung emphasized how self-knowledge gives meaning to our suffering and joys. More recently, research by Mahoney and his colleagues has found that clinical psychologists from a broad spectrum of therapeutic approaches agree on the importance of self-examination and exploration of the self in relation to personal change.

Behavioral coaches certainly recognize the centrality of self-knowledge in the process of development and change. Not only does self-knowledge help us to accept ourselves, but it makes it possible for us to evaluate our qualities and abilities. We can know ourselves as the subject and also as an object to others. In our second book, *The Coaching at Work Toolkit*, we discussed coaching techniques to encourage self-knowledge in the form of self-awareness. Some of these techniques included exercises for being aware in the present, owning our feelings, being aware of our choices and taking responsibility for our choices. In this book, we look at self-knowledge from another viewpoint, namely in relation to the mechanisms by which we protect ourselves against knowing about our true selves and others.

Self-knowledge and defense mechanisms

We all recognize that at times our behavior is inexplicable, even irrational, although we are probably more aware of this kind of behavior in others. Occasionally we may become filled with rage over what may be a relatively trivial matter. Similarly, events can trigger anxiety that seems greatly disproportionate to the situation. We may inexplicitly react to another person with intensely negative or positive feelings that we cannot explain either to ourselves or others. These behaviors may be defending us against anxiety.

Freud believed that the mind contains processes and purposes of which we know nothing at all and that the goal of psychoanalysis is to bring the unconscious into consciousness. Clearly, it is not the role or mandate of the coach to uncover these processes and purposes. Nevertheless, there may be certain defense mechanisms at work that could explain irrational feelings and behaviors. Understanding these benefits the coach, coachee and organization.

By definition, a defense mechanism is an enduring pattern of protective behavior, the purpose of which is to protect against the awareness of something that is anxiety-provoking. Some defenses are unconscious, while others are conscious. Furthermore, some defenses are limiting, while others are positive. We have chosen to discuss, briefly, several of the most common defense mechanisms that behavioral coaches encounter in themselves, their clients and coachees.

"Negative" defense mechanisms

Rationalization is the defense whereby we deal with anxiety by concealing our true motivation from ourselves by reassuring or self-serving statements. Typical rationalizations include: "I didn't want that job, anyway" (in response to an unsuccessful job application), or "No one could work with that coachee" (in response to a failed coaching intervention).

Intellectualization involves the excessive use of abstract thinking or generalizations to control or minimize unpleasant feelings. Some individuals hide their feelings behind jargon or philosophical discussions. The coach may recognize that this is a coachee's pattern and that by refusing to acknowledge certain feelings, the coachee will remain blocked and not be able to achieve his or her stated goals. In such cases, the coach can persist in asking the coachee how he or she *feels*, rather than what he or she *thinks*, about a situation.

Help-rejecting complaining is a defense mechanism whereby an individual deals with anxiety by complaining, making repeated requests for help but never following through on any suggestions. These requests frequently disguise covert feelings of hostility or reproof toward others. Coaches, like most people, find such behavior frustrating. If such a pattern continues, it tends to augur poorly for a successful coaching outcome. The behavior has to be confronted. A firm action plan has to be agreed on and the coach should consider ending the relationship if the coachee continues to complain and seek assistance, but does not attempt to reach a solution by carrying out the steps in the action plan.

Passive aggression is a pattern of aggressive behavior whereby the individual deals with anxiety by indirectly or unassertively expressing hostility toward others. Sometimes it can take the form of over-compliance. Some typical examples of this behavior include obstructionism, pedanticism, procrastination, "forgetting" to give critical information to a colleague or "losing" an important document. At all times, though, the behavior is such that the individual remains blameless and refuses to understand why the "victim" of the passive-aggressive behavior is so upset. Behavioral coaches frequently work with coachees who have to deal with passive-aggressive behavior in a colleague. Such a situation can prove exceedingly stressful to the coachee, who may even consider leaving his or her job.

Several strategies (McGrath and Edwards) that behavioral coaches encourage coachees to use when dealing with passive-aggressive behavior in others include:

- Document the pattern of the passive-aggressive person's behavior.
- Refuse to play the game; that is, don't get angry or upset.
- If possible, go to a higher authority.
- Be assertive and insist that "forgotten" or delayed tasks be completed within a time frame.
- Whenever possible, don't work with such people.

Reaction formation is a defense mechanism whereby we think, feel or act in a way that is diametrically opposed to our true, unacceptable feelings. For example, if we have unacceptable feelings of resentment and hostility toward a colleague, we may treat that person with exaggerated respect and affection.

Displacement is a defense mechanism whereby we transfer unacceptable feelings to a person, group or organization even though the feelings were triggered elsewhere. For example, anger at the way we are being treated by an organization may be displaced on to a friend for some minor infringement of the rules of friendship.

As well as these defenses, we employ methods of resistance to protect ourselves against anxiety. These include procrastination, wishful thinking, excessive busyness, resignation and boredom.

Procrastination, or the avoidance of implementing an intention or plan, is a common issue in coaching. Research suggests that antecedents of procrastination include fear of failure, aversion to the task, aversion to risk taking, rebellion against control, dependency and difficulty making decisions.

Wishful thinking is a form of resistance that involves longing for something other than what actually is. Individuals who experience wishful thinking to the degree that it distracts them from engaging in the "real" world are avoiding life and its demands.

Excessive busyness, although encouraged in many workplaces, is a distraction technique whereby individuals devote equal attention and energy to everything and so fail to emphasize what is essential. Such busyness leads to tiredness and exhaustion, which dulls perception, so that the person is unable to see what is missing in life.

Resignation refers to a fatalistic attitude or apathy that prevents individuals from taking up opportunities. Such individuals experience habitual boredom, feel empty and apathetic and see any action as futile, as it would inevitably lead to boredom.

Boredom can be based on meaninglessness or self-directed anger. Individuals who experience "life boredom," that is, boredom generalized beyond a situation or situations, adopt passive and resistant stances toward their own lives. These may manifest in depression and aggressive behaviors. Such individuals may experience an identity crisis because they are not working toward a future of their own making.

"Positive" defense mechanisms

Altruism is a defense mechanism whereby individuals dedicate themselves to meeting the needs of others rather than experiencing unpleasant feelings or conflicts. Altruism may involve helping a colleague rather than attending to a difficult and anxiety-provoking work task of one's own, or one may choose a career that involves helping others to deal with their problems while avoiding one's own.

Humor is a somewhat underrated defense strategy whereby individuals deal with stress and conflict by focusing on the amusing or ironic aspects of a situation.

Curiosity involves dealing with emotional conflicts or stressors by reflecting on or processing one's thoughts, experiences, needs, motivations and emotions. These are then able to be accepted and expressed appropriately.

Implications for behavioral coaching

Here we have discussed only a few defense mechanisms that coaches might benefit from recognizing within themselves, coachees and organizations.

Being able to recognize these patterns of behavior does not mean that a coach has the knowledge, qualifications or skills to investigate them in a "therapeutic" sense. Rather, this knowledge helps coaches gain insight into behaviors that are counterproductive or self-sabotaging. Coaches can then explore the behaviors, not in terms of their origins, but how they may be affecting current performance and goals. Likewise, coaches can encourage and promote the use of "positive" defense mechanisms to further coachees' self-knowledge and personal development.

Finally, many coaches report that a working knowledge of defense mechanisms is invaluable when giving (and receiving) feedback. It is generally accepted that receiving feedback is critical to learning, and certainly coaching revolves around feedback from the coach, the coachee, the coachee's peers and management. Yet we don't always respond gracefully to feedback, particularly if it is construed as being negative. Generally we react in a defensive manner. Research suggests that we like to hear positive things about ourselves and that we accept negative feedback only if it confirms what we already believe about ourselves.

It is useful for coaches to bear this in mind when they are met with an enthusiastic coachee who claims to love feedback, both positive and negative, viewing it as a learning experience. While this may be true, it might also be a defense mechanism that guards the coachee against rejection and hurt. While we are not suggesting that the coach necessarily explores this with the coachee, it certainly calls for diplomacy, even gentleness when giving negative feedback. Pointing out that most of us don't particularly welcome negative feedback can "normalize" the experience for a coachee who may be feeling angry or defensive.

COACHING AND SELF-KNOWLEDGE

J. C. has been referred to a behavioral coach because of an apparent inability to deal with the company's restructuring and his new role in it. Basically, the company has grown and J. C. is not able to meet the increased demands of the new position. The company has employed another manager to work with J. C., but J. C. has refused to cooperate with his colleague and insists that he is able to manage alone. During discussions with the coach, it became evident that J. C. frequently "rationalized" his failures. For example, he had recently alienated an important client. His response was that the company no longer needed to deal with those kinds of clients. On another occasion, J. C. failed to complete and submit a critical proposal on time. He claimed that the company wouldn't have won the tender anyway. Rather than confront these "rationalizations" directly, the coach focused on exploring the competencies for J. C.'s position and his strengths and weaknesses in relation to these. The coach believed that encouraging J. C. to discuss the challenges and anxieties around the new work situation allowed him not only to enhance his performance skills but also to develop more effective strategies for dealing with his insecurities. The initial goal was for J. C. to arrange a meeting with his new colleague and to gain a consensus on their respective roles and responsibilities. The second stage of the coaching program involved the coach and J. C.

working together to develop and enhance the specific competencies associated with his new role. Measurable outcomes were set against each of these competencies.

Self-responsibility

On the subject of self-responsibility, it is possible to become prescriptive and moralistic. Behavioral coaching does not adopt this attitude toward the issues discussed here. The authors' aim is to outline the broad parameters of self-responsibility, and to show how self-responsibility affects the coaching relationship.

In *The Coaching at Work Toolkit*, we emphasized the critical role of making choices and taking responsibility for them. Many coaching situations involve the coachee making a choice, whether this is to follow a new career path or to choose to feel, think or behave differently. Individuals may choose to be more self-aware, or to think outside the box, whether it is one's own, one's peers or the organization's. Behavioral coaching encourages the individual to make more choices, to be more authentic. This may include choosing to embrace challenges and confrontation. Always, it includes being responsible for one's choices.

The approach behavioral coaching adopts toward self-responsibility echoes that of Maslow, according to whom taking responsibility is self-actualizing. Furthermore, as mentioned earlier in this chapter, we have found it useful to view self-responsibility in the context of existentialist thought. Existentialists such as Jean-Paul Sartre, for example, claim that "existence precedes essence," that is, humans have no fixed essence except as it is revealed through their moment-to moment behavior. We are defined not by our personality, but by our choices. Our choices define us and create us from one moment to the next and we choose what is meaningful to us. It is in this choosing that our freedom lies, but, as Sartre claims, "we are condemned to freedom" because our choices are always accompanied by loss of opportunity (what we didn't choose) and the possibility of bad outcomes. We may not be able to choose our circumstances, but we can always choose our response to these circumstances.

Finally, Nathaniel Branden emphasizes the importance of self-responsibility, which he claims is one of the six pillars of self-esteem. He states that who we are may be understood as a function of what we are willing to take responsibility for. This includes being responsible for:

- the level of consciousness we bring to our activities
- our choices, actions and decisions
- the fulfillment of our desires
- the beliefs we hold and the values we live by
- how we prioritize our time
- our choice of companions
- how we deal with people
- what we do about our feelings and emotions
- our happiness
- our life and well-being.

Implications for behavioral coaching

Behavioral coaches generally find that simply asking coachees how much responsibility they assume in certain areas of their lives is not an effective form of inquiry. Sometimes we may genuinely believe that we are assuming full responsibility, even though our reactions and behavior suggest otherwise.

Rather than directly asking coachees about self-responsibility, it is helpful if the coach adopts the concept as an overriding principle to inform her or his questioning, regardless of the topic. For example, when working with individuals on time management, the coach may suggest strategies to help prioritize and organize time more efficiently. These strategies can be discussed within the context of the coachees' responsibility for how they choose to prioritize or with whom they choose to spend time. Similarly, self-responsibility can be built into every goal and action plan that derives from a coaching conversation. By encouraging a coachee to add the words, "I take responsibility for..." at the beginning of every list of goals or objectives, the coach can underscore the centrality of self-responsibility in coaching.

Self-responsibility is closely linked with accountability, a term frequently bandied around in organizations. Today, there is broad acceptance that the command and control style of management is outmoded. Businesses demand self-managing and self-responsible individuals. Leaders and managers frequently ask coaches how they can develop their staff to be more accountable. These individuals themselves, however, may only function and flourish within a culture of accountability. If leaders and managers are not perceived as self-responsible and accountable, then these qualities will remain in the realm of wishful thinking and rhetoric.

Behavioral coaches working with leaders and managers explore the following questions:

- In what ways does the leader or manager take responsibility for his or her choices and decisions?
- In what ways are responsible and accountable behaviors modeled and communicated in the organization?
- Does the organization truly value independent thinking and self-management or are these qualities punished? For instance, Richard Sennett (1998) makes the interesting point that prejudices against older workers are partly related to their being more judgmental and more likely to speak up against poor management than younger workers, who are more tolerant and more likely to exit in the face of poor management.

Finally, as coaches we have to guard against using models of self-responsibility and accountability as weapons or means of expressing our own displaced self-righteousness, even hostility. Individuals are not responsible for everything that happens to them and often, as many authors have pointed out, a person's options are limited. To deny this is both cruel and destructive. Coaches can maintain empathy with and compassion for coachees while still exploring, challenging and encouraging self-responsibility.

COACHING AND SELF-RESPONSIBILITY

N. L. is a successful small business owner. Her business is performing well, but her life–work balance is causing her some distress. She has raised this issue with the business coach she employed to work with her on strategic initiatives and product development. After several discussions, it became clear to the coach that N. L. was harboring considerable resentment against some friends and acquaintances that she felt made unreasonable demands on her time and emotional resources. At first, N. L. was unable to recognize her role in these unsatisfactory relationships. However, rather than exploring the dynamics of the friendships and what needs of N. L.'s were and were not being met, the coach approached the problem from the standpoint of self-responsibility for our choice of companions. At first, N. L. was reluctant to accept the notion that she was responsible for her current choice of friends. She believed that once friendships were made, they should continue for life, during both the good times and the bad. The coach explored and challenged some of her beliefs around friendship, and together with N. L. devised strategies to limit the demands placed on her. Although the process was quite painful for N. L., she finally accepted that she was responsible for choosing her companions. Despite initial feelings of loss, she established a series of measurable goals around severing ties with certain companions and embarking on building relationships with positive, supportive individuals.

Self-esteem and self-efficacy

No discussion of personal development would be complete without addressing the ubiquitous concept of "self-esteem." Definitions of the construct abound and there is disagreement as to its importance in the life of the individual. For some psychologists, such as Nathaniel Branden and Albert Bandura, self-esteem and self-efficacy are central to personal growth and development. However, others, such as Martin Seligman, view self-esteem as an epiphenomenon. Seligman claims that self-esteem is a reflection of one's relationship with the world and it will be low if that relationship is not going well. If this is changed, and the person no longer feels and acts helplessly and passively, then self-esteem will improve indirectly. In a similar vein, in reality therapy being able to meet one's own needs in a way that does not deprive others of their ability to meet their needs is linked with self-worth. Finally, Albert Ellis and RET emphasize self-acceptance rather than self-esteem. In this view, individuals are encouraged to rate and accept their behaviors, not themselves in totality.

There are, as mentioned, numerous definitions of self-esteem. One of the most widely accepted is that of Stanley Coopersmith, who considers self-esteem to be the evaluation that we make and customarily maintain with regard to ourselves. It expresses an attitude of approval or disapproval and indicates the extent to which we believe ourselves to be capable, significant, successful and worthy.

Closely related to the notion of self-esteem is Bandura's concept of "self-efficacy." Essentially, this refers to the belief in our capability to organize and carry out the actions necessary to manage prospective situations. Our degree of self-efficacy influences our choices, efforts, feelings and persistence. Self-efficacy clearly influences our motivation. For example, we work harder and more persistently at tasks we believe we are good at, and vice versa.

Implications for behavioral coaching

Behavioral coaching approaches self-esteem as a heterogeneous concept that is always changing and developing. The following types of self-esteem as defined by Nancy Leonard and colleagues provide a useful framework for coaches to explore with coachees.

- *Chronic self-esteem* is a relatively stable, dispositional state that occurs across situations. It tends to focus on one's competencies and is the result of past experiences.
- *Task-specific self-esteem* is the perception of confidence regarding a particular task. It is the result of direct feedback from observing the results of one's efforts.
- *Socially influenced self-esteem* is a function of the ability to meet the expectations of others, such as feedback and communication from reference group members or society as a whole.

COACHING AND SELF-ESTEEM

L. G. is receiving coaching as part of an organizational initiative for senior managers. Initial assessments, feedback from the sponsor and L. G.'s demeanor and speech indicated to the coach that L. G's self-esteem was low. Rather than assuming that L.G. was experiencing chronic low self-esteem, the coach employed the three-part model described above and explored the coachee's experiences in the three realms. Careful questioning and feedback from colleagues suggested that L. G.'s self-esteem was related to his performance as a newly appointed manager of a senior team. Specifically, L.G. was feeling demoralized about his ability to conduct efficient and productive team meetings. Frequently, certain members of the team would not appear, others would not complete agreed-on tasks and morale generally was low. Having isolated the specific task that was contributing to L. G.'s negative feelings, the coach and coachee were able to focus on strategies to improve L. G.'s competence in this area. The first action L. G. agreed to take was to develop a specific agenda for the meeting, including expected outcomes. Second, he was to personally speak to each team member about the importance of attending the meetings. The measures of success were the number of attendees at the meeting, and the completion of tasks as agreed at the meeting. As L. G.'s team-leading skills developed, so did his feelings of self-worth.

In Chapter 5 we discuss these types of self-esteem, particularly in the context of organizations. The behavioral coaching model provides guidelines for questioning, as well as effective strategies for coaches to employ when working to explore and enhance these domains of the self.

Self-regulation of emotions

Managing or regulating our emotions is increasingly recognized as an important aspect of personal growth and development. Over the past two decades there has been a wealth of research into the neurochemical and physiological bases of emotions. For instance, we now know that some emotions register in the amygdala, or the emotional seat of the brain, before the neocortex, or rational, conscious part of the brain. As a result, our emotional reactions can be formed without our thinking participation and we can be "flooded" by emotion.

However, research into the functions of emotions, how they are related to our thoughts and how we can manage these more effectively has also led to increased knowledge and interest in the area. Research suggests that through a process of self-awareness, we can maintain a reflective or monitoring stance toward our emotional states. We can name them and choose whether or not to act on them.

In our previous books we discussed emotions, and in *The Coaching at Work Toolkit* we provided exercises for coaches to use when working with emotions. These included locating the emotion, recognizing emotional coping styles, getting "unstuck," accepting responsibility for our feelings, managing our emotions and developing healthy emotional states. Rather than reproduce these exercises, we have chosen here to focus on the self-awareness aspect of emotional growth and development. An awareness of emotion and an ability to let emotion inform reasoned action is needed for emotional intelligence. Being alert to our emotions, then, allows us to use them to facilitate our thoughts and maintain our self-awareness even when we are in the grip of emotional states.

Implications for behavioral coaching

Behavioral coaching emphasizes the importance of:

- assessing our emotional states
- differentiating between emotions
- identifying triggers for these states
- understanding the signals our emotions are giving us
- learning to tolerate our emotions
- learning to regulate our emotional experience and emotional expression.

In line with RET, behavioral coaching accepts the notion of a "fully functioning person" as one who is:

- aware of her or his own feelings
- doesn't try to repress feelings
- often acts on feelings
- acknowledges feelings but doesn't necessarily act on them.

COACHING AND SELF-REGULATION OF EMOTIONS

A. K. is experiencing difficulties with a particular colleague at work. Not only is this affecting her work performance, but it is spilling over into her personal life. She constantly complains of feeling "stressed," "bad," and "unable to cope." The HR department has employed the ongoing services of an external behavioral coach and A. K., on the advice of friends and the HR manger, has decided to request coaching. As the coach listened to A. K.'s experiences, he realized that she categorized all her emotions under the umbrella of "stress" or "feeling bad." The coach decided that unless A. K. could differentiate her emotional states, it would be difficult to attempt to regulate them. Consequently, the initial goal of the coaching sessions was for A. K. to monitor and put a name to her "intense" emotional states during a working week. For example, she would attempt to distinguish between anger and anxiety and between boredom and depression. Once A. K. was able to name her feeling states, she and the coach began to work on identifying triggers and how these could be recognized and behavioral change techniques employed to regulate A. K.'s responses.

While there are clearly benefits, both personal and professional, to be gained from the regulation of emotions, coaches and coachees should also be alert to the costs of self-regulation. For example, research suggests that all acts of self-regulation, including the regulation of emotions, deplete limited cognitive resources within the individual. In turn, this affects subsequent performance on a range of unrelated tasks. These negative effects remain in place until the new learning or skills are practiced enough to become automatic. We discuss strategies to regulate emotion in Chapter 5.

A sense of control

Several authors, such as Bandura, claim that we strive to control events that affect our lives and this permeates our existence. Indeed, a considerable amount of research over the past forty years or so has demonstrated the importance of control in an individual's life. Several studies on self-accuracy suggest that typically, non-depressed people tend to overestimate their control and underestimate their vulnerabilities, in contrast to depressed people, whose sense of control is more realistic. Interestingly, depressed people have a more realistic view of their own skills than non-depressed individuals, who tend to overrate them. Clearly, having an inflated sense of control can help us deal with difficulties and illnesses. On the other hand, it might also set us up for disappointment and self-recrimination when we fail.

Behavioral coaching highlights the importance of control in our lives. Acknowledging our need for control and understanding the strategies we use to gain control are critical elements of personal awareness and self-knowledge. Obtaining insight into these areas therefore is crucial to personal development.

Implications for behavioral coaching

When working with coachees, the question of control frequently arises. It may present in the aspect of an over-controlling individual or one with a diminished sense of control. For example, control is often a core issue for top performers. Indeed, research has established that "top performers" score high on the need for unilateral control. Such individuals attempt to gain and maintain control through various strategies, some of which can have positive outcomes, while others are destructive, both personally and organizationally. Clearly, it is helpful for behavioral coaches to have a framework within which to assess and explore control issues.

The literature, academic and self-help, abounds with suggestions and methods to control anger, binge eating, anxiety, panic, cigarette smoking, drinking and children. The concept of self-control, however, is multifaceted and involves our need for control, the confidence we have in our control (self-efficacy), the reality of how much control we actually have and the methods we employ to gain control. Clearly, a detailed discussion of this subject is beyond the scope of this book.

The following four styles proposed by Shapiro, however, provide a useful framework for behavioral coaches when investigating how individuals seek to gain control:

- A *positive assertive style* implies active control whereby individuals attempt to alter themselves or their environment. These efforts result in effectiveness, competence and the ability to make decisions with authority.
- A *positive yielding style* involves letting go of active control and accepting oneself or the situation while still feeling in control.
- *Negative assertive* is an over-controlling style whereby individuals are excessively self-sufficient and use active control excessively or inappropriately. These people may be possessive, emotionally restricted and dominating in their personal and work lives.
- *Negative yielding* implies the inability or unwillingness to use active control when it is necessary or useful. Such a style results in resignation, denial of the self, helplessness and feeling manipulated and dependent. Indecision, procrastination and passive-aggressive behaviors are negative yielding.

Understanding a coachee's control mechanisms can be especially informative for the coach, particularly in an organizational setting. For instance, behavioral coaching does recognize that working with a "negative assertive" individual, for instance, is particularly challenging and working with a "negative yielding" individual is often frustrating and draining. Nevertheless, simply because an individual generally acts in a certain manner does not mean that the behavior cannot be changed. As with many behavioral styles, it may be that the individual's mechanisms of gaining control are a function of a lack of self-awareness and a lack of skills to behave differently. Assessing, either formally or informally, a coachee's style of gaining control, and educating him or her about the other options can open up avenues for insight, new behaviors and growth.

COACHING AND SELF-CONTROL

R. H. has been referred for coaching because of his domineering and over-controlling manner with his colleagues and clients. During his first encounter with the coach, R. H. was demanding and controlling and the coach felt somewhat intimidated. Although clearly extremely intelligent and competent, R. H. appeared to lack self-awareness. The coach reflected back R. H.'s behavioral style in the sessions and her response to it in order to suggest how others might respond to him. At first, R. H. insisted that the coach's reaction was atypical and that his style was not intimidating. Nevertheless, he agreed to the coach obtaining written feedback from his colleagues about his manner. The feedback confirmed the coach's impression and R. H. reluctantly accepted that his controlling style was working against him. The next step was to suggest alternative methods of gaining control to R. H. The coach reported that discussing Shapiro's styles with R. H. opened up avenues for exploring various strategies that could meet R. H.'s need for control in a more appropriate and acceptable manner. For example, one of the actions R. H. took was to determine which current events he could address in a "positive assertive style," how this style might play out and what the desired outcomes of his new behavioral style were.

Mindfulness

Related to self-awareness in general, and awareness of our emotions, is the concept of mindfulness. In a broad sense, mindfulness refers to being in the present, being aware of our physical body, our thoughts and our emotions as they are occurring. Mindfulness is, of course, closely associated with Buddhist teachings.

One of the best known authors on mindfulness is Thich Nhat Hahn. He encourages us to be conscious of our every breath, every movement, each thought and feeling and everything else that has any relation to us. To do this involves bare attention, or the ability to separate out our reactions from the core events themselves. While recognizing that this is not a task that is easily mastered, Thich Nhat Hahn believes that we can learn to be mindful when we are at work, when we are doing the dishes and when we are walking in the park. Mindfulness at work, for instance, involves keeping our attention focused on our tasks and being alert and ready to competently and intelligently deal with any situation that arises.

Another approach to mindfulness was developed by Ellen Langer, who sees it as necessary for increased self-control and self-direction. She notes how many of our actions are carried out mindlessly; that is, we perform them automatically, without first weighing the pros and cons or their rationality. Langer sees mental fluidity as a way to free ourselves of these automatic or unconscious ways of behaving. According to Langer, we all have "premature cognitive commitments" and we tend not to allow new information or new meanings into our experience. Mindful individuals, however, are able to create new categories, are open to new information, are aware of more than one perspective, attend to the process rather than the outcome and trust their intuition.

Although Langer recognizes parallels with her theory and Buddhist ideas of mindfulness, she states that the major difference is in the way one develops this capability. For her, the most efficient way for people to develop and learn mindfulness is to consciously and actively draw novel distinctions about things and situations. By doing this, we can break through the rigid categories that trap us into thinking and behaving mindlessly.

Implications for behavioral coaching

Behavioral coaching does not advocate that all coaches become expert meditators and teach coachees to do likewise. Nonetheless, self-observation or self-monitoring (which we discuss in Chapters 3 and 5) is critical to effecting behavioral change. The powers of observation a coachee brings to a situation she or he is monitoring are very much in line with those of mindfulness. While coachees typically monitor specific episodes or events for the purpose of collecting data, there is no reason why mindfulness on a broader scale cannot be encouraged.

Examining a coachee's self-limiting beliefs or fixed ideas can reveal rigid categories and reveal how the coachee is cut off from new information or new experiences. As a form of self-monitoring, the coach can conduct the following exercise.

An exercise on mindfulness

Ask the coachee to observe a typical (preferably problematic) situation and to notice three new aspects of it. These three aspects can then be explored in the following session in relation to:

- how they changed the coachee's perspective
- how the change in perspective can lead to behavioral change.

The technique of centering is a form of mindfulness. Many coaches report that beginning each coaching session with a brief centering exercise or ritual enables both coach and coachee to focus on the present and be truly mindful of the coaching interaction.

COACHING AND MINDFULNESS

R. R. always arrives at his coaching sessions feeling under stress. He complains about traffic conditions and is restless and distracted. The coach, F. K., feels that R. R. is only ever partially engaged in the coaching sessions, and consequently is not deriving any real benefit from them. A colleague introduced F. K. to a "mindfulness" or centering exercise that he was using to good effect in his own coaching sessions. The exercise involved the coach and coachee sitting quietly together, eyes closed and feeling themselves present in the room, listening to sounds, and focusing on their breathing for several minutes. F. K. introduced this exercise at the beginning of each coaching session with R. R. He also employed a scaling technique to obtain a measure of R. R.'s level of stress immediately on arrival at the office and after the exercise in order to measure the benefits. Although he was initially skeptical, R. R. came to appreciate the benefits of the exercise and on his own initiative, introduced it into his work day whenever he became aware of being distracted and unfocused.

Self-transcendence

The concepts of "peak experiences" and transcendence are familiar to all of us, although our definitions of these phenomena may differ. Behavioral coaching nominates self-transcendence as integral to personal development, and, therefore, to coaching. As mentioned earlier in this chapter, we view self-transcendence as a loss of self-consciousness, rather than as an altered state.

Maslow is probably most frequently associated with the notion of transcendence, which, according to him, involves the same kind of self-forgetting that comes from being spontaneously absorbed, fascinated and focused. The phenomenon is the highest and most inclusive form of human consciousness and entails behaving and relating, as ends rather than means, to oneself, to significant others, to human beings in general, to other species, nature and the cosmos.

In his research with his students, Maslow found that peak experiences (their happiest moments, moments of rapture or creativity) resulted in:

- a tendency to view themselves in a happier way
- changes in their view of the world
- attempts to repeat the experience
- a release of creativity and spontaneity
- a tendency to view life as more meaningful.

The peak experience, or transcendence, to a great extent echoes Erich Fromm's views on spontaneity and freedom. To Fromm, spontaneous activity, such as a fresh perception of a landscape, the dawning of a truth, creative work or the welling up of love for another is the answer to the problem of freedom. He claims it is the one way a human being can overcome the terror of aloneness without sacrificing the integrity of the self. Through spontaneous, or peak experiences, we are united anew with the world— with humankind, nature and ourselves. These experiences are similar to Victor Frankl's notion of happiness as a by-product of forgetting ourselves in a task that draws on all our imagination and talent.

More recently, Csikzentmihalyi's concept of the "flow experience" synthesizes notions of peak experiences, transcendence, meaning and self-forgetting. According to Csikzentmihalyi, we are in the flow when we are in control and feel a sense of mastery. From this we derive meaning because, as discussed earlier in this chapter, meaning comes from what is meaningful to us personally and subjectively. When we are in the flow we are mindful and focused, not distracted by thoughts and feelings. Our sense of time is distorted and there is a harmonious focusing of our physical and psychic energy. We lose our sense of self-consciousness because we are at one with what we are doing. Such an experience can occur in sport, at work or while doing our daily tasks. It is, as Albert Ellis noted, similar to what RET labels "a vital absorbing interest."

Implications for behavioral coaching

Exploring a coachee's peak experiences or periods of being in the flow is highly informative for both the coach and the coachee. It establishes those activities the coachee finds most enjoyable and rewarding. Strategies can then be put in place to increase the possibility of these experiences becoming more frequent. At the same time, an opportunity is created to examine self-limiting beliefs or fears that may be sabotaging the coachee's capacity to generate and experience flow states.

Many behavioral coaches concur that the following questions or discussion points generate useful and valuable information.

- When are you at your happiest?
- When do you feel most creative?
- When do you feel most spontaneous?
- How can you increase the frequency of these experiences?
- What beliefs might be getting in the way of having these experiences? (e.g., an exaggerated work ethic)
- What fears might be holding you back from these experiences? (e.g., fear of disapproval, fear of feeling childish)

COACHING AND SELF-TRANSCENDENCE

M. D. is the CEO of a national manufacturing company. He is approaching his fifties and feels that he is preoccupied with work to the detriment of enjoyment and self-fulfillment. He spends his weekends on his farm and loves gardening and horse riding. However, even when involved in these activities, he is highly structured and goal-focused. The coach asked M. D. to complete the above six questions by writing in a journal for two weeks. Surprisingly, M. D. reported that he was an amateur, though not untalented painter, and it was painting that gave him his greatest feelings of spontaneity and creativity. M. D., however, had not "indulged" in this pastime for more than twenty years. His journal comments revealed that he was held back from these "peak experiences" by an exaggerated sense of duty and a belief that life was all about work. Furthermore, M. D. feared that his family and friends would consider his painting to be a childish indulgence and a waste of time. Exploring and challenging these beliefs and recalling the pleasures of painting allowed M. D. to begin to incorporate this activity into his weekends. One of his goals was to spend at least an hour each weekend on his artwork.

Motivation and stages of development

Exploring an individual's motivation is critical to coaching as personal development. Many of our colleagues find it useful to examine motivation within a framework of "stages of development." Although there are numerous "adult stages of development" theories, feedback from coaches working within and outside organizations suggests the following approaches to be the most relevant: Adler's "tasks" and life goals, Erikson's adult stages of psycho-social development, Jung's individuation theory and Levinson's "seasons of man" categories. We will outline each of these briefly and then detail how each one is applied in behavioral coaching.

Alfred Adler (1870–1937)

Adler, along with Freud and Jung, is associated with the development of psychoanalytic theory. Unlike Freud, Adler believed that individuals are motivated more by social urges than sexual urges. He considered consciousness, rather than unconsciousness, to be the core of personality. To Adler, choice and responsibility, meaning in life and striving for success are critical to human existence and the ways in which these elements play out are unique to each individual. It is this uniqueness that is reflected in Adler's designation of his theory as individual psychology

Adler believed that our motivation or main goal is to move toward a better way of life, to move from *feelings of inferiority* to *feelings of superiority*. By superiority, Adler meant self-improvement and striving for our personal best, not superiority over others. Related to this is the idea of what our perfect self would look like. Adler called this "fictional finalism," which helps give us clearer directions about our decisions and choices. According to individual psychology, unless we understand the individual's "fictional finalism," we will never understand the individual. Furthermore, our conscious and unconscious work toward this imagined goal, even though many of us are not really clear about it.

Adler nominates the following "life tasks" of healthy individuals:

- relating to others (friendship)
- making a contribution (work)
- getting along with ourselves (self-acceptance)
- developing our spiritual dimension.

Carl Jung (1875–1961)

Jung also believed we are motivated to reach our full potential and develop all of our unique capabilities. Like Adler, Jung claimed that our behavior is motivated by our goals. He claimed that the unconscious contains strivings other than sexual ones, such as spiritual or religious ones. He wrote at length about "the collective unconscious," which is made up of archetypes, the most important being the Self. It is the Self that represents our striving for balance, meaning and wholeness.

According to Jungian theory, our personalities are not fixed, but continue to change and grow over our lifetime. Jung postulated three stages of life: youth, middle age and old age. Youth is a period of expanding consciousness, while in middle age there is a questioning of long-held convictions. Around the age of forty the individual undergoes a transformation whereby many external goals and achievements lose their value, and, consequently, a person may feel unfulfilled and at a stalemate.

This is a period of *individuation,* which involves owning and integrating parts of the self that previously were not acknowledged or were disowned. There may be lack of conformity to the goals and values of society and the individual may adopt a new career, new hobbies and different friends and interests. Finally, old age is characterized by increasing introspection and preoccupation with self-evaluation. There is some research to support Jung's stages of development.

Jung, like Maslow, believed that we often don't achieve ideal functioning until our mid-forties. Some characteristics of well-functioning individuals include:

- a high level of self-knowledge
- acceptance of one's strengths and weaknesses
- acceptance and tolerance of human nature
- acceptance of the unknown and a willingness to heed intuition.

Erik Erikson (1902–94)

Erik Erikson was the first Freudian to propose stages of psycho-social development. In our first book, we discussed the various "tasks" associated with stages six, seven and eight of Erikson's model. Here, we will list the eight stages of development and the tasks individuals face at each stage. Later in this chapter we discuss some of the issues or behaviors that behavioral coaches might encounter in individuals at various adult life stages.

Stage one: Infancy (first year), during which an individual develops trust or mistrust toward the world and interpersonal relations.
Stage two: Early childhood (1–3 years), during which an individual's task is to develop a sense of autonomy or shame and doubt.
Stage three: Preschool age (3–6 years), when an individual's task is to develop initiative rather than guilt.
Stage four: School age (6–12 years), when the child's task is to develop industry rather than a sense of inferiority.
Stage five: Adolescence (12–18 years), during which the main task is to achieve a sense of identity rather than role confusion.
Stage six: Young adulthood (18–35 years), during which the developmental task is to develop intimacy rather than isolation.
Stage seven: Middle age (35–60 years), when the task is to go beyond the self through an interest in younger people or stagnate.
Stage eight: Later Life (retirement to death), when the individual is faced with a sense of integrity or despair.

Levinson's seasons of life

Levinson's research into midlife crisis suggests four stages of development and accompanying tasks at each stage. According to Levinson, adult development consists of stages of relative stability interspersed with periods of transition. During the periods of stability we create "life structures," a network of roles and relationships including family ties, views about ourselves and others, and dreams and aspirations. During transition periods, we are likely to re-examine these structures, and this is when change is most likely to occur.

These four stages are:

1 *Early adult transition* (17–22 years), during which the individual leaves home and seeks independence.
2 *Early adulthood* (22–40 years), when the individual seeks to achieve autonomy and emotional stability, establish a career, seek intimacy and develop an identity.
3 *Middle adulthood* (40–60 years), which involves coming to grips with aging, adjusting to physiological change, finding career satisfaction, developing social networks and leisure time and finding new meaning in life. Around forty to forty-five, a midlife transition occurs, during which the individual re-evaluates his or her life to this point.
4 *Late adulthood* (60 years to death) includes letting go of commitments, but maintaining identity and social status and achieving integrity through accepting one's life. The major transition here is the confrontation with the self.

Implications for behavioral coaching

Adler highlighted the importance of exploring an individual's fictional goal. Asking the coachee to describe such a goal can open up discussion around strategies towards its realization. Likewise, many coaches explore the "life tasks" nominated by Adler. One effective method to generate thought and discussion about life tasks is to use the wheel shown in Figure 2.3.

The coachee then nominates which "task(s)" she or he wishes to work on and together, the coach and coachee generate goals and strategies to achieve greater satisfaction in this area(s).

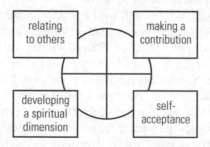

Figure 2.3 The tasks wheel

COACHING AND ADLER'S "TASKS"

S. W. is a 50-year-old woman who has recently retired from her position as national sales manager for a multinational IT company. Although initially excited about her increased leisure time and freedom, S. W. has begun to feel dissatisfied and "a bit useless." She has resumed coaching with a behavioral coach who had previously worked with her on managing a particularly difficult sales team. The coach asked S. W. to complete the "tasks" wheel. Of the four areas, S. W. was least satisfied with "developing a spiritual dimension." She stated that this realization was quite surprising to her, as she had always minimized the importance of spirituality in her life. The coach encouraged S. W. to write down her definition of spirituality, its dimensions and how she might develop these. In the ensuing sessions, S. W. set goals to read at least an hour a day on spirituality, attend one lecture a month on diverse spiritual topics and to record her experiences on a weekly basis for ongoing discussions with the coach. S. W. completed the "tasks" wheel at a three-monthly and a six-monthly interval in order to compare her ratings and evaluate the changes in her life.

Jung's approach to life stages is particularly relevant to coaches working with individuals in transition. As we well know, although a great deal of literature testifies to the issues associated with midlife crisis, individuals are frequently left to their own devices when it comes to dealing with these. Coaches are in an excellent position to explore transition issues such as:

- Which aspects of my "self" or personality do I wish to develop further?
- Are there aspects of my "self" I am only vaguely aware of?
- Where in my life do I feel unfulfilled?
- What is truly important to me now?
- How satisfied am I in my current career? What needs of mine are being met? What needs are not being met?
- How satisfied am I with my current friends and relationships?
- What are my individual strengths?
- What are my individual weaknesses?
- To what extent am I bound by convention?
- How frequently do I trust my intuition? What prevents me from doing this?
- How are my spiritual needs being met?

COACHING AND JUNG'S INDIVIDUATION PROCESS

S. E. reports to her coach that she feels her personal development is lagging behind her career achievements. Although at first S. E. is not able to clearly articulate her vague feelings of disquiet, writing down responses to the above questions has helped her articulate her concerns. She and the behavioral coach explored her personal strengths and weaknesses and set goals around areas such as developing a wider network of friends and acquaintances, and expanding her career options. However, S. E. reported a series of troubling dreams in which she was visited by demons of various kinds, or in which she herself manifested as a demon. S. E. had experienced such dreams occasionally in the past, but they were now increasing in intensity and frequency. The coach referred S. E. to a therapist to work with these dreams.

In relation to Erikson's stages of life, coaching is typically more relevant at stages five through eight. In our experience, many coaches find it helpful to view each of these stages in terms of specific problem behaviors or difficulties that might be encountered. The following list of behaviors, nominated by Hamachek, provides a useful guideline for coaches:

Stage five: Identity versus role confusion

- unstable self-concept
- difficulty establishing long-term goals
- low level of self-acceptance
- poor decision-making skills
- fatalism.

Stage six: Intimacy versus isolation

- intolerance of others
- no firm sense of identity
- lack of trust in others
- competitive rather than cooperative
- difficulty committing to relationships.

Stage seven: Generativity versus isolation

- self-concerned
- focus more on what one gets rather than what one gives
- self-absorbed in own needs
- self-centered attitudes and values.

Stage eight: Integrity versus despair

- shame, mistrust and guilt
- external locus of control—belief in fate rather than oneself
- blaming others
- lots of regrets.

Many coaches have found that using the above clusters of behaviors can help coachees to recognize how certain beliefs, attitudes and responses are holding them back on the path of development. When these behaviors are explored within the context of a particular "task" at a specific stage, a coach and coachee can work together to develop strategies that may result in altering the behaviors and moving closer to achieving the stated task.

COACHING AND ERIKSON'S STAGES OF DEVELOPMENT

D. E.'s career aspirations are suffering because he is unable to function effectively as a team player. In group coaching sessions, his colleagues have reported that he is intensely competitive and is constantly engaged in power struggles with them. The coach decided to address this issue with D. E. in one-on-one coaching sessions. Working within an Eriksonian framework, the coach approached the matter from the viewpoint of intimacy and isolation (stage six). D. E. expressed beliefs that indicated a lack of trust in his fellow workers. Because of this, he was unwilling and unable to develop meaningful relationships with them. The coach did not explore the origins of this mistrust, as he believed this belonged to the realm of therapy. Instead, the coach focused on challenging

D. E.'s fixed belief that people could not be trusted. The task was difficult, as D. E.'s lack of trust was long-standing and integral to his world view. Nevertheless, over a series of sessions, D. E.'s goal was to be able to recognize when he was acting on automatic feelings of mistrust and to look for objective evidence to confirm or dispute his beliefs. Over time, D. E. became less competitive (e.g., he no longer needed "to have the last word" in every discussion) and there was a measurable improvement in his relationships with his colleagues (e.g., fewer arguments and increased social contact outside work hours).

Similarly, working through Levinson's stages of development and the specific transitions involved in each of these can assist coachees in recognizing life structures, reevaluating relationships and careers, and maintaining dignity and status in old age.

COACHING AND LEVINSON'S "LIFE STRUCTURES"

A. T. is a 40-year-old lawyer who has recently been headhunted to a prestigious law firm. Part of his role is to "grow the business" by attracting clients. Although his knowledge of the specific area of corporate law is extensive, A. T. experiences considerable difficulty in selling the services of the law firm. This difficulty manifests in procrastination and poor time management, for which he has sought assistance from a behavioral coach. Despite agreed-upon goals and strategies to deal with these issues, A. T. has failed to meet the performance criteria of the firm. The coach explored A. T.'s "life structures," particularly in relation to his views about himself and his dreams and aspirations. These discussions revealed that A. T. viewed the law as something almost sacred, and that "selling" the services of the firm somehow contaminated the purity of the law. On the other hand, A. T.'s aspirations were to be a partner in the law firm and to have a financially rewarding career. The coach recognized that A. T. was in a transition stage, during which he needed to re-evaluate his "life structures" and patterns. Initially, the major goal of the coaching sessions was for A. T. to reconcile his feelings about the law, his own ambitions and dreams and to make choices about these.

These models offer frameworks whereby behavioral coaches can understand an individual's reality and challenges at various life stages. While it is useful to understand these challenges or tasks, however, it is important that the coach also appreciates what each of these means to the individual. How, if at all, do these challenges present themselves to the individual? Is it feasible that a coachee be capable of, or even want to achieve, the implicit and explicit demands of each stage? Are some models, for example that of Erikson, gender biased as has been claimed?

Exploring stage-of-life issues with a coachee is not necessarily an end in itself, particularly within a business context. It is a starting point for exploring the coachee's unique meaning and interpretation of his or her place in the world, as well as his or her goals, ambitions, challenges and triumphs.

Behavioral coaching is a developmental process. It is about learning and growth. It therefore emphasizes the importance of the coach being aware of the individual's current stage of development, or "proximal zone" of development. Otherwise, the coach may be working at a level below where the coachee is and may appear patronizing or simply lacking in insight. On the other hand, the coach may focus on issues and concerns that are not relevant to the coachee's current stage of development and so the coach's interventions, suggestions and explorations may be premature. Either way, little learning and much frustration ensues. Of course, it is helpful if coaches, too, are aware of their own stage-of-life development.

Finally, many of the theories we have discussed have been criticized for being static. It is true that there is a wealth of research suggesting that our responses to similar situations vary a great deal. Indeed, throughout this book we discuss some of the factors that may dictate our behavior, including reinforcement, expectancy, attribution style and cognitive dissonance. While it may be true that our behavior is not always or only motivated by unfulfilled needs as the stage-of-life theories suggest, this in no way detracts from the usefulness of exploring these stages with coachees.

The following table summarizes some of the major coaching issues that are relevant to each stage of development according to Adler, Jung, Erikson, Hamachek and Levinson.

Table 2.1 Stages of development and coaching issues

Stage	Theory	Tasks/coaching issues
Young adulthood Youth	Erikson Hamachek Jung	Developing self-concept Developing sense of identity Developing trust Developing cooperation Commitment to relationships Expanding life's possibilities and consciousness
Early adult transition	Levinson Adler Levinson	Achieving emotional stability Establishing a career Establishing intimacy Reworking, modifying roles/relationships
Middle adulthood	Erikson Adler Levinson Jung Adler and Jung Levinson	Going beyond self-interest Guiding/mentoring others Leaving a legacy Re-examining life goals and values Seeking spiritual meaning Re-evaluation of life goals/meaning Career satisfaction/change Developing social networks/leisure time
Late adulthood	Erikson Jung Levinson	Acceptance of life path Re-evaluation of self Maintaining social status and worth Acceptance of one's life

Personal development goals in behavioral coaching

As we note throughout this book, behavioral coaching is an integrative model. In this chapter we have discussed coaching as a form of personal development that derives from and integrates principles from numerous sources. The following table summarizes some of the main goals of personal development in coaching and the major theoretical influences on each of these.

Table 2.2 Major influences on personal development goals in behavioral coaching

Personal development goals of behavioral coaching	Major influences
To live an authentic existence	Fromm, Adler, Frankl, existentialism
To find new purpose and meaning	Jung, Adler, existentialism, Frankl, logotherapy, Gestalt
To promote self-knowledge	Freud, rational emotive therapy (RET), Adler, Jung
To increase self-responsibility	Branden, logotherapy, existentialism, RET, cognitive behavioral therapy (CBT)
To increase feelings of self-worth	Branden, Bandura, RET, reality therapy, Leonard et al., Adler, CBT
To promote self-regulation of emotions	Mayer & Salovey, Greenberg, RET, CBT
To develop a sense of control	Bandura, Shapiro
To increase capacity for joy and pleasure	Maslow, Fromm, Jung, RET, Csikzentmihalyi
To live more fully in the present	Buddhism, existentialism, logotherapy, RET, Langer
To review life's achievements and goals	Adler, Jung, Erikson, Levinson
To develop realistic and meaningful goals	Adler, RET, CBT

In conclusion, behavioral coaching recognizes that significant changes in personal development typically do not occur overnight and can evolve over a period of time well beyond the coaching relationship. The role of the coach is to provide coachees with questions, processes and strategies to continue along their own developmental path. Effectively, coachees will then have a blueprint for self-coaching.

3

Learning and Behavioral Change

Behavior is extremely complex as it is a function of many factors. These include environment; perception; consequences of behavior, past experiences and learning; emotions; needs; and motivation. Our knowledge base, intelligence, values, and goals and expectations also contribute to our behavior. Biological and genetic factors, as well as unconscious processes, likewise play a significant role in the way we behave.

As mentioned, the behavioral coaching model is based on the behavioral sciences, which seek to explain why people behave the way they do. It presents replicable, reliable and validated methodologies for managing behavior and effecting lasting change. Behavior and learning are inextricably connected. For example, learning is generally defined as a relatively permanent change in a person's behavior due to experience. In this chapter, we explore the relationship between learning and behavior, especially in the context of changing unwanted behaviors and enhancing desired behaviors.

Behavior refers to any measurable response of an individual. That is, it includes anything the individual does in response to external or internal events. These responses can be *overt* or observable, or *covert* and not shown openly. Covert behaviors include thinking and reasoning by which we generate ideas, plans and expectations. They also include beliefs and rules or guiding principles that act as antecedents for our behavior. For example, if we believe that everyone should be as honest as we are, then we are likely to respond angrily or with disappointment when we encounter dishonesty.

The importance of understanding behavior

We are all aware that many change initiatives fail to produce the desired results. One of the major reasons for this is that change agents and organizations don't pay sufficient attention to behavior. The focus is usually on changing systems and processes, while the impact of the behaviors of those involved in and affected by the changes is rarely taken into account. Yet leaders, managers, individuals and teams have to change their behaviors in order to align with the changed objectives of the business or organization.

How people behave in the workplace is a major factor in an organization's overall growth and profitability. However, behavior also affects the workplace in numerous other significant ways, including the following:

- Behavior affects morale, customer service and productivity.
- Behavior determines how strategies are implemented.
- Behavior determines whether an organization's demands for self-learning, self-management and accountability will be met.
- The behavior of leaders directly affects the behaviors of all individuals in an organization. As well as setting strategies, leaders need to model the desired behaviors to others. Importantly, desired behaviors must also be rewarded.
- How individuals and teams behave when having to work cooperatively with former competitors, for example in a merger, will determine the success of the merger.
- Technological implementations are shown to be more successful when individuals are coached through the behavior changes needed to manage the new information.
- Individual and team behaviors affect how successfully businesses adapt to the requirements of "cross-selling" among their business units and departments.

Behavior analysts have gathered a significant body of research and knowledge about human learning and behavior. The purpose of this chapter, then, is to explore and assess how people learn. It examines how individuals acquire, perform, and, importantly, sustain behaviors critical to personal and professional success.

While understanding the laws of behavior is essential for coaches in their work with coachees, it is equally important to share this information with clients and coachees. If individuals, teams or organizations wish to change certain behaviors, they have to recognize how their current behaviors are affecting and being affected by the work environment. Furthermore, they need an understanding of how to reward or strengthen existing desired behaviors.

Adult learning

The principles of adult learning

It is widely accepted that adults have different needs and requirements as learners compared with children and teenagers. Despite this, there is not a great deal of research in the area. Behavioral coaches underscore the importance of incorporating adult learning needs into their work with both individuals and teams. They are guided by the following principles of adult learning, which are adapted from the work of Malcolm Knowles.

- Adults are self-directed and learn best when the coach facilitates and guides them in the acquisition of their own knowledge.
- Adults need to connect their new learning to their life experiences. That is, what coachees learn has to relate to their work life and/or personal life. Adults learn skills and behaviors more easily when these are informed by and integrated with their own life experiences and knowledge.
- Adults are goal-oriented and need to clearly understand the benefits and value of coaching. It is therefore imperative that coaches clearly explain the elements of the coaching program and how each session will move coachees forward to reach their goals.
- Adults learn when they have a reason to do so. The content of coaching sessions, therefore, should always be tailored to the individual's or group's work requirements and other responsibilities.
- Adults tend to be pragmatic and focus on those aspects of a learning situation that are most useful to them in their daily work and personal lives.
- Adults demand respect for their knowledge and experience. Coaching, being a democratic process, insures that coaches and coachees are equally involved and equally free to voice their opinions about the structure, content and progress of coaching sessions.

Adults' motivation to learn

In addition to adult learning principles, motivational factors play an important role in adult learning. Adults are motivated to learn for varied and individual reasons. However, behavioral coaches explore the following four motivational sources that research and experience show affect learning in the coaching relationship.

1 *External expectations* For example, a coachee complies with the requests of senior management or the CEO to undertake coaching.
2 *A sense of urgency* As well as highlighting the benefits of coaching, behavioral coaching establishes a moderate sense of urgency and emphasizes that the changes entailed in coaching are relatively difficult for the coachee. However, this sense of urgency and difficulty has to be tempered by the understanding that individuals do not learn if their stress levels are too high.
3 *Personal advancement* Many coachees undertake coaching to develop and enhance their career prospects and/or to increase business growth.
4 *Stimulation* Ideally, coaching is a stimulating experience. Coachees learn new, sometimes quite complex and demanding skills and behaviors. Furthermore, when coaching is transformational, they learn new ways of viewing themselves and the world.

Learning styles

Coaching is an interactive and cooperative partnership, and within this relationship coaches employ a variety of learning techniques. As we all know, coachees hail from many diverse backgrounds and coaches have to adapt their learning techniques to satisfy these various styles and demands. By learning style we refer to an individual's disposition to approach, manage and achieve learning. For example, some research suggests that women approach learning in a way that highlights "connectedness" or empathy, active listening and collaboration. Cultural factors also affect preferred learning styles. Some evidence suggests that certain cultures, for example African-Americans, prefer learning in a group situation in order to achieve their goals. Clearly, coaches have to be cognizant of the individual's or team's learning style in order to maximize the learning experience.

In this section we discuss four approaches to learning styles that are employed by behavioral coaches in both individual and team coaching. These are Kolb's learning cycle and the learning styles inventory, Honey and Mumford's learning styles questionnaire, the Myer–Briggs Type Indicator and a learning profile (Zeus & Skiffington).

Kolb's model of learning

David Kolb's (1984) learning model remains one of the most influential and widely used descriptions of the adult learning process. The model was developed from Kurt Lewin's cycle of adult learning and involves four stages, as shown in figure 3.1.

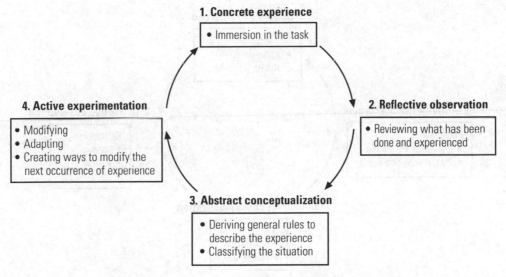

Figure 3.1 Kolb's cycle of learning

It is critical that coaches attend to each stage of the process during the learning experience. Behavioral coaches insure that the following questions are addressed at the four stages, respectively:

Stage one: Why are we learning this?
Stage two: What are the key points of the issue?
Stage three: How do I use the knowledge?

Stage four: What are the implications of this information for other situations?

Although learning involves a cycle of four learning modes, one of the assumptions of this four-stage model is that individuals are likely to feel more comfortable in one of the four modes. Kolb and colleagues have conducted extensive empirical research using the learning styles inventory (LSI), whereby the individual's learning preferences are measured along two dimensions: perception (concrete/abstract) and processing (active/reflective). The LSI is employed by behavioral coaches working with individuals and teams.

The learning styles questionnaire

Another popular learning styles questionnaire employed by behavioral coaches is Honey and Mumford's (1982) learning styles questionnaire (LSQ). It assesses and assists coachees to understand their preferred learning styles and weaknesses.

The typology of learning styles assessed by the LSQ is built around the four sequences or stages of learning, as outlined in Kolb's model. These four styles, as shown in Figure 3.2, are activist, reflector, theorist and pragmatist, respectively.

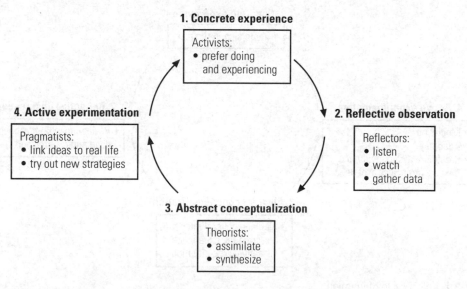

Figure 3.2 The learning styles questionnaire model

Recognizing an individual's preferred learning style allows the coach to tailor teaching and learning exercises to match the coachee's way of learning. It also helps the coach and coachee to understand the coachee's learning weaknesses. In turn, this provides the coach with vital information to help structure learning situations that help the coachee develop and enhance other learning styles.

The learning profile

Many formal psychometric assessments of learning styles require licensing and accreditation. However, the learning profile, developed by the authors and published, along with a series of assessment profiles, in *The Coaching at Work Toolkit*, is available to all practicing coaches. The learning profile can be administered in the form of a structured interview or given to the coachee to complete in her or his own time. The profile (see #3) explores the coachee's learning history, her or his preferred style of learning and potential obstacles to learning. It, too, is widely used with both individuals and teams.

The learning profile

1 When was the last time you sought out a new learning experience?
2 What obstacles might prevent you from learning?
3 When faced with a completely new area of learning, do you usually view it as an exciting challenge or just something else to contend with?
4 Do you learn best from material presented in a visual form or in a written text format?
5 Are you more likely to remember what you see or what you hear?
6 Do others describe you as logical and analytical?
7 Do you have any existing models of hypothesis testing and problem solving?
8 Do you prefer a lot of detailed information and preparation time before you begin work on a project?
9 Do your feelings play a significant role in your actions?
10 Do you consider yourself to be pragmatic?
11 When presented with new ideas, are you quick to adopt them?
12 Do you think a great deal about an issue before you act?
13 Are you more excited about "the big picture" than details?
14 Do you learn better through theory or practice?
15 Would you prefer to "give something a go" and learn from your own experience or seek advice from others?
16 Do you learn best when you're "thrown in the deep end"?
17 When you acquire new information, do you try to synthesize it and explore links with your existing knowledge?
18 If you are acquiring a new skill, do you prefer written instructions, watching a training video or being actively involved in a role play or simulation of the task?
19 What do you most need to learn right now?
20 What might inhibit you?

The Myer–Briggs Type Indicator (MBTI)

The Myer–Briggs Type Indicator (MBTI) assesses an individual's personality profile in sixteen categories based on preferences along four dimensions: orientation to life (extraverted/introverted); perception (sensing/intuitive); decision making (thinking/feeling); and attitude to the outside world (judging/perceiving). Of these dimensions, the individual's preferred orientation to life and perception are particularly relevant to his or her learning style.

In summary, it is impossible to accommodate all learning styles. Experienced behavioral coaches, however, are aware of their own preferred style of learning and how this affects their style of teaching and coaching. Additionally, as with all assessment, no one instrument "fits all." Coaches require access to a variety of learning style measures that meet the needs of the individual coachee or team. Finally, assessment for its own sake is a waste of time. Regardless of which instrument a coach employs, it is how the individual or team is debriefed that is critical. Knowing one's preferred style of learning is not in itself especially helpful. The coach has to insure that preferred styles are explored and discussed in the context of how they affect the individual's or team's work and life performance.

History of the behavioral approach to learning

In the seventeenth century, the British philosopher John Locke (1632–1704) claimed, as had the Stoics, that at birth the mind is a blank tablet or clear state (*tabula rasa*) upon which experience "writes." We learn and gain knowledge through associations. In the early twentieth century, the notion that virtually all behavior is the product of experience became the cornerstone of behaviorism.

Prior to this, behavior was considered to be the result of internal drives, instincts and conflicts. For instance, Freud believed that in order to change or remove unwanted behaviors (e.g., panic, phobias), it was necessary to explore and resolve childhood conflicts around sexuality and aggression.

The new approach to learning and change that developed in the early 1900s remained a major force in psychology for more than half a decade. The most influential names associated with behaviorism are Ivan Pavlov, John Watson or "the father of behaviorism," and B. F. Skinner. Both Watson and Skinner emphasized the study of observable events and believed that psychology should eschew any reference to internal events (e.g., ideas, goals) and focus on observable and measurable behaviors.

Learning through classical conditioning

Ivan Pavlov, famous for his conditioning work with dogs, is associated with the development of classical or respondent conditioning. Essentially, classical conditioning is a learning process whereby a conditional stimulus (e.g., a tone) gains the ability to elicit a conditional response (e.g., salivation) through repeated associations with an unconditional stimulus (e.g., food) that already elicits the response. That is, after hearing a tone at the same time as food was presented, Pavlov's dogs eventually salivated to the tone alone. They had learned the association.

It is also possible to elicit a fear response through classical or respondent conditioning. For instance, if we have a very frightening experience in an elevator, we henceforth may experience fear whenever we approach an elevator. This is a conditioned fear response. Many coachees report having had a distressing experience speaking in front of a group. As a result, the thought of public speaking makes some of these individuals afraid of doing so again, and they avoid such situations even to the detriment of their careers.

It is only by "coping" in the feared situation that individuals overcome conditioned fears. Such "coping" involves using relaxation techniques, employing cognitive techniques such as "self-statements" to counter fearful, catastrophic thoughts, and systematically exposing oneself to the feared situation. An understanding of this process is critical for behavioral coaches. If a coachee's fear of a particular situation, such as public speaking, is extreme or long-standing, then the coach should refer the person to a therapist.

Learning through operant conditioning

Another explanation for how we learn is known as *operant* or *instrumental conditioning*. B. F. Skinner refined the ideas of Pavlov and Watson and developed the basic terminology and methodologies to study behavior. Operant conditioning is the learning process by which behavior is changed by the consequences of that behavior. That is, if we are rewarded, or reinforced for a behavior, we are more likely to perform it again. On the other hand, if the consequence of our behavior is punishment, we are less likely to repeat it. For example, if a coachee self-discloses an embarrassing event and the coach listens attentively and empathically (reinforcement), the coachee is more likely to self-disclose in future sessions. If, on the other hand, the coach trivializes or minimizes the embarrassing event (punishment), the coachee is unlikely to engage in further disclosures or support-seeking behaviors.

Typically, operant and classical conditioning occur together in everyday life. For example, a senior executive reported that as a child he had made a speech in front of a group of adults who had laughed at him (operant conditioning). Thereafter, whenever he had to make a presentation he felt apprehensive and threatened (classical conditioning).

Behavioral coaching and the new thinking

A recent approach to learning, known as accelerated metacognition or the new thinking, is employed successfully by behavioral coaches in personal and organizational coaching. According to this model, traditional training, teaching and coaching approaches simply involve retraining and practice of behaviors, but do not bring about sustained change because they do not bypass the interference of old habits.

When we learn a different way of behaving, we often feel uncomfortable because we have been acting in the old way for a long time. We usually have to concentrate so hard on the new skill or behavior that we feel robotic and it drains our energy. Furthermore, whenever we lose concentration or feel fatigued or under pressure, we revert to our old ways.

A significant body of research shows that our old habits and old learning can get in the way of new learning. The phenomenon responsible for this is known as proactive inhibition (PI). Essentially, PI is the interference with learning that occurs whenever the way we currently perform conflicts with the new knowledge and skills we are trying to learn. That is, the pre-existing incorrect learning interferes with the new, correct learning by slowing it down. PI doesn't prevent learning from occurring, but it does prevent the association of conflicting ideas, which slows down change and improvement. If there is no conflict between the new and pre-existing knowledge and skills, then traditional training, teaching and coaching methods are appropriate.

All our learned knowledge and skills are protected by PI, whether they are correct or incorrect. PI causes accelerated forgetting within minutes or hours, which is why we revert to the old ways of thinking or performing. Even though we know what we are doing is incorrect and want to act differently, PI gets in the way. This is one of the major reasons why learning and changing can be so difficult. Nevertheless, it is critical that this phenomenon is not seen as a form of resistance. PI is a knowledge protection mechanism that is involuntary and universal, even though it seems to exist to greater or lesser degrees in individuals.

One of the major differences between the new thinking and traditional ways of training and learning is that the new thinking requires the individual to think about and "mediate" the differences between the old and the new behaviors. Mediation refers to the individual's ability to "stand between" the old and new behaviors and to sort out their differences.

Accelerated metacognition demands that the individual "think through" the old behavior before learning a new one. Such reflection is a means of bypassing the interference from prior learning and allows old behaviors to be replaced faster and more effectively. In this respect, new thinking or accelerated metacognition belongs to the neo-constructivist tradition because it is the learner who is responsible for learning, understanding and changing.

Studies on the effectiveness of the new thinking, especially in sports, including Olympic settings, show that after one "correction" session lasting for twenty minutes to one hour, there is an 80 per cent probability of a person performing in the new way and a 20 per cent chance that she or he will perform in the old way compared with conventional skills training. There is also a 90 per cent probability of self-detecting an old way of performing and self-correcting it. Achievement of full correction and eradication of old ways is a function of practicing the new skill. The new thinking has also proved effective in coaching individuals for anger control and presentation skills.

COACHING AND THE NEW THINKING

S. M. is a 30-year-old manager undergoing coaching for development as part of an internal coaching initiative for junior and middle management. One of S. M.'s major issues is that she becomes extremely anxious when dealing with the CEO or anyone on the senior executive team. She feels that this behavior was a factor in her not gaining a recent promotion, for which she was highly qualified. S. M. has attended two workshops on assertiveness, but has been unable to maintain the gains she made, soon reverting to her old apprehensions and feelings of inadequacy. The coach decided to use a new thinking approach and employed the following, validated strategies:

1   In line with the principles of reflection and "thinking through" old behaviors, the coach explored any self-limiting beliefs S. M. had about dealing with authority. S. M. reported that her father was extremely autocratic, impossible to please and that she was always somewhat intimidated by him. One of her core beliefs was that "anyone in authority will be critical of me." S. M. and the coach disputed this belief, and, over time, S. M. replaced it with the belief that "authority figures are not my father and I am a competent, skilled professional."
2   The coach asked S. M. to demonstrate how she usually behaves in front of her senior colleagues and boss.
3   The coach then nominated the specific errors in the presentation. These included poor eye contact, fiddling with her hair, a soft voice and sentences that trailed off at the end.
4   The coach explained why these behaviors were incorrect and the impression it was leaving on her boss and colleagues.
5   The coach then requested S. M. to again demonstrate how she typically behaves in such situations.
6   The coach then spent a considerable amount of time heightening awareness of the "wrong" behaviors S. M. was performing. This is a critical step in new thinking.
7   The coach modeled exactly how S. M. should behave.
8   The coach showed and explained to S. M. the differences between the "old" behaviors and the "new" correct behaviors.
9   Together the coach and S. M. broke down the elements of the new skills and systematically and repeatedly rehearsed these differences, with S. M. doing it the old way first, then the new way, comparing the two and describing the difference.
10 When S. M. had the two different ways clearly sorted out, then, and only then, did they proceed to practice the new ways systematically.

Although S. M. became frustrated and somewhat impatient with the systematic rehearsal of both the old and new ways, the results were impressive. After five sessions she was confidently and assertively communicating with her boss and senior colleagues. She had learned how to self-correct whenever she fell back into "the old ways." Furthermore, her changed beliefs and self-statements were positively affecting several other areas of her personal and professional life.

Transfer of learning

As noted throughout this book, the ultimate goal of behavioral coaching is achieving learning that endures. As mentioned earlier in this chapter, the amount of learning retention is associated not only with the style of learning (e.g., new thinking), but with the amount of practice a coachee does during and after the learning. Behavioral coaches encourage, even demand, that a coachee practices the new skills and continues to self-monitor and self-correct until they are firmly entrenched and become "second nature."

Another critical aspect of sustained learning and change is that coachees can transfer what they learn in coaching sessions to other situations. Transfer of learning refers to the extent to which the knowledge, skills and abilities acquired in the coaching situation are applied, generalized and maintained over some time in the work or personal environment.

Studies have demonstrated that the organizational culture (e.g., situational cues and consequences) in a chain of fast food restaurants and supermarkets was a powerful predictor of whether trainees transferred learned skills.

The transfer of knowledge, skills and abilities is more likely to occur under the following conditions:

- *Association* When coachees can associate the new information with something they already know.
- *Similarity* When the information is similar to material coachees already know; that is, it fits into an existing logical framework or schema.
- *Degree of original learning* If the amount of original learning and knowledge is high, it is more likely that new learning will transfer.
- *Critical attribute element* When the information contains elements that are extremely critical or beneficial to individuals in the workplace and/ or their personal life, learning is more likely to transfer.
- *Organizational culture* New behavior is more successfully learned if the organizational culture supports it.
- *Opportunity* There must be opportunities to perform the new learning.
- *Minimal delay* There is minimal delay between acquisition and actual use of the new behavior on the job.
- *Support* New learning is more successful if coachees receive social, peer, supervisor and subordinate support.

Reinforcement and coaching

As mentioned previously, new behaviors have to be reinforced or strengthened if they are to recur. Reinforcement is an event that, when presented after a behavior, causes the behavior to increase or decrease in frequency. Positive reinforcement is synonymous with reward and increases the likelihood of a behavior occurring again. For example, if we smile at someone who returns the smile, the behavior has been rewarded and we are likely to smile at that person again or at other people.

There are six features of reinforcement coaches need to consider when working to alter a coachee's behaviors.

1 *Select a specific behavior to be increased* For example, a new team leader's goal was to engage and align his four team members. The behavior that was targeted for increase was to engage in conversation with each team member once a day on non-related work issues.

2   *Select a reinforcer* Different things are reinforcing to different people. Generally, positive reinforcers are categorized under consumables (e.g., chocolates), activity (e.g., watching television, sport), the opportunity to do something pleasurable (e.g., time to read a novel) and social rewards (e.g., hugs, praise, smiles). Attention from others is a powerful reinforcer for most of us. Clearly, a coach and coachee have to choose a reinforcer that is meaningful to the coachee. For example, the new team leader was an avid reader but recently had lacked time for this activity. As reinforcement for spending time with his team members he chose to reward himself by reading a novel for thirty minutes every day that he met his goal of personal interaction with each of his four colleagues.

3   *Select a reinforcer that the coachee is relatively deprived* For example, a senior project manager was regularly praised for the quality of her work. However, she believed that she was taken for granted and that her colleagues didn't really appreciate the amount of time she spent to produce such quality work and the sacrifices this entailed. She required reinforcement for her hard work and dedication, rather than the end product. She and the coach devised a plan whereby the manager would seek out acknowledgment for her efforts.

4   *Reinforcers should be given immediately following the event* Of course this is not always possible. Strictly speaking, it is necessary to establish a rule that "when you (do or say something), then you can (state the reward)." The rule then becomes a cue that performing a behavior as specified will result in reward. For example, the team leader was encouraged to say to himself: "When I spend this time chatting with a colleague, then I can spend some time reading a novel."

5   *The reinforcer should be contingent upon the specified behavior and not given for other behaviors* For instance, if the coachee has three goals or three behaviors to be increased or decreased, then each of these should be associated with separate rewards. For example, a senior executive set three goals: to delegate more, to meet more frequently with his executive team and to give positive rather than critical feedback. The rewards he chose were to leave the office an hour earlier than usual whenever he successfully delegated a major project, to spend at least an hour reading sports magazines whenever he had met with his team twice weekly and to spend several minutes relaxing and doing abdominal breathing exercises each time he gave positive, constructive feedback.

6   *Natural reinforcers can be very effective* These include such behaviors as listening, formally or informally recognizing another's efforts, paying compliments and smiling. Most coaches employ these behaviors in coaching sessions. For example, a recently appointed junior manager was being coached for her abrasive, dismissive style. The coach and coachee enlisted the coachee's manager and the coaching program manager in the reinforcement process. Both agreed to acknowledge the coachee (either verbally or non-verbally) whenever she exhibited active listening or asked for opinions from her staff.

Negative reinforcement refers to taking away something unpleasant. It is frequently confused with punishment. Anything that strengthens behavior is a reinforcer (whether positive or negative), whereas punishment serves to weaken the behavior. For example, a recently promoted middle manager was experiencing distress about a project he did not have time to complete, but was reluctant to delegate. After examining some of his beliefs around responsibility and control, he and the behavioral coach agreed that he would hand over the project. Once the coachee had delegated the task, he experienced considerable relief, which was a negative reinforcer in that it reduced his stress levels and therefore made it more likely that he would delegate again in the future.

Schedules of reinforcement refer to the rules that state how many or which specific responses will be reinforced. Such a schedule determines how effective a reinforcer will be. There are two main types of reinforcement schedules. Continuous reinforcement occurs when a response is rewarded every time it happens. On the other hand, intermittent reinforcement occurs when a response is rewarded only some of the time.

During the acquisition stage of behavior, continuous reinforcement is best, but behaviors tend to become extinguished faster once the reward is withdrawn. It is therefore more effective to move to intermittent reinforcement. For example, a business owner was being coached to enhance her presentation skills in relation to prospective clients. A major area of focus was her voice, which was loud and "intimidating." Initially the coach reinforced the coachee (verbally and sometimes with a smile or nod) every time she modulated her voice. Gradually, however, the coach only responded in this way on an intermittent basis.

Extinction is a law of learning that states that if a person is not reinforced for a behavior that was previously reinforced, he or she is less likely to act the same way when faced with a similar situation. For example, a coachee was continually complaining about his colleagues in an unproductive manner. After almost two sessions of not being able to break the cycle of complaint, the coach did not pay attention to the critical remarks but moved on to another topic. As well as working to extinguish the complaining, the coach combined this with positive reinforcement by acknowledging the coachee whenever he spoke non-critically of his colleagues. An important aspect of extinction to be aware of is what is known as "an extinction burst," which means that the unwanted behavior actually increases in intensity and frequency before it decreases. In this case, when the coach first began to shift the topic of conversation, the coachee complained even more and became quite angry. The coach persisted, however, and eventually the coachee spent less time complaining and more time trying to understand work relationships from a collaborative rather than a combative point of view.

Punishment is considered the least effective (and potentially unethical) form of attempting to change behavior. As well as generating undesirable emotional side-effects, it does not generally elicit new behaviors.

Analyzing behavior

On a strict behavioral level, any behavior can be analyzed in terms of three sets of events: antecedents or the stimuli that occur just prior to the event (e.g., sitting at one's desk); behavior or what the person does or says (e.g., reading a magazine); and consequences or what follows from the behavior (e.g., feeling guilty because one should be working).

Consequences tend to have the greatest effect on learning and behavior. Table 3.1 details an example of a behavioral analysis.

Table 3.1 An example of a behavioral analysis (ABC)

(A) Antecedents	(B) Behavior	(C) Consequences
Sitting at desk	Reads a magazine	Feels guilty about not writing an overdue paper.
Feels insecure (covert)	Reads a magazine	Feels non-threatened because doesn't have to commit to opinions that can be reviewed unfavorably by peers.
Sitting at desk	Writes half a page	Feels relieved that the procrastination cycle has been broken.
Feels more confident (covert)	Writes two pages	Feels better about self.

The purpose of examining the ABC framework is to help a coachee understand why behaviors occur; that is, what precedes them and what follows them. Knowing this allows the coach and coachee to work together on behavioral change processes to manage the antecedents, behavior and consequences.

The following table summarizes the behavior change techniques behavioral coaches employ at the three stages of behavioral analysis.

We will now briefly discuss each of these groups of change techniques in relation to the ABC model.

Table 3.2 Behavior change techniques (adapted from Sarafino, 2001)

Managing antecedents	Managing behavior	Managing consequences
Modeling	Shaping	Positive reinforcement
Prompting/fading	Alternative responses	Negative reinforcement
Self-instructions	Relaxation	Self-reinforcement
Stimulus control	Coping statements	Extinction
• controlling antecedents	Practicing new behaviors	Self-monitoring
• widening antecedents	Booster sessions	Promoting generalization
Reframing	Reframing	Reframing
Self-regulation	Self-regulation	Environmental support

Techniques for managing antecedents

1 *Modeling* is the learning process whereby we observe someone and then act in a similar or imitative manner. For example, new recruits in an organization often imitate the dress code of established seniors. We will discuss modeling as a form of learning in greater detail in the section below on social learning.

2 *Prompting* involves the use of a stimulus that reminds us to perform a behavior we already know how to do, or that helps us to perform a behavior we don't do often or well. Prompts can be verbal, pictorial, gestural or auditory. For example, an executive who was being coached to enhance her performance at interdepartmental meetings was prompted verbally by the coach to "relax" every time her speech accelerated and she fidgeted with her papers.

3 *Fading* involves gradually removing any prompts used in the coaching sessions that won't occur in everyday work life. For example, after the executive's presentation skills had reached a certain level of competence, the coach refrained from prompting her to relax. Then, after another two sessions, the coach removed himself from the session room and the coachee rehearsed directly to video.

4 *Self-instructions* are antecedent statements we make to ourselves that describe, direct or guide the behavior we will perform. These can have a positive or a negative effect on our performance. For example, a team leader who was being coached for leadership skills usually prefaced his performance at team meetings with negative self-statements, such as, "I'm hopeless at running meetings." He and the coach developed a replacement, positive self-statement, namely, "I've carefully prepared the agenda so I can run this meeting successfully."

5 *Stimulus* control is the term used to indicate that a certain behavior (e.g., yelling) occurs in the presence of certain stimuli (e.g., a football match) and not in others (e.g., in church). A considerable amount of our behavior is under stimulus control. It is important to ask coachees to list the stimuli that trigger certain behaviors, whether these are behaviors to be increased or decreased. Understanding how stimuli control what we do can be the first step in changing our behavior. There are various types of stimulus control. Two of these are:

   - *Controlling antecedents* It is generally accepted that old habits die hard. We have learned them very well and even though we know the correct, new responses, we still persist in the old ways. A significant body of research shows the importance of controlling the antecedent (what leads up to or cues the old behavior). For example, an executive whose old behavior pattern included yelling and abusing colleagues at staff meetings was likely to fall back into this habit unless she learned to control the antecedents of the behavior. She recognized, for instance, that she was more at risk of the undesired behavior when she was feeling stressed. Practicing a centering exercise regularly, and especially prior to a meeting, as well as positive self-talk helped reduce her stress and therefore the likelihood that the behavior would occur.

- *Widening stimulus control* This technique involves the coach and coachee working together to increase the number of antecedents for the desired behavior. For example, rather than just working on being relaxed and communicating clearly in formal presentations, a coachee also learned to act in this way when talking to colleagues, when giving feedback to staff and when conducting a team meeting.

6 *Reframing situations* is a technique that helps us to redefine an unpleasant situation or event, thereby making it easier to manage. It is a useful strategy when managing behavior as well as the consequences of the behavior. For example, a middle manager was rarely acknowledged for his efforts. He initially interpreted this as a slight and inferred that the senior manager did not like him and did not appreciate his efforts. However, after careful analysis of the situation with the coach, the manager reframed the event in terms of the senior manager not being skilled at giving feedback. The senior manager, in fact, rarely acknowledged anyone's efforts and when he did it was perfunctory and vague. Reframing the situation in this way removed a great deal of resentment and allowed the coachee to generate a plan to actually ask for specific feedback and acknowledgment from his boss.

7 *Enhancing self-regulation skills* refers to the coach's work in increasing the coachee's ability to recognize, direct and modulate her or his own behavior. Increasing a coachee's self-regulation skills has been shown to increase generalization and maintain the gains made in coaching sessions. Self-regulation techniques are also effective for managing behavior as well as antecedents. For example, a coachee who was prone to anxiety when carrying out performance appraisals, and, consequently, avoided doing them, learned to recognize the triggers for anxiety and how it first manifested physiologically. Once she was aware of her bodily reactions, she was able to perform a calming exercise and use positive self-instructions to decrease the likelihood of the anxiety escalating and resulting in avoidance of the desired behavior.

Techniques for managing behavior

1 *Shaping* is the development of a new behavior that is not presently performed by an individual. The coach reinforces a response that at least remotely resembles the final desired response. For example, a coachee was presenting a research paper to a large group for the first time. Together, he and the coach broke the elements of the presentation into three segments: voice modulation, non-verbal skills and mind mapping the contents. Each of the segments was practiced and mastered separately and then combined into the overall performance of the behavior.

2 *Alternative or competing responses* are actions that interfere with or are incompatible with other, desired behaviors. For example, a line manager received 360-degree feedback that her own feedback to staff

invariably contained criticism and rarely praise or acknowledgment. The manager learned a competing response, which was that, in feedback sessions, she would acknowledge each staff member for at least three accomplishments. She combined this with another competing response, which was smiling rather than frowning.

3   *Relaxation* is any response that induces calmness or lowers a person's level of physiological arousal. It can include deep-muscle relaxation, which involves clenching and relaxing all the muscle systems in the body; ten rounds of abdominal breathing; or a meditation technique whereby the individual focuses attention on the breath, a mantra or an image. All of these techniques have to be learned and practiced regularly if they are to be effective, and they must be practiced when the coachee is not in a distressed state. Once the skill has been learned, it can be effectively employed in difficult or challenging situations.

4   *Coping statements* are statements we make to ourselves that emphasize our ability to tolerate unpleasant situations. These can be positive or negative. For example, saying, "This is difficult but I can get through it" has a positive impact on our behavior, whereas a statement such as "I can't handle this" has a negative impact.

5   *Practicing the new behaviors* makes them stronger and reduces the likelihood of the person falling back into old patterns. The coachee has to practice, practice and practice the new behaviors. Some skeptics of coaching claim that, in their experience, people always revert to type or habit when they are under pressure or in a crisis. These comments aren't necessarily cynical or dismissive. Such regression frequently occurs and one of the reasons for this is that the new behaviors are not strong enough to replace the old.

6   *Booster sessions*, during which new skills are revisited and practiced, have been shown to help coachees maintain the gains made in coaching sessions. Booster sessions should occur periodically, over a few months, after the coaching intervention has ended.

Techniques for managing the consequences of behavior

1   *Reinforcement* serves to strengthen new behaviors, and must be undertaken if new behaviors are to replace the old ways and last. An effective technique used in behavioral coaching is to insure that new behaviors are positively reinforced on an intermittent basis, rather than every time they occur. Intermittently reinforcing behaviors has shown to enhance persistence after the coaching intervention has ended. For example, a coachee who displayed the new behavior of listening to colleagues rather than talking at them, was encouraged to monitor the occurrence of the listening behaviors and reward himself every now and then. The coach too, reinforced the behaviors through recognition or praise on an intermittent basis. Furthermore, the coaching program manager was informed of this strategy, and likewise reinforced the coachee's listening behaviors intermittently.

- *Self-reinforcement* involves a coachee feeling free to reward himself or herself at any time when a particular response is performed. The individual decides when to deliver the reward and for what behaviors. For example, a hard-driven, time pressured Type A executive self-monitored her "frantic" behavior and then set a goal for two ten-minute relaxation periods each day. The reinforcement or reward she chose for the new behavior was swimming for half an hour every second day, an activity she thoroughly enjoyed but had not found the time for during the past two years.

- *Extinction*, as discussed above, entails not reinforcing a behavior that was previously reinforced and thereby causing that behavior to lessen and finally, to cease to occur.

2 *Self-monitoring* or *self-observation* entails systematically observing one's own behavior, on several occasions in an ongoing manner. Through a self-regulatory process, the process of observation can lead to a change in the desired direction, although the results are usually transient. The technique is usually employed along with other methods of behavior change. For example, a coachee who had anger outbursts at work monitored these events (when they occurred, how frequently, how intense the feelings were, what she or he was thinking and said or did). The coachee and coach then decided on a baseline for the behavior and they instituted strategies such as relaxation and self-statements to reduce the number of outbursts. Meantime, the coachee continued to observe and record the angry outbursts until they had significantly decreased.

3 *Promoting generalization* involves the use of techniques that allow the coach to insure that the new behaviors practiced in the coaching sessions will generalize, or also occur, in the coachee's work environment. Typically, coaching sessions are conducted in a very different environment from that at work. It is widely known that the greater the difference between the intervention setting and natural settings, the less likely it is that the behavior will generalize. There are three ways to help generalize the new behavior:

- *Fading or removing the prompts* for a behavior, as discussed above.

- *Conducting coaching sessions in the work environment* is a very powerful technique, although it is not always possible due to environmental constraints or confidentiality issues. However, for example, when a coachee is working on team-leading skills, the sessions could be conducted in the room where the team meetings are held.

- *Bring aspects of the coachee's everyday life into the coaching sessions*; for example, as a coachee continued to practice skills to build his team, two of the team members were invited to the coaching sessions. Of course, this is only possible in a culture that is open about and receptive to coaching and where the team leader has trust in the team members.

4 *Insuring environmental support for the new behaviors.* Research and experience show that if a person whose behavior has changed or improved returns to an environment that doesn't reward the improved behaviors, the gains will be lost. While praise and recognition are powerful reinforcers, the environment has to allow for the behavior to occur so that it can be reinforced. The environment should also provide *natural reinforcers.* For example, the coach encouraged a sales representative to seek feedback and reinforcement from two trusted colleagues regarding her "new" style of relating to her clients. The sales manager was also enlisted to watch for specific new or improved behaviors and reinforce these with comments and recognition.

Finally, as we mention throughout this book, the aim of behavioral coaching is for the coachee to self-coach and manage her or his own life. Together, the coach and coachee work on a plan for the individual to manage his or her own responses. For example, a self-management plan for an executive who experienced frequent angry outbursts at work included:

- Learning and substituting a calm response instead of yelling.
- Using self-instructions to encourage the use of the alternative response, for example, "I can handle this calmly."
- Practicing a calming technique, such as centering, every day.
- Rewarding or reinforcing himself for practicing centering and for using the calm response.

In summary, there are numerous behavioral and cognitive techniques behavioral coaches employ to insure that coachees have learned the desired skills and will be able to maintain this learning and new way of behaving long after the sessions have ended. There may be some resistance from coachees who assume that because they "know" how to behave and have tried it once or twice, the behavior is entrenched. Hence, it is critical that coaches are familiar with the research and the techniques so that they can provide a solid rationale for their use and can employ them appropriately and effectively.

The social learning approach—an integrated model

In the previous section we discussed two major approaches to learning, operant and classical. We then detailed numerous behavioral change techniques employed by behavioral coaches. The operant and classical conditioning models alone, however, do not account for all the ways in which we learn and behave. For this reason, the approach to learning in behavioral coaching is underpinned by what is known as social learning theory (SLT).

The social learning approach, developed and expanded on by Albert Bandura, integrates reciprocal interactions among environmental factors, cognitive factors and behavior itself. It incorporates an understanding of the cognitive complexities of human behavior with the practicalities of operant learning.

We learn and then display behavior through:

- operant conditioning, as in environmental antecedents and consequences as discussed above
- modeling or vicarious learning
- self-efficacy
- self-regulation and self-evaluation.

Modeling, a term sometimes used synonymously with observational learning, vicarious learning, imitation and social learning, refers to the process by which the behavior of a model (an individual or the group) acts as a stimulus for similar thoughts, attitudes and behaviors on the part of observers. Modeling has three effects: the acquisition of new responses or skills and the performance of these; inhibition of fear responses, such as watching someone perform a prohibited act and not being punished; facilitation of responses, in that the model provides cues for others to emulate. Models can be live, such as a coach, team leader or manager. They model appropriate behaviors and influence attitudes and values. For example, coaches model honest, empathic, non-defensive and clear communication to coachees. Similarly, coachees can learn a variety of new behaviors by observing successful peers and colleagues.

Symbolic models are the behaviors shown by an individual or group of individuals on television or film. For example, an individual being coached for presentation skills could observe a video of someone who is an excellent speaker.

It is important that coaches know which models are most likely to be imitated. These would include models of similar sex, race and attitudes as the coachee. Furthermore, models with high prestige and status but not too high as to seem unrealistic, and those who are competent and warm, are the best facilitators of modeling effects.

Modeling relies on four processes:

1 *Attentional processes* Models often attract because they are distinctive and prestigious. As well, the degree of modeling depends on how much one likes or identifies with the model. The observer's expectations and emotional state also influence how much attention is paid to the model. If the coach is modeling behavior, then it is likely to be effective only if she or he has a solid, trusting and "respecting" relationship with the coachee.

2 *Retention* Naturally, coachees have to recognize and remember the observed behavior. Mentally and physically rehearsing new behaviors is critical if coachees are to retain the learning.

3 *Production* Simply observing a behavior doesn't mean that it can be produced by others. Coachees may not have the required skills to perform the behavior and may require skills training to master it.

4 *Motivation* Unless coachees can clearly recognize the rewards of performing the modeled behavior, there will be no motivation to attain it.

Self-efficacy is an important concept for Albert Bandura, who, as mentioned, developed this construct. Self-efficacy refers to the judgments individuals make about how well they can perform a task. It depends on the performance standards we set or are set by others. In behavioral coaching, it is especially important to consider this concept when there are no externally set performance standards or other task-related modeled or learned behaviors, for example, when coaching for career development.

How we judge ourselves derives from a variety of sources. These include how we performed previously; our prior failures and successes; how successfully these behaviors or strategies have been employed by others; how much encouragement we receive from others; and our emotional state at the particular time. Coachees' levels of self-efficacy affect their choice of goals, how much effort they will expend and how much they will persevere in their efforts to change their behavior.

Research shows that self-efficacy mediates a number of variables, including job satisfaction, organizational commitment and intention to leave a job. It is also significantly related to health outcomes, academic outcomes, and enhanced work performance.

Self-regulation and self-evaluation processes act on what we learn through experience or modeling. The individual sets performance standards, such as a performance goal, as a part of self-evaluation and self-efficacy. Behavior feedback is then tested against these standards. If there is a discrepancy, the self-regulation system adjusts its behavior. For instance, when the individual creates a higher performance standard, there is a performance discrepancy, which is reduced by increasing performance. The feedback on the adjusted behavior provides new input and the system continues until the input matches the higher standard.

Finally, self-efficacy is also used as an outcome measure in coaching. It is an effective evaluation measure of a coachee's performance, especially of "soft skills." For example, behavioral coaches measure a coachee's self-efficacy regarding a particular skill, such as leading a team meeting, at the beginning of the coaching sessions, halfway through, and at the end.

Self-regulation of emotions

Although behavioral coaching, by definition, implies an emphasis on behavior, it does not negate the role emotions play in our personal and professional lives. Emotions can affect a wide variety of phenomena in the workplace, including learning and memory, social interaction, self-evaluation, evaluation of others, decision making and irrational or limiting beliefs.

According to Mayer and Salovey (1995), who developed the construct of emotional intelligence, individuals need an awareness of emotion and the ability to allow it to inform reasoned action. Regulation of emotion refers to the process whereby individuals influence which emotions they have, when they have them and how they experience and express these.

There are numerous methods of working with emotions. The following approach is employed by behavioral coaches in a variety of coaching situations.

Step one: Help the coachee become aware of his or her emotions and the physiological responses and thoughts that accompany them.

Step two: Ask the coachee to name the emotion(s).

Step three: Together, identify any beliefs that may be triggering the negative emotions.

Step four: Use the A-F model to challenge the belief(s). That is, establish:

> A— The activating event, e.g., giving a presentation
>
> B— The self-limiting *belief* about the event, e.g., "If I don't give a perfect presentation, my boss will think I'm stupid."
>
> C— The consequences, e.g., anxiety and avoidance
>
> D— Dispute the belief, e.g., Is it realistic to expect to give a perfect presentation? Is it logical that if my presentation falls short of "perfect" my boss will think I'm stupid? How is believing this helping me?
>
> E— An effective new belief(s), e.g., "Giving a perfect presentation is probably impossible, and there is no evidence to suggest that my boss will think I'm stupid if my presentation isn't perfect. Holding on to this idea is making me more nervous and is not helping."
>
> F— New feelings, e.g., more confident, less intimidated.

Step five: Employ, where appropriate, other behavioral change techniques. These include *stimulus control*, whereby a coachee avoids a situation that generates anxiety or distress (e.g., working with a particular colleague on a project) or modifies an existing situation (e.g., corresponds with an angry colleague by email or only in the presence of others); and *attentional deployment*, which is using distraction to draw attention away from the emotional experience (e.g., focusing on something bright or colorful in the environment), or focusing on the physiological facets of the emotion (e.g., heart rate, posture or muscular tension).

COACHING AND SELF-REGULATING EMOTIONS

R. M. is receiving coaching to "groom" him for a new position that involves increased contact with an administration person with whom he has difficulties. Almost every encounter with this person results in R. M. becoming frustrated and upset and storming out of the room. He identifies anger as the core emotion, which first manifests in a tightening of his neck muscles. The behavioral coach examined R. M.'s beliefs around these incidents. At first, R. M. dismissed his co-worker as "just stupid." However, further exploration and disputing of the belief revealed that the administration person was, in fact, very competent, highly regarded and had good working relations with R. M.'s colleagues. R. M. conceded that his behavior may well have been in response to his demanding, impatient manner. As well as establishing a new belief about the relationship, the behavioral coach and R. M. worked on change strategies to manage his behavior. R. M. agreed to correspond with his colleague as much as possible by email, and to use a calming self-statement and a brief muscle relaxation exercise prior to any face-to-face contact.

Learning in organizations

Although definitions of learning organizations abound, it is generally agreed that while individuals learn, the organization provides a holding environment for knowledge. Organizations are places where people learn and accumulate knowledge, and they control the processes by which knowledge is created, acquired, distributed and used to reach long-term business objectives. Organizations, then, learn through the learning of their members or by introducing new members with new knowledge. However, it has been suggested that the terms "corporate knowledge" and "corporate intelligence" seem to imply that knowledge is more than the sum of knowledge of an organization's individual members.

The traditional view of learning organizations is that they are responsible for keeping people happy and informed, but have little responsibility and accountability for making changes themselves. This attitude, according to Argyris, can actually impede learning. On the contrary, true learning organizations need people who have learned to take active responsibility for their own behavior, develop and share information about their jobs and have and use genuine power to shape and effect lasting solutions. One of the goals of behavioral coaches is to promote accountability and initiate discussion around learning and responsibility in an organization.

Behavioral coaching subscribes to the concept of a learning organization as one where individuals are supported by a culture that values and promotes learning. By fostering learning, an organization allows individuals to achieve behavioral change and transformation. Importantly, behavioral coaching acknowledges that learning organizations do not occur spontaneously. They have to be developed through conscious interventions, such as coaching, which insure that individuals learn information that can be systematized and passed on to the team. In turn, the team's knowledge is available to the organization as a whole in an ongoing cycle.

The characteristics of a learning organization

There is some agreement on the characteristics of a learning organization. An understanding of these features is essential for any organizational change agent. It allows the change agent to understand an organization's culture; find out whether it truly values learning and development, and, if so, how it does this; and develop a checklist of desired characteristics to set goals and objectives around when coaching people in the organization.

There is consensus that the defining characteristics of a learning organization are that it encourages:

- creative problem finding and solving
- critical thinking

- reflection and "generative learning," which involves a capacity to create the vision the organization holds
- trust between all members
- open communication at all levels
- risk taking
- creative conflict around work-related issues rather than personality and emotions
- accountability and self-responsibility
- recognition of members as "units of free will" who are responsible for their own learning
- continuous enquiry
- appreciation of its own and its members' strengths
- individuals to act according to their own values and to align these with corporate values rather than imposing corporate values
- diversity in its composition and points of view
- a collective, communicated vision and objectives
- teamwork
- reflection that is non-judgmental and encourages different perspectives and paradigms
- intuition and emotional learning.

The organization's environment and learning follow-through

Most of us would agree that economic, sociocultural and technological factors are demanding that organizations pay attention to their "human capital." Businesses and organizations recognize that workplace learning on a continuous basis is essential if they are to survive, least of all compete. To meet this need, organizations invest from 50 billion to 200 billion dollars annually.

Nevertheless, a great deal of research shows that a significant amount of this investment is wasted and that much learning and training is never followed through in the workplace. For instance, only 15 per cent of managers who attend a course, management meeting or conference or receive 360-degree feedback actually take any action to put this learning in place. As we note throughout this book, substantial follow-through is critical to any successful coaching program.

It has also been shown that the most important factors influencing postlearning follow-through are often outside the context of the learning situation. For example, competing priorities or commitments are a major reason for lack of follow-through on initiated learning and change. Some of these commitments include incoming work demands, distraction and a short-term rather than a long-term focus. Lack of follow-through is frequently attributed to time pressures, with individuals feeling there is not enough time and that they have no control over their own time.

In addition, when members perceive that organizational support is lacking, there is a absence of motivation or willingness to devote the time and effort to follow-through learning. Typically, in the face of a perceived lack of commitment from managers or senior executives, follow-through efforts are abandoned. When a coachee's learning and change efforts are not reinforced by approval, praise or recognition, new behaviors, as mentioned above, are less likely to recur.

Behavioral coaches need to insure that there is organizational support for follow-through on what is learned in coaching sessions. Prior to the commencement of a coaching program, senior executives have to be aligned to the process. One way to increase the probability of such alignment is to tie the individual coachee's development plan to the organization's objectives. These development plans, of course, have to be in synchrony with the individual's values and objectives. Moreover, available resources and any organizational constraints on the transfer of knowledge, skills and abilities have to be discussed openly and honestly in a forum that engenders creative problem solving.

What individuals learn in the coaching sessions is frequently reinforced in the workplace. Reinforcers or rewards, as noted, must be meaningful. Some rewards include promotions, corporate financial incentives, and personal and professional recognition. Ideally, in a true learning organization, a coachee's goals and objectives are made visible to others and their impact on business objectives are recognized by team members and the organization. As well as acting as positive reinforcement, these factors can serve as a negative reinforcer because coachees arc more likely to adhere to their commitments in order to alleviate any guilt or discomfort associated with not following through.

Another critical factor regarding follow-through is accountability. Ideally, a coaching program manager or senior manager can be appointed to insure that learning continues after a program has ceased. This person is responsible for guaranteeing that coachees have the opportunity to continue to practice their new skills. In turn, coachees report to that person on what they have done to follow through on their learning. These arrangements should be agreed on by the coach, coachees and third party during the course of the coaching program. In this way, any changes to the process can be addressed while the coaching is still taking place. Otherwise, it will probably be too late and the follow-through plan will flounder. We discuss these issues in detail in Chapters 5 and 6.

Coaches cannot create a learning organization. Nevertheless, understanding the qualities of such an organization can help them generate conditions that foster self-learning and accountability. Understanding the factors that impede follow-through and educating the client and coachees about these can insure that learning is not wasted, that the goals and objectives of the coaching program are achieved and that behavioral change and transformation occur.

Motivation in organizations

Over time numerous theories have been developed to explain what motivates or propels individual behavior in a particular direction. In Chapter 2, we discussed motivation in terms of drives and goals and in relation to developmental stages. Here, we are focusing on "self-concept based motivation," which explains some of the diversity of behaviors found in an organizational setting, according to Nancy Leonard and colleagues.

The concept of self is composed of four interrelated elements: self-perception, the ideal self, social identities and self-esteem.

1 *The perceived self* includes self-perceptions of actual traits (relatively permanent patterns of behavior, e.g., conscientiousness), competencies (knowledge, skills, abilities and talents) and values (behaviors that guide selection and evaluation of behavioral events).

2 *The ideal self* represents the traits, competencies and values a person would like to have. The ideal self develops in early interactions with the family or a work group. If the individual receives positive feedback, she or he becomes inner-directed and traits, competencies and values are internalized. If the feedback is negative or conditional, however, the individual becomes other-directed and may withdraw or seek constant feedback from other group members.

3 *Social identities* are our definitions of self in relation to the social categories to which we belong. The reference groups define the role expectations and norms that guide the individual within each of his or her social identities. We have two sets of identities: a global identity, or one that is portrayed across all situations; and role-specific identities.

4 *Self-esteem* is the evaluative component of the self and is a function of the gap between the perceived self and the ideal self. As mentioned briefly in Chapter 2, there are three types of self-esteem:

   • *Chronic self-esteem* is a relatively stable, dispositional trait occurring across situations. It is the result of past experiences and focuses on our competencies.
   • *Task-specific self-esteem* refers to self-perception and confidence concerning a specific task.
   • *Socially influenced self-esteem* is a function of the expectations of others. It is a result of communication and feedback from an individual's reference group or from society as a whole regarding the value of an identity and the ability to meet the expectations of the reference group and society.

These four aspects of self-concept determine how an individual is motivated to behave in an organizational setting, and behavioral coaches assess coachees in relation to these elements. We outline a working model for assessing self-concept in Chapter 5.

Motivational processes and self-concept

Behavioral coaches are cognizant of four other motivational processes that play out in organizational settings and are related to self-concept. These are expectancy, attribution, cognitive dissonance and reinforcement.

1 *Expectancy* is a cognitively based approach to motivation and the management of human behavior. It considers motivation to be a function of three components:

- *Expectancy*, or the perceived possibility that effort will lead to the desired result.
- *Instrumentality*, or the perceived probability that an effort will lead to the desired result.
- *Valence*, or the value or attractiveness of a given reward or outcome to the individual.

Coachees, therefore, assess the likelihood of certain actions leading to types of task and/or social feedback that are consistent with their self-concept.

2 *Attribution* focuses on the way individuals attempt to account for the causes of behavior. Typically, we make external attributions (e.g., that someone's behavior is due to situational factors) or internal attributions (e.g., that behavior is the result of a personality or values). In relation to self-concept, outer-directed individuals want the traits, competencies and values of the reference group to be attributed to themselves. They may seek control over group projects so that the outcomes are attributed to their own efforts and skills. On the other hand, inner-directed individuals seek control over task outcomes for their own, personal satisfaction.

3 *Cognitive dissonance* refers to the state of tension that exists when a person holds inconsistent beliefs or attitudes and is motivated to reduce this dissonance. Understanding a coachee's self-concept helps a coach to appreciate how feedback from herself or himself and peers will affect the coachee and which strategies the coachee might adopt to reduce inconsistency. Such knowledge is powerful because, as we know, giving feedback is at the core of coaching and coaches sometimes struggle with a coachee who seems determined to reject it. The following is a brief list of how coachees sometimes respond to feedback that is inconsistent with their self-concept. They may:

- make a greater effort to improve future feedback
- discredit the source of feedback
- argue against the feedback
- dissociate from the outcome of the project; that is, publicly show that he or she wasn't really trying or isn't really responsible. The individual cannot therefore be judged on the traits, competencies and values associated with the outcome.
- try to convince self and others that a particular trait, competency or value is not important
- avoid the opportunity for feedback.

4 *Reinforcement* refers to task and social feedback that confirms self-perception. Where it is lacking, vague or inconsistent, coachees are motivated to obtain greater task or social feedback.

Motivation and the "referred" coachee

Motivation is frequently an issue in relation to coachees who have been "referred" for coaching. Behavioral coaches find it helpful to view the individual's situation in the light of self-determination theory, which introduces a continuum from "controlled behavior" (or taking action because you have to) to autonomous behavior (doing something because it is one's choice). Essentially, people are more likely to take action when they choose to do so.

For example, it can happen that managers and others in an organization who have assumed a coaching role are very action-oriented and take a confrontational approach to an individual's need to change. They set themselves up as experts with a prescription for change. Even if the coachee does change, she or he may do so under pressure and feelings of coercion. On the other hand, the coachee who operates within a framework of autonomy believes that he or she has personal control and that initiating, performing and maintaining behavioral change is an internal matter. The individual has identified the value of coaching and chooses to become involved in the partnership.

Behavioral coaches, whether functioning in an internal or external role in an organization, have to increase coachees' level of autonomy, and, therefore, motivation. Employing a decision balance in order to weigh up the benefits of changing and of not changing increases motivation.

For example, a coach was working with a senior manager who had been "referred" for coaching and was initially skeptical and uncommitted. In order to work through these obstacles, the coach employed the following questions as discussion points:

- What are the gaps between where your business unit is now and where it wants to be?
- What are the advantages of coaching and changing?
- What are the disadvantages of coaching and change?
- Do the advantages outweigh the disadvantages?

After considering these questions and engaging in dialogue with the coach, the coachee decided that the benefits of coaching outweighed the disadvantages. Because the coachee had made her own decision about undertaking coaching, she had moved further along the autonomy dimension and increased the probability of long-term success.

In summary, motivation is a complex and multifaceted phenomenon. Coaches are faced with numerous frameworks and theories within which to view the individual coachee's behavior. We agree that certain approaches are more suited to certain coaching issues. One of the tasks of the behavioral coach is to determine which theory or approach best guides their work with a specific coachee. For example:

- If an individual is faced with making choices, exploring the expectancy or the self-determination approach is useful.
- Examining a coachee's attributions is relevant to interpersonal difficulties, especially where there is a gap between the coachee's explanations of the behavior of others and his or her own attributions.

- If a coachee is not being reinforced adequately, the coach can explore how this is affecting the coachee's self-concept. Furthermore, they can work together so the coachee receives consistent task and social feedback in the workplace.

Guiding principles of behavioral coaching and learning

In summary, the behavioral coaching model emphasizes the following aspects of learning and behavior:

- Much human behavior is learned. Biochemical, genetic and unconscious factors play a role in our behavior, but it is through learning and cognition that we acquire and change most of our responses.
- Recognizing and working with an individual's motivation is critical to any successful learning initiative.
- Defining individuals' current status and developmental progress in terms of their behavior, rather than personality traits or personality styles.
- Specifying the target behavior.
- Measuring the targeted behavior.
- Assessing covert behaviors (e.g., limiting beliefs, anxiety) in relation to overt actions (e.g., speaking at a board meeting).
- Accessing and assessing emotional events.
- Accessing and assessing cognitive events.
- Assessing environmental events and the interactions between behavior and environment.
- Analyzing antecedents, behavior and consequences.
- Validated behavioral techniques are effective in managing antecedents, behavior and consequences on both an individual and an organizational level.
- There are limitations to changing the antecedents and consequences of behavior. For example, if these are strongly entrenched, either socially or culturally, they are extremely difficult to alter.
- Lack of follow-through is the greatest impediment to learning and change.
- Humans actively build or make meaning out of their experiences. By reflecting on these experiences, coachees can construct new meanings.

Coaching can facilitate transformational learning, which not only affects what we know but the way we know. It can shift paradigms and allow us to reflect and view situations from an objective, rather than a subjective, perspective.

4

The Behavioral Coaching Approach

The nature, elements and process of change

Although the term "behavior" is seen more and more frequently in the training, leadership, management and coaching literature, it is generally employed very broadly. As already noted, the definition of behavior to which behavioral coaching subscribes is: the actions, responses and reactions of an individual, team or organization.

Not only is the term frequently misused, but little attention is paid to methods of actually changing behaviors and insuring that these changes are lasting. Behavioral coaching bridges these gaps on both an individual and an organizational front. The purpose of this chapter, then, is to review and discuss validated behavioral change techniques that are employed by coaches on the micro (personal) and macro (organizational) level.

Today, the principles of behavior change are widely applied. They are used in education, medical and other health care settings, business, sports and everyday life. Indeed, the application of these principles is virtually limitless. As we discuss in this chapter, these principles and techniques provide the framework for behavioral coaching. One of the major reasons why behavioral and cognitive techniques are so widely accepted is that they allow for data to be gathered on specific, targeted behaviors so these can be measured and evaluated in a rigorous, scientific manner.

Essentially, these principles and techniques are employed by behavioral coaches because they not only effectively change behavior but insure that changes are maintained. That is, behavioral coaches employ validated behavioral and cognitive techniques because they allow coachees to self-manage and self-coach after a coaching program has ended.

It is generally agreed that many of us resist changing our behavioral patterns. Unfortunately, changing is a process that rarely occurs overnight. Behavioral coaching, with its emphasis on research and evidence, offers individuals and organizations a system that greatly increases their chances of effecting lasting behavioral change. As emphasized frequently in our work, a coach is an agent of change. Nevertheless, coaches do not make the changes. Our role is to teach methods of self-change, then facilitate these changes in coachees and organizations.

The behavioral coach's mandate is also to guide and support those involved in the change process, whether this is on an individual or team basis or at the broader organizational level. Otherwise, as we discuss in detail later in this chapter, coachees and organizations will revert to old behaviors. Although there may be some measure of change, which may or may not be sustained, they will not meet all of their objectives or fulfill their potential. The coach, in these instances, has failed to meet her or his contractual obligations.

One of the critical roles of the behavioral coach is that of a drill master. The coach exhorts, encourages and insists that coachees practice their new skills. It is true, as noted in the previous chapter, that lasting behavioral change comes through repetition.

Personal change

Some catalysts for change

- A career promotion demands new skills and competencies.
- Feedback from others suggests that change is necessary, perhaps even urgent.
- The need to redefine oneself, either personally or professionally.
- Something in the individual's personal or professional life is not working.
- Critical incidents, such as physical or psychological trauma.
- Being "stuck" in a situation and not knowing how to get out or where to go.
- The need to deal effectively with life stages, such as midlife crisis.
- The individual is faced with the necessity of becoming self-defining and self-responsible.

Certainly, some individuals change because their current situation, personal or professional, is untenable. Indeed, many coaches proclaim that a person has to be "in a crisis" of some sort in order to recognize the need for change and to work toward this. Clearly, however, this is not always the case. For instance, an individual may have already achieved significant gains in his or her personal and professional life. Because of the resultant security, the person may feel ready to take new risks and embrace significant changes. Life stages, as mentioned above, often usher in the call to change. Again, these changes can be seen in the context of human development; they do not necessarily result from crisis.

What can we change?

Before embarking on a discussion of the necessary conditions for change, barriers to change and the behavioral coach's role as an agent of change, it must be established what we can change and what is immutable. As noted previously, behavioral coaching presents research-based and scientifically validated means of instilling new optimism about achievable change. Here we summarize the results of a number of studies that looked into what is able to be changed and what is stable in human beings.

- Many behaviors shown by children between the ages of three and six are good predictors of their behaviors at age twenty-nine. This is particularly true of aggressive behavior in boys and dependency behavior in girls.
- There is quite remarkable consistency from young adulthood into later life on three dimensions of personality:
  - *Introversion and extraversion.* Introverted or solitary, quiet young adults tend to remain so in later life. Similarly, longitudinal studies have shown that extraverted, outgoing, excitement-seeking young adults display these behaviors later in life.
  - *Neuroticism*, which includes depression, hostility, anxiety and impulsiveness, tends to be stable over a lifetime. Typically, "neurotics" are likely to be miserable and complainers all their lives.
  - *Openness to experience*, including willingness to take risks and make major life changes, tends to be stable throughout an individual's life. However, this effect is not as strong as for the previous two dimensions.
- Pessimistic, self-blaming, helpless individuals tend to have more physical and psychological health problems later in life.
- Old age, typically, does not bring with it "new problems" but brings to the fore or highlights existing issues or problems.
- As we age, behavioral patterns tend to stabilize and we become more resistant to change.
- Feelings of alienation, morale and satisfaction can change dramatically within an individual's lifetime.
- Our intelligence, musical abilities, religiousness, conscience, politics and exuberance are significantly influenced by genetics.
- We are born with varying degrees of hardiness and adaptability.
- We are born with varying levels of "frustration tolerance" and resilience in the face of adversity.
- Difficult, painful early experiences can result in unusual maturity and resilience in adults.

What hinders our efforts to change?

Some individuals are reluctant to change at all. However, these are the minority. Most of us embrace change, although to varying degrees. This may, as mentioned, be partly a function of our biological makeup. Nevertheless, as so many broken New Year resolutions show, it is not initiating the change that presents the greatest difficulty. Rather, it is our inability to persist with these changes, particularly in the face of discomfort, that causes many good intentions to go astray.

A considerable body of research suggests some of the following reasons for the lack of perseverance when it comes to change.

- *The belief that our behavior is inevitable* For example, a manager may have a tendency to become anxious and avoidant when he has to conduct performance appraisals. Because he has always felt and acted this way, he may conclude that he will always have to act this way. The coach has to insure that the client is educated about the difference between a tendency to act in a certain way and the real possibility of working successfully against this tendency.

- *We don't see the results soon enough* Coaches, indeed all change agents, are continually faced with the desire of individuals for immediate change. Even when we understand that change is a process that tends to occur gradually and unevenly, we still want to see immediate results. The coach has to educate the client about the nature of change and how our enthusiasm and motivation peak and waiver during the change period. The coach has to be supportive, be able to contain a coachee's impatience and frustration, and be able to build in "small wins" early in the process.

- *Low frustration tolerance* Some individuals have a limited ability to deal with frustration or setbacks. They find it difficult to manage present unpleasantness or discomfort for the sake of future gains. Coachees with a low tolerance for frustration are likely to focus on immediate or short-term benefits, rather than long-term goals. For instance, an employee may be in a boring position but have very good promotion prospects. However, rather than managing the current boredom and frustration, the person gives up the position and takes on another that does not offer any career prospects at all.

- *Fear of failure or success* An individual may not persevere with changes because she or he feels unworthy of the success these changes will bring. On the other hand, an individual's fear of failure may be so strong that she or he will not continue trying to change.

- *Imposed goals* If an individual feels that the objectives or goals of the coaching program belong to the organization but not to him or her, then persistence with change is unlikely. Individuals are more likely to change their behavior and persist with these changes when they attribute their effort and behavior to their own inner dispositions rather than to external circumstances.

- *Feelings of loss* Frequently, change requires an individual to review his or her past experiences. The new way of behaving may cause the person to experience feelings of regret for wasted or negative time. For example, a coachee who is striving to achieve a good balance between her or his work and personal life can experience considerable feelings of remorse and anger about the years lost when she or he focused on career to the detriment of family or other personal relationships. A coach has to be especially supportive at this time, and encourage the individual to move ahead rather than focusing on the past.

- *Inadequate skills* Although coachees may be well intentioned, they may not have the requisite skills to deal with obstacles that arise on the path of change. We discuss the critical importance of maintaining coaching gains and behavioral changes later in this chapter.

- *Lacking belief in the need for change* Although coachees might initiate changes in their behavior, if they are ambivalent about the need for change or don't trust the source of the feedback on this need, they tend not to persist.

- *Wanting the outcome, but the costs are too high* Although a coachee may genuinely desire the outcome of developmental coaching (e.g., a promotion), during the coaching sessions it becomes clear that the costs (e.g., financial, study time, loss of time with family and friends) are too great.

- *Perception of the changes made* Changes in our behavior are related to our self-concept, or how we view ourselves. Sometimes, individuals believe and say they have changed in terms of how they see themselves. If their self-concept has changed sufficiently, they may no longer feel the need to persist in changing their actual behavior. It is therefore necessary for behavioral coaches to not only measure changes in self-perception, but to measure actual behavioral shifts.

- *Sabotage from self and others* From a systems perspective, changes in one person disrupt the patterns of interaction within the entire system. Everyone has to adapt and adjust. If others in the system are unwilling to adjust, they can sabotage the individual's attempts to change. Moreover, if an individual who has strong needs for affiliation and belonging recognizes this resistances in others, he or she may be inclined to give up on making changes for the sake of harmony and unity. Again, we underscore the importance of support from the coach and the work environment if individuals are to persist in their efforts to change.

Change methodology in behavioral coaching

In order to effect sustainable change in behavior we need to know who responds to what types of behavioral methods and when. Most change models focus on action, and coaches, too, can move into action before they have explored in sufficient detail what precedes this. Additionally, they may not have put in place validated methods of maintenance.

Behavioral coaching employs the change methodology developed by James Prochaska and his colleagues John Norcross, Carlo DiClemente and Wayne Velicer. In an attempt to understand the process of human change, Prochaska first isolated the principles and processes of change from more than four hundred therapies. His research showed that all of these therapies produced change by applying two of ten processes, which we will discuss below.

Prochaska and his colleagues then conducted studies to determine how frequently people use these processes when attempting to change on their own. In this case, they found that change unfolds through a series of five stages. The first four stages were first identified in a 1982 study that compared smokers attempting to quit on their own with smokers in two smoking cessation programs. A fifth stage was developed and validated in 1991–2.

Prochaska's change methodology, then, was initially presented as a theory that incorporated change methods from many diverse theories and practices. However, since its development, it has been validated as a robust, practical change model across a wide range of populations and issues. For example, it has been shown to effect lasting change in various areas of addiction, personal growth and organizational change. It is also used successfully in psychotherapy, leadership programs and education.

The methodology we discuss in this chapter is the only approach to change that, to date, has been empirically shown to produce lasting results. It is for this reason that behavioral coaches have adapted this methodology of learning and change. While other coaching models emphasize the importance of change, they do not operate within a scientifically validated change framework.

Prochaska's methodology as adapted to coaching emphasizes change as a temporal process involving four stages. At each of these stages, behavioral coaches employ validated processes and change strategies to alter coachees' behavior. Furthermore, the emphasis on maintenance and processes to insure that learning and change are sustained is in line with one of the major objectives of behavioral coaching.

The four stages of change in behavioral coaching are:

- the reflective stage—phase one and phase two
- the preparation stage
- the action stage
- the maintenance stage.

During phase one of the *reflective stage*, individuals are not intending to change their behavior in the near future. They simply may not want to change, or they may be uninformed about the consequences of their behavior, lack confidence in their ability to change and be defensive about others wanting them to change. Individuals at phase two of the reflective stage are aware that a problem or issue exists, but have not yet made a commitment to move ahead and change.

During the *preparation stage*, individuals intend to take action in the near future. They have goals and an action plan and have learned, practiced and rehearsed skills and strategies to put in place. They then move to the *action stage*, which is when behavioral changes are put in place and are measured and evaluated.

The *maintenance stage* typically lasts from six months after the behavioral change. The important issue here is the use of tools and techniques to prevent regression until the behavior is no longer problematic or important.

Whereas regression occurs when an individual reverts to an earlier stage of change, relapse refers to regression from the action or maintenance stage.

Coaches and coachees should be aware, though, that regression can occur at any stage during a coaching program.

Coaching change processes

As mentioned, Prochaska's methodology proposes ten processes of change a coachee has to apply during the change process. A change process is any activity that individuals initiate to help modify their thinking, feelings or behavior. Here we will discuss nine of these change processes, which behavioral coaching has relabeled coaching change processes (CCPs). These processes, which can involve numerous behavioral change techniques, include:

- *Increased awareness,* or giving information to heighten the coachee's recognition of the issue(s) she or he is facing.
- *Emotional awareness,* which refers to the coachee experiencing and expressing feelings about the issue or problem.
- *Reviewing the impact of behavior on the people in the coachee's environment,* such as colleagues, friends and family.
- *Reappraising the self* in relation to feelings about the issue.
- *Environmental control,* or changing or avoiding triggers for the old behavior.
- *Developing support networks,* which includes enlisting the coach, colleagues, mentors or others in the coachee's environment to support the new behaviors.
- *Developing alternative behaviors* refers to substituting new responses, thoughts and feelings for the old behaviors.
- *Rewarding changes* includes any reinforcement for the new, desired behaviors from the coachee (self-reinforcement) or others in his or her environment.
- *Commitment* occurs when the coachee chooses and commits to actions that will bring about change. It also relates to the coachee's self-efficacy. Self-efficacy, as noted earlier, refers to the individual's degree of confidence in her or his ability to perform the tasks related to the particular goal or change.

We will now discuss each of the five stages of change and the CCPs in the context of case studies.

Stage one: The reflective stage—phase one

Many individuals who are recommended for coaching are at this stage. They may choose not to think about the problem or gather any information about it. Often, they underestimate the benefits of changing. Although on the surface their behavior appears as resistance, there are several reasons why coachees may be reluctant to embrace coaching. For instance, they may have tried to change on previous occasions, but were unsuccessful and have become demoralized. Likewise, they may have had skills training but no follow-up to insure they maintained the behavioral gains, and so reverted to old behaviors.

COACHING AT PHASE ONE OF THE REFLECTIVE STAGE

P. J. is a senior manager in the finance department of a large national company. One of his functions is to be team leader of a group of six managers. Although the team is underperforming, P. J. seems unaware of the role his leadership style plays in this. He attributes delays in project delivery to scarce resources and time constraints and believes team conflict to be a function of a "very difficult" manager on the team. The coach explained and showed P. J. the change model, and P. J. agreed that he was at the reflective stage of change. The behavioral coach employed the CCP of "increasing his self-awareness." She presented P. J. with a list of the team's achievements and its failures to deliver. Also, in keeping with the goal of increasing P. J.'s awareness of the issue, the coach reminded him that he had recently been overlooked for promotion because of a perceived lack of leadership qualities. In order to help P. J. "reassess the impact of his behaviors on the workplace," she drew his attention to a recent 360-degree appraisal indicating that his team did not rate his leadership skills very highly. Next the coach explored the organization's key performance indicators for P. J. and discussed how his behavior as a role model was negatively affecting the team. Importantly, throughout this session, the coach did not suggest action. Because P. J. was "referred" for coaching, she had to tread a fine line between confronting the behaviors and not wanting P. J. to feel coerced. P. J.'s homework was to reflect on his situation, read material on the benefits of coaching, and list five potential benefits of coaching for his development.

The reflective stage—phase two

As noted, individuals at phase two of the reflective stage accept that there is a problem or an issue to be addressed, although they haven't yet made a commitment to change. Although these people may be aware of the benefits of coaching, they are also aware of the negative consequences of changing their behavior. They may contemplate changing, but procrastinate about making any actual behavioral changes.

COACHING AT PHASE TWO OF THE REFLECTIVE STAGE

Over the two-week period following the previous sessions, P. J. came around to acknowledging that the team's performance was lacking and that his leadership style could be a contributing factor. Although P. J. was aware of the benefits of adopting a less "laissez-faire," more interactive and decisive leadership style, he was also ambivalent about it. For example, although he functioned well on a one-to-one basis, he had always been apprehensive about working with groups or teams. Also, a more interactive style of leadership involved his making regular presentations to the team and to members of other departments. He was extremely apprehensive about these presentations and either performed them badly, avoided them or delegated them. In keeping with the appropriate CCPs, the coach worked toward "increasing P. J.'s emotional awareness" and "reappraising his self-image." P. J.'s role models, as established in a structured interview, included his father, who had built a solid reputation as an industry leader in a different area. P. J. became quite emotional when talking about his father, so the coach used this heightened emotionality to help move P. J. to the next change stage. The coach was also able to help P. J. link his emotional state to a reappraisal of his self-image as a dynamic leader. P. J.'s homework task was to complete a decision chart (see below) about the pros and cons of changing his leadership style.

Prior to the following session, P. J. emailed the following completed decision chart to the coach.

A decision chart about change

Consequences to self

Pros	Cons
Increased self-esteem	Have to face fears about presentations
Greater chance of promotion	Time spent with team will take away
Be more respected by team members	from own work

Consequences to others

Pros	Cons
Team more productive	"Difficult manager" will resist and
Projects in on time	create conflict, which could spread to
	others

Stage two: Preparation

At this stage, the coachee has realized that the benefits of changing his or her behavior through coaching outweigh the negative consequences or losses. The coachee is ready to structure a plan for action.

COACHING AT THE PREPARATION STAGE

P. J. and the coach collected data and identified concrete behaviors to be changed. They also established valid and reliable measures of these behaviors. Time frames and measurements were set against the following behaviors: announcing the changes at a team meeting and to the CEO; meeting individually with each team member to discuss the proposed changes; being more decisive and working with the team to draw up specific team objectives for the next six months. The CCP that the coach focused on at this stage was strengthening P. J.'s "commitment" to changing, which included making public announcements about the changes. Second, P. J. and the coach discussed "support networks" for P. J. As well as the coach, P. J. agreed to enlist the support of a colleague who was not a team member. He would tell his colleague of the proposed changes and seek feedback on his progress (especially regarding his decisiveness) on a regular basis. In order to measure P. J.'s self-efficacy or belief in his ability to change on an ongoing basis, the coach asked P. J. to list a number of situations where he would be likely to fall back into old ways of behaving and nominate how confident he felt about dealing with these in new ways. He regularly reviewed and rated himself on this list (see below) throughout the remainder of the coaching cycle and beyond. P. J. learned and rehearsed several behavioral change techniques, including self-statements and stimulus control of antecedents in the coaching sessions.

P. J. listed the following areas where he might be "tempted" to regress to his old style of leadership, as well as his level of confidence in instituting the new behaviors.

A self-efficacy rating chart

Risky situations	Confidence rating (out of 10)
When he was under time pressure	5
When staff didn't respond positively to his initial overtures	6
When a client presentation was due	5
Dealing with the difficult manager	4

Stage three: The action stage

At this stage, the coachee looks to implement the agreed-upon and practiced behaviors in the workplace and to measure these according to established criteria.

COACHING AT THE ACTION STAGE

As P. J. began to put the new behaviors in place within the work environment, he and the coach worked on several CCPs. Commitment was revisited every session, with P. J. being free to honestly assess when his commitment wavered and when it peaked. Having established P. J.'s "risky situations," the partners worked on "stimulus control" methods to avoid or manage these most effectively. These included time management and delegation to ease his work load so that he would be less likely to feel under pressure, and "alternative behaviors" such as positive self-talk and relaxation/breathing techniques when dealing with the team. Substituting these new behaviors involved practicing what he would say to the team at the initial meeting. He drew up a formal written agreement for each team member, outlining the broad objectives of their weekly meeting and including a clear time frame to replace the previous easy, relaxed style of "chatting" and achieving very little. Finally, P. J. agreed to attend a workshop on presentation skills and to follow through and practice the newly acquired skills in the coaching sessions and in the workplace. P. J. also established a system of "rewards" for himself for changing nominated behaviors. These included positive self-statements, asking for team recognition and allocating thirty minutes a day to his gardening hobby.

Stage four: The maintenance stage

As mentioned frequently throughout this book, many changes are initiated but not sustained. A major reason for this is that change agents and the individual, team or organization do not pay adequate attention to maintenance or fail to use validated strategies and techniques to insure that new behaviors are maintained. The maintenance stage is perhaps the most difficult. It can last for long periods, certainly well after the coaching program has ended. Some issues facing coachees during this stage include overconfidence, being regularly faced with antecedents that trigger the old ways of behaving, lack of self-efficacy or confidence in their ability to maintain the changes and self-blame for perceived failures.

COACHING AT THE MAINTENANCE STAGE

When P. J. initially approached his team about his proposed changes in his leadership style, some of the team responded less than enthusiastically. The coach provided support to P. J. by commenting on and praising his efforts. She also reminded him that it can take a long time for people to trust that someone's changes are permanent and not just a passing fad. Fortunately, P. J.'s colleague had given favorable feedback on two occasions regarding P. J.'s decisive handling of the difficult manager. The coach encouraged P. J. to focus on his successes. The coach and P. J. continued to assess the conditions under which P. J. was most at risk of falling into his old style of leadership and together practiced alternative ways for P. J. to respond to difficult situations. P. J.'s self-limiting beliefs were examined and alternative, more helpful beliefs were explored and practiced. Stimulus control methods and self-regulation techniques were explored and put in place so that P. J. was able to self-manage once the coaching sessions ended. Finally, the coach arranged for two postcoaching "booster" sessions for P. J. at a three-month and a six-month interval, with ongoing evaluation of the coaching outcome.

Reflective	Preparation	Action	Maintenance
Increased awareness ———▶			
Emotional awareness ———▶			
Review impact on environment ———▶			
Reappraising self ———▶			
	Commitment ——————————————————▶		
	Alternative behaviors ——————————▶		
	Environmental control ——————————▶		
	Rewarding ——————————————————▶		
	Support networks ————————————————▶		

Figure 4.1 A summary of coaching change processes at each stage of change (adapted from Prochaska and colleagues)

We have discussed the change methodology and the various change processes behavioral coaches use at these different stages. However, within these processes, coaches also employ several behavioral change techniques. In Chapter 3 we outlined and discussed several techniques that insure new behaviors are learned and become entrenched. These include controlling antecedents, promoting generalization, widening stimulus control, reinforcing new behaviors and enhancing self-regulation skills.

We also discussed a model that behavioral coaches employ when working with emotional self-regulation. Change, as we know, always involves an emotional response on some level. Research, for example, suggests that if an individual recognizes a difficult emotion when it emerges (via the amygdala in the brain), the "message" is switched off and the higher, reasoning levels of the brain (the cortex) come into play. When this happens, the individual will no longer feel the need to try to control or flee from the emotion, and will be in a much better position to work with it.

The behavioral coaching model addresses emotional arousal and how it can be best regulated. Behavioral coaches work with individuals, teams and organization members to identify and label emotions, such as enthusiasm, excitement, anger, anxiety and general distress. Individuals learn to put a distance between themselves and negative feelings. They also learn to better tolerate the feelings of unease and discomfort that frequently accompany change.

Behavioral coaching and change in organizations

It is widely recognized that technological advances and globalization have been pushing businesses and organizations toward change. Indeed, this is so much the case that ongoing change is currently recognized as an inevitable, if not a defining, feature of the business world. In turn, organizational learning and development priorities dictate the need for a vehicle to effect these changes.

As part of this impetus, different competencies have emerged for managers and leaders, such as the need for new and more effective means of managing people in the workplace. A by-product of this broad impetus for change is an increased emphasis on performance measurement. Because change programs, including coaching, can be costly and time-consuming, businesses and organizations are demanding that changes in performance be measurable.

Behavioral coaching in organizations is a significant contributor to this changing and challenging landscape. It is a vehicle for individuals and organizations to adopt changes that are measurable and clearly related to business or organizational goals. It is the science and art of facilitating performance, learning and development of the individual, team and organization to assist the growth of the organization.

Behavioral techniques have been employed to enhance the performance of individuals in a wide variety of organizational and corporate settings. Behavioral coaching is the application of behavioral and cognitive principles and techniques to assess, measure, change and evaluate individual and group behavior within organizational settings. These settings include small and large businesses, as well as public and private organizations and corporations.

The objective of behavioral coaching, essentially, is to change the organization. Behavioral coaches work with leaders, managers, HR personnel and others to develop a climate in which people embrace change. Such a climate generates, fosters and rewards behaviors that are necessary and essential for success and growth. For example, how the leader embraces change affects how individuals in the organization react to change. In turn, this attitude affects customers, and, ultimately, profit.

Any organization can be viewed as an organism, or a living thing. Like individuals, as discussed earlier in this chapter, organizations and businesses also differ on several constructs relevant to change. These include:

- readiness to embrace change
- knowledge, skills and abilities to introduce and manage change
- forces of resistance or barriers to change.

There is a vast array of literature, research, models and prescriptions on actual change management processes. This is not our focus, however. Behavioral coaches address the behaviors of individuals and organizations within these change processes. As mentioned, one of the frequently cited reasons for the failure of so many change processes is that they did not focus on the behavior of the individuals involved. The behavioral coaching model leverages on these change processes and strategies by focusing on behavior.

Examples of behavioral coaching in organizations

Change in organizations can begin at any of seven levels. These are: changes in the type of work done; changes in how work is done; changes in roles and relationships; changes in the organization's identity in the marketplace; change in the relationship to customers and the outside world; and change in mission, culture and values.

Within these seven broad areas of organizational change, behavioral coaches typically work on the following three levels:

1 The individual level
2 The group or team level
3 Organizational outcomes.

On an individual level, behavioral coaches target the following areas:

- performance, or work-related behaviors and productivity
- career development
- organizational identification and commitment.

On the group level, coaching interventions focus on:

- productivity (planning, project development and delivery)
- team performance, which includes team dynamics, team behavior, team cohesion and unity, shared vision, roles and responsibilities, and accountability.

On the organizational level, areas addressed by coaching include:

- leadership
- attitude change
- productivity
- organizational growth
- enhancing learning and development.

Within these three levels, coaches provide leaders, managers and teams with a perspective and set of tools to carry out their jobs more efficiently and more effectively. Through the use of behavioral coaching techniques, the members of an organization enhance their personal and professional growth and development, and meet organizational objectives as well. Some specific coaching areas include:

- recognizing and understanding personal values and needs
- understanding motivation, both one's own and that of work colleagues
- bringing about attitude change
- improving decision-making skills
- improving conceptual and abstract-thinking skills
- enhancing people management skills
- communicating more effectively
- managing change more effectively
- understanding and working with team dynamics
- better diagnosing of problems and developing creative, more effective solutions
- maneuvering through organizational politics to improve career prospects.

The coach's role in changing attitudes

In organizations, a great deal of time is spent attempting to alter attitudes and values. It is true that people embedded in a particular social context will often change their views to conform with those of the group. Persuasion and social influence, therefore, can effect attitude change regarding a coaching program. A coach needs to be aware of specific methods and processes that can effect changes in attitude, and hence foster alignment and enthusiasm for the coaching initiative.

Cognitive dissonance is a process whereby individuals align their conflicting beliefs with the beliefs of others. For example, a middle manager might have negative views about a coach as an effective agent of change. The manager, however, discovers that her or his peers like and value the coach. As a result, the manager may experience tension or dissonance. In order to reduce this, the manager is likely to shift her or his viewpoint toward that of peers and the group, and consider the coach in a more favorable light.

Reframing is a method whereby individuals alter the ways in which they interpret or label their experiences. For example, a significant body of research from sport psychology shows that elite athletes, compared with non-elite performers, interpret pre-performance cognitive and somatic anxiety as facilitating rather than debilitating. Performance anxiety, for instance, was labeled as "psyching up" and "energizing arousal." It is a question of language.

Behavioral coaches find this technique useful when working with individuals who react negatively to the changes that coaching demands. Changes that are perceived as threatening or extremely taxing can be reframed as challenges, a new opportunity or a chance to get out of a rut.

While there are methods that can contribute to attitude change, it is generally recognized that these are time-consuming. Furthermore, a great deal of research and experience shows that an effective way to change attitudes and values is to first change behaviors. Behavioral changes can bring about changes in attitude.

Coaches generally work with leaders and managers to change behaviors in the direction of an organization's desired goals and objectives. The behaviors have to be targeted and clearly established and communicated performance standards and expectations put in place. These new, desired behaviors need to be rewarded or reinforced. Ideally, the new ways of behaving should be owned by coachees, so that they become intrinsically motivated rather than extrinsically motivated behaviors. When this occurs, not only is there a shift toward acceptance of the organization's goals, but the behaviors are more likely to be maintained.

Organizational culture

Behavioral coaches require a working knowledge of an organization's structure, processes and behavior. Each of these constructs can be understood in the context of the organization's culture. It is commonly recognized that culture plays a critical role in an organization's strategic planning, leadership style and accepted ways of accomplishing tasks and responsibilities. For example, research indicates that an organization's culture is one of four major factors that influence how management development programs are conducted. In fact, organizational processes depend on organizational culture, and at the same time these processes create the culture. Clearly, the coach has to be cognizant of an organization's culture and how it affects learning and development.

There are numerous approaches to explaining and understanding organizational culture. For instance, culture has been examined within an anthropological context, from a sociocultural viewpoint, from a systems perspective and from a mechanistic point of view. Clearly, a detailed description of these approaches is beyond the scope of this book. Our broad intent is to explore culture in terms of existing patterns of behavior within an organization and to discuss culture as a determinant of these behaviors. These aspects of culture are examined from a systems perspective in the following section.

A systems approach to understanding culture

As we emphasize throughout this book, coaching never occurs in a void. The individual is always part of a larger system and changes that occur within coaching sessions affect this system. Similarly, organizational systems affect coachees and their behavioral changes.

Behavioral coaches adopt various systems approaches. Because of the complexity of systems theories and for the sake of economy, we have chosen to discuss several essential principles of a systemic approach to organizations and coaching change. Essentially, the behavioral coaching model considers an organization as a sociocultural system that operates within chaos and increasing complexity, as described by Jamshid Gharajedaghi.

According to this perspective, behavior can be understood only in terms of its context or environment. Individual behaviors, therefore, are a function of, and affect, organizational culture. Additionally, a systems approach suggests that although a great deal of what occurs within an organizational environment cannot be controlled, it can be influenced. Behavioral coaches have to work with leaders and individuals to help them recognize what they can control, what they can influence and how best to do this.

Closely related to this is the need to understand the purpose of a system and why it behaves in a particular way. This, in turn, entails understanding the choices made within the system. Unless leaders, coaches and coachees have this knowledge, it is impossible to change the purpose and objectives of the organization.

Behavioral coaches have to recognize the many structures, functions and processes within a multidimensional organizational system. Focusing on only one process, for example, can lead to missed opportunities. Furthermore, doing so increases the probability of unforeseen resistance or forces of regression from within the ignored processes, structures and functions of the organization.

Finally, behavioral coaching underscores the importance of regarding the organizational system as an interaction, rather than just the sum of its parts. The broad goals of coaching are generally development, success and well-being. However, these factors only emerge as an interaction between parts. For instance, an individual's motivation, competencies or opportunities to practice new behaviors alone are not sufficient to produce development. Development is an emergent property of the interaction of the three factors.

In summary, a systems approach to organizations allows the coach and the organization to understand the many influences on planned change programs. For instance, delayed effects, circular dependencies, multiple effects of a single event and resistance to the effects of change can result in unpredictable and undesirable outcomes. A systems approach arms the coach and coachee with knowledge of these variables and a context within which to manage them.

The profile of an organization

Many behavioral coaches hold to a particular model of organizational culture and work satisfactorily within this framework. There is no one all-inclusive, comprehensive model that is mandatory for coaches. Nevertheless, there are key elements of culture that coaches have to recognize and understand if they are to work successfully and effectively in an organization. This profile includes the components of the culture, its character, its power structure, whether the orientation is team-based, how person-focused the organization is and how conflict is managed.

The components of organizational culture

Typically, culture refers to the shared patterns of belief, assumptions and expectations of its members. This includes values, norms and roles as they exist outside of the individual. The subjective culture of an organization consists of shared values and beliefs, myths about the organization, and taboos and rituals.

Within the dominant culture, there may be subcultures. These subcultures may oppose the dominant culture, particularly during times of change and stress. For example, members of a certain business unit may consider themselves to be the technical experts and therefore not in need of any of the "soft skills" that coaching embraces. Although these beliefs and cultural values may not be explicitly stated, a coaching initiative is doomed to failure if the coach is not aware of them. On the other hand, another unit or department may be proud of the manner in which it deals with staff issues, and, accordingly, may promote coaching as a developmental tool. The coach has to be attuned to these cultural nuances in order to successfully seek alliances and manage resistance.

The character of an organization

Individuals working within organizations as well as outsiders recognize that organizations have a "character." Such character can be conceptualized in different ways. One methodology, developed by William Bridges, that some behavioral coaches find useful involves viewing an organization within the framework of the Myer–Briggs Type Indicator (MBTI). According to this approach, an extroverted organization, for example, would be outwardly focused on markets and competition. In contrast, an introverted organization is more likely to be orientated toward its leader's dreams and vision. Of particular interest in this, and indeed any typology, is how organizations deal with change. Intuitive organizations are typically easily bored and always looking for new ways to accomplish their objectives. Sensing organizations, on the other hand, are more conservative and tend to introduce changes incrementally.

Regardless of which classification system is employed, it is critical that coaches have a clear understanding of an organization's approach to change. Coaches need this knowledge so that they can alter and tailor their approach to meet the strengths and weaknesses of the organizational character.

Culture and the individual's style

There is a relationship between the personality style of the organization and that of the individual. Some evidence indicates that individuals, especially leaders, attempt to change the organization to fit their preferred style. Consequently, behavioral coaches can find it extremely helpful to assess a leader's personality style and how this interacts with different types of organizational character.

The methods employed by coaches to assess an individual's style include the following:

- *The Social Styles Inventory* assesses individuals on four dimensions (amiables, analyticals, drivers and expressives) and suggests a "goodness of fit" between these types and certain organizational cultures.
- *The Fundamental Interpersonal Relations Orientation Behavior (Firo-B)* measures individuals on three dimensions (inclusion, control and affection). Scores on these dimensions can indicate why individuals are motivated to join, stay or leave certain organizations.
- *The Big Five Personality* model assesses individuals on five dimensions (negative emotionality, extroversion, openness, agreeableness and conscientiousness). Each of these five factors has six dimensions, which include compliance, excitement seeking, trust and order. Many of these characteristics can be either undervalued or nurtured by an organization's culture.

The power structure in the culture

In some organizations, especially small-to-medium businesses, power and influence spread from a central figure or group. Behavioral coaches have to be cognizant of the source of power. In this type of organization emphasis typically centers on the following areas: developing political savvy, gaining prestige and power and increased risk taking.

In contrast, some organizations are bureaucratic, with power residing in structured, rational authority. It is this authority that defines rules, role definitions and procedures. Such organizations often find it difficult to change because of their cumbersome structures. In such a culture, individuals who are innovative and risk takers may become frustrated and demoralized. They may also have issues around the cultural demands for deference to authority and the rigid chain of command.

Team-based cultures

In some organizations, small groups work together to deliver a project. Individuals are given resources and control over their work and performance capability is more important than status. Evidence for a team-based culture, or, indeed, how highly teams are valued, can be found in how decisions are made. Are they handed down from the CEO or are major decisions the result of executive team participation? Furthermore, while the virtues of team playing may be espoused, some organizations actually reward individualism. Teams may be under-resourced and unsupported. In this case, a coach's mandate frequently is to bring about lasting change in team structure and team performance. If, however, teams are not truly valued and the organization is unconcerned about this, management has to be closely involved in setting team performance goals and committing the necessary resources.

Person-focused culture

Some organizations are more people- and relationship-oriented than others. Although the rhetoric might suggest that all organizations care equally for their people, this is not manifested in their behavior. Usually, the bottom line is profit, and people are vehicles for increasing profit. A coach, when developing a profile of an organization, looks for evidence that people matter. For instance, he or she may look at how seriously learning and development is promoted.

In the previous chapter we examined organizations in relation to their priorities and methods of learning and development and how these affect a coaching initiative. It is widely agreed that another aspect of culture a behavioral coach needs to assess is how truthfully it informs its members of "failures" or mismatches between predicted and actual outcomes. If a coachee is not aware of "what went wrong," then learning new skills and strategies will be virtually impossible. For example, does the culture allow or encourage mistakes? When mistakes are made, do the members receive reliable information about these? The coach working with individuals or teams has to know, for instance, whether the undesired outcomes were a function of poor decision making, incorrect data gathering or poor implementation of strategies. A culture that truly values learning and development and change will make this information available, so that the culture can adopt new, more effective methods of behaving.

The issue is not so much whether a coach chooses to work with an organization that does not value its people to the extent it claims. There is, after all, a self-selection process that determines which organizations are more likely to adopt the services of a coach. What is critical is that the coach tailors the coaching program to meet the organization's business objectives. If the organization focuses on task accomplishment, then coaching to enhance performance will be more appropriate. Alternatively, coaching for development is more suited to organizations whose concern is for people and relationships.

Conflict management and culture

There are several methods cultures use to manage conflict. These include collaboration, coercion, avoidance, compromise and accommodation. A culture may ignore or neglect conflict, or it may redesign processes and procedures as a means of dissolving conflict.

Coaches frequently work with individuals and teams to manage conflict at various levels of an organization. In order to teach, promote and practice the most effective strategies, both coaches and coachees need to understand how the culture deals with conflict.

Finally, culture change is frequently a critical component of successful coaching programs. Coaches typically work with behavior to help individuals become aligned with the changes that coaching entails and to manage these changes on an individual, team or organizational level. Behavioral coaches apply the following methods to gain a deeper understanding of an organization's culture.

- Observing the interaction of the members. This can be done formally at team meetings or may simply involve observing informal dialogue.
- Using questionnaires and surveys relating to values and morale.
- Conducting focus groups on coaching.
- Interviewing key stakeholders and individuals involved in the coaching change program.

In summary, understanding the culture or profile of an organization is critical. Apart from the areas discussed above, a coach must be cognizant of the organization's emotional profile as it manifests in morale, rates of absenteeism, levels of enthusiasm and commitment. Recognizing an organization's spiritual dimension, its stated meaning and purpose also presents the coach with the data necessary to determine where and how sustainable change and growth can be accomplished.

Managing resistance to change in organizations

Behavioral coaches, like any change agents, may face resistance from within organizations. Understanding where this originates, how it manifests and ways to manage it are vital skills for a successful coach. Change is typically resisted when people hear about it from a secondary source, such as rumors. Top-down proclamations of change are frequently met with cynicism. Changes need to be announced at ground level; that is, where people are actually working. When this occurs, the line manager can clearly explain the changes and how these will translate into actual behaviors to be put in place. Importantly, discussions can then occur around the specific behaviors and how they will be measured and rewarded.

Reluctance theory offers an explanation for why individuals in an organization resist change. Frequently, people act counter to pressures put on them to change. They do so because of the emphasis and value they put on freedom and control. When these are threatened, they cling even harder to the behavior despite increasing pressure and evidence for the need to change. Essentially, the amount of resistance will increase as a function of the number of freedoms threatened. The implications of this for coaches are to:

- understand what freedoms are being threatened from the viewpoint of the individual, team and organization
- work with those concerned to try and meet the need for freedom in other ways
- include the individual or team in the early stages so they feel they are initiating the change rather than having it imposed on them. Sometimes we resist sound ideas simply because they aren't ours
- work with individuals and teams to clearly understand their sphere of influence; that is, what they can and cannot change
- provide a forum that is supportive and allows for free discussion about the shock, denial and anger individuals may be experiencing
- look for immediate and small wins for the individual, team and organization.

Barriers to change in organizations

Although every business and organization is unique and boasts a unique culture, there are commonalities among the factors that impede behavioral change. Research shows that the following present the greatest and most common obstacles to coaching for change within organizations:

- Organizational cultures are based on emotion and these emotions intensify when changes are perceived as threatening.
- Cultures are based on and emerge from a platform of historical continuity and change involves some degree of loss of this continuity.
- Cultures, despite their regression forces or resistance, are always changing. Energy is frequently dissipated in fighting rather than embracing or managing change.
- Coaches may lack familiarity with the organizational culture.
- Failure to educate and inform individuals about the need for change, and hence the benefits of coaching.
- A lack of support from senior management for the coaching program.
- Opposition from employees and middle management.
- Attempting to roll out a large project without first conducting a pilot.
- Coachees' competing commitments may interfere with the coaching program.

The psychological contract

Behavioral coaching emphasizes the significant role of the psychological contract between the individual and the organization. When a coach works in an organizational setting, it is critical that she or he is aware of the contract between the coachee and the organization. Otherwise, expectations may not be met and the coach can find herself or himself at odds with the coachee, the organization or both.

The individual is not the organization and the individual and the organization have separate needs and obligations. There has to be a two-way agreement on what the individual and what the organization will provide. For example, individuals are usually hired because of the skills they bring to the organization. They are also, however, obligated to enhance and develop these skills and competencies. Individuals can also contract for loyalty and ongoing effort. Loyalty is perhaps the most difficult or complex of an individual's contractual obligations because the scope and strength of loyalty depends, to a great extent, on the individual's values.

Loyalty from organizations is increasingly under question. It is commonly accepted that job changing, estimated to occur up to eleven times in a lifetime, is now a feature of the contemporary and future workplace. Moreover, increasing numbers of organizations and corporations engage short-term, contract or episodic labor. As a result of this trend, some experts in the field encourage young professionals to work as consultants to, rather than inside, corporations. Some also speak of the conflict between short-term, limited loyalty and security within an organization and the human needs for long-term commitment, loyalty and stability in relationships.

Organizations exist to serve the purposes of its members while serving the purpose of the organization as a whole. The exchange system between the organization and its members is the means by which both the individual and the organization gain from belonging. Therefore, the organization has to provide inducements to employees such as adequate monetary compensation, job security, promotion opportunities and career development. In relation to coaching, the organization should commit to supporting, training and coaching its members, not only for positional skills but for personal skills such as values, motivation and balance.

Organizations also have to appreciate that individuals with a high sense of "psychological safety" in their organization are more likely to embrace change than individuals with less security. Clearly, coaches are not in a position to dictate business trends, which, as we all know, are subject to the vagaries of the marketplace. Nevertheless, they can insure that a mutually agreeable contract is set up between an organization and its employees. They can help the organization to establish and manage psychological contracts. The organization has to insure that it is getting value from its members. In turn, employees have to be provided with the opportunity to develop and enhance their skills, both professional and personal. Behavioral coaching is a twenty-first century tool for insuring that organizations develop and maintain strong, healthy and productive psychological contracts with their members.

In summary, the end result of any behavioral coaching program, whether at the individual, team or organizational level, is to introduce and maintain changes of some kind. Behavioral coaches focus on the behaviors involved in change. They apply validated and reliable behavioral change techniques within a change model that is tailored to an organization's culture to introduce, implement and maintain new ways of responding.

5

The Behavioral
Coaching Model

Behavioral coaching, as we have noted throughout this book, is an integrative model founded on the behavioral sciences. Although behavioral change techniques play a crucial role in behavioral coaching, the model is not simply based on behavioral modification methods. It encapsulates personal development, beliefs, values, emotions, motivation and social learning, as well as personal and organizational dynamics and defenses.

Many of the components of the model, however, do derive from the behavioral approach to learning and change. The following aspects of behavioral coaching, in particular, are grounded in behavioral methodologies:

- Targeting and focusing on specific behavior.
- Analyzing the behavior in relation to its antecedents and consequences.
- Applying valid and reliable methods of assessment, data collection and data analysis.
- Developing goals in the context of goal theory and related research.
- Employing validated behavioral change techniques.
- Managing and maintaining behavioral change.

One of the aims of behavioral coaching is to eliminate the duality between the theory and practice of coaching. In this chapter, we present a general model of the conceptual and practical elements of behavioral coaching within an accessible and useful framework for coaches.

Because coaching is still in the early stages of its development, there is no agreed-upon, all-embracing model of the coaching process and practice. To date, most efforts to construct a comprehensive coaching model have emerged from sports coaching. The model we present is one attempt to relate the components of the process to the practice of executive, business and organizational coaching.

A coaching model cannot be procrustean. It requires an in-built flexibility and adaptability so that coaching programs can be tailored to fit the specific needs of each client and coachee. For example, coaches need to take into account their own, as well as coachees', differences in personality, knowledge, skills and abilities. Coachees also vary in motivation and preparedness for change.

As well as individual factors, each coachee exists within various systems, both personal and professional. These affect how a coaching program is conducted, as do factors such as the organizational culture and structure, available resources and the organization's business objectives. Therefore, we cannot expect, or even hope, that every client and coachee will "fit" perfectly with our model and methodologies.

The model we present is not static, but remains open to input and change from research, from experienced professionals working in the field and from successful outcome studies. The model can be constantly refined and new theories and knowledge will continue to build on the framework presented here, adding to and expanding the knowledge base of coaching.

Constructing the model

A model, by definition, is a representation that mirrors, duplicates, imitates or illustrates a pattern observed in nature or data. We also use the term "model" in the sense of an ideal or a standard that is worthy of imitation. The construction of the behavioral coaching model was guided by research that suggested a useful and valuable model meets the following criteria:

- It presents a comprehensive, complete description of the process.
- It builds toward an outcome and is, therefore, predictive.
- It applies to all (coaching) situations.
- It establishes the nature of the component parts.

For the purposes of clarity we are presenting the model in the following format:

1 We discuss the assumptions about coaching on which the model is based.
2 We revisit Prochaska's methodology and outline the stages of change (reflective, preparation, action and maintenance) that serve as the linchpin for the behavioral coaching model.
3 We describe the five forms of coaching (coaching education, skills coaching, rehearsal coaching, performance coaching and self-coaching) as they are practiced across the seven coaching process steps.
4 We outline and discuss the seven steps in the coaching process (education; data collection; planning, including goal setting and action planning; behavioral change; measurement; evaluation; and maintenance). We also nominate the requisite coaching competencies, both knowledge and skills, for each step of the process.
5 We discuss some of the core competencies of coaches across the entire coaching process.

Assumptions of the behavioral coaching model

The assumptions upon which the behavioral coaching model is built include the following:

- Coaching is widely accepted as a powerful tool for personal and professional growth.
- Successful coaching programs focus on individual, team and organizational business objectives and goals.
- Change is at the heart of any coaching program. For this reason, behavioral coaching employs proven behavioral change techniques.
- Changing behavior involves learning. Behavioral coaching, therefore, incorporates principles of adult education and psychological laws of learning.
- Coaching outcomes are more likely to be successful when coachees are voluntary, understand the fundamentals of behavioral coaching, and, through the coaching partnership, develop a strong commitment to the change process.
- Although procedural knowledge is critical for coaches, the model is situated within the context of interpersonal relationships between the coach and client, and the coach and coachees. The model can be successfully implemented only in a safe, open and trusting climate.
- Coaching outcomes can and should be measured against the stated objectives of the individual, team or organization.
- Within the nominated stages, processes and coaching competencies of the model, there is scope for differences in coaching styles and techniques. There is also scope for individual differences (e.g., in personality, values, belief systems and philosophy) among coaches and coachees.
- Coaching is a demanding and challenging profession. As the distinctions between coaching and similar disciplines (e.g., consulting) become increasingly blurred, the range of knowledge and competencies required by coaches will expand.

The matrix in Table 5.1 (Zeus 2000) is designed as a road map for behavioral coaches and all other stakeholders to insure a common understanding of what behavioral coaching entails. It makes explicit the interaction between the stages of change, as well as the forms of coaching

Table 5.1 An overview of the behavioral coaching model as developed by Zeus (2000)

Stages of change	Five forms of coaching	Seven-steps coaching process
Reflective	Coaching education	EDUCATION
Preparation		DATA COLLECTION
		PLANNING (target; goals; action plans)
	Skills coaching Rehearsal coaching	BEHAVIORAL CHANGE
Action	Performance coaching	MEASUREMENT
		EVALUATION
Maintenance	Self-coaching	MAINTENANCE

relevant to each stage and to the seven process steps of the behavioral coaching model. It is not possible for any model to delineate all the contextual variables that exist in coaching. Although the model situates coaching within a linear process, each coach's and coachee's path is unique. The model displayed here, therefore, is necessarily a working model only. We expect it will be subject to changes and refinements over time and we welcome comments and revisions from practitioners.

Stages of change and the coach's role

In this section, we revisit Prochaska's methodology as discussed in detail in Chapter 4. Adapted for the behavioral coaching model, there are four stages of change that interrelate with the forms of coaching and the seven coaching process steps. These are: the reflective stage; the preparation stage; the action stage; and the maintenance stage.

The reflective stage

At the reflective stage, clients and individuals are in one of two states. Either they are in a state of unknowing, and, at least consciously, are unaware that there is an issue to address (phase one), or they may accept that changes have to be made but have not yet made a commitment to move ahead (phase two). As discussed in detail below, it is at this stage that a coach functions as an educator.

The preparation stage

At the second stage of change, the client and/or coachees appreciate that there is a need for change through coaching, but they are unsure how to proceed and are not totally committed to coaching. Here, the role of the coach is to collect data, conduct assessments, target specific behaviors for change, set goals and develop action plans. These are the necessary preliminary steps before the coach institutes behavioral change and other coaching techniques in order to change the selected behaviors. During the preparation stage, the coachee learns new skills and rehearses these in preparation for action in the workplace.

The action stage

Here, coachees actually put the skills into place in the workplace. These are monitored, measured and evaluated on an ongoing basis.

The maintenance stage

The emphasis at this stage of change is on sustaining the behavioral changes and overall gains and making sure that coachees do not revert to earlier behavioral patterns.

The five forms of coaching

As noted in Chapter 1 and mentioned above, throughout any coaching program, whether it be executive or business, the coach practices five distinct forms of coaching. These are coaching education, skills coaching, rehearsal coaching, performance coaching and self-coaching. As shown in Table 5.1 above, these five forms of coaching occur at various stages of change and the seven-step coaching process.

Coaching education

Coaching education situates the coach in the role of teacher. At the reflective stage, the coaching education role involves informing potential clients and coachees about relevant generic issues that all organizations face today, as well as industry-specific challenges. Coaching services are presented as a means of facing and overcoming these concerns. Such education can be conducted via the written word in industry-specific journal articles, newspaper articles or books. A particularly effective means of disseminating information and knowledge about coaching is through seminars or workshops.

Coaches present such seminars or workshops to organizations or business groups, emphasizing the types of coaching interventions that would address their specific issues and the resultant benefits. If an organization decides to go ahead with a coaching program, the seminar or workshop will be followed by meetings with key stakeholders, a coaching needs analysis and a proposal documenting the identified needs, how changes will be measured and evaluated and suggested services. During all these stages, the coach is acting in an education role.

As discussed in Chapter 6, the client and key stakeholders require specific information about coaching. Some areas of requisite knowledge involve the nature of coaching, its applications, its benefits and the methodologies employed, including methods of measurement and evaluation. Coachees also require education regarding these facets of a coaching program. Additionally, they need to be educated about the nature of the coaching relationship, coachees' responsibilities, the role and accountabilities of the coach, the nature of behavioral change and the need for ongoing measurement.

Other clients and individual coachees may be at the reflective stage, but are undecided about how to move ahead. In this case, the information provided by the coach is similar to that mentioned above. However, the coach may progress faster in terms of discussing and clarifying individuals' or an organization's specific issues and conducting a coaching needs analysis.

Education and teaching continue throughout the seven coaching process steps. The coach is a resource provider and supplies information relevant to coachees' development plans. These resources include recent research findings, videos, articles, books and information about action strategies and their advantages and disadvantages. Obstacles to progress and how others manage to overcome these, as well as other insights from the behavioral sciences, are provided by the coach as required.

Skills coaching

At the preparation stage, coachees accept that the benefits of changing outweigh the costs and are preparing to take action. The coach collects data and conducts assessments and together the coach and coachees target behaviors to change, set goals and develop action plans. Once these are in place, the coach begins to teach coachees the requisite skills. For example, the coach may teach coachees planning skills, presentation skills, assertiveness skills, communication skills, methods to manage difficult colleagues, assertiveness skills, networking skills and sales skills, to name a few. Coachees also learn behavioral change techniques that facilitate the acquisition and maintenance of such skills.

Rehearsal coaching

Once a coachee has learned new skills, he or she has to rehearse these before performing in the workplace. Rehearsal occurs within the coaching sessions and involves video rehearsal, role plays and analogue situations. These rehearsals are monitored and measured. It is at this stage that practice and "drilling" are most critical. Later, rehearsal also takes place within the work environment.

Performance coaching

The coachee is now at the action stage of the change model; that is, she or he is fully applying the learned skills in the workplace. During this phase, the coach supports the coachee, as do the aligned manager and coaching program manager. The new behaviors are measured by the coachee and peers, and the coach also observes or shadows the coachee as he or she executes the new skills.

As noted in Chapter 1, performance coaching involves a considerable amount of measurement, so that the coachee's behaviors can be compared with her or his precoaching performance. The coach employs 360-degree or other multirater assessments and the coachee self-monitors to obtain the comparative data. This data plays an important role in the final evaluation of a coaching program.

In performance coaching, the coach has to manage fluctuations in a coachee's performance and deal effectively with resistances within the coachee or the work environment. The coach provides ongoing, effective and constructive feedback on the coachee's performance of the learned skills.

Self-coaching

At the maintenance stage and step seven of the coaching process, the emphasis is on maintaining the gains made during a coaching program. During coaching education, skills coaching, rehearsal and performance coaching, the coach is the key driver. Nevertheless, each form of coaching aims to make the knowledge and skills accessible to the coachee so that, ultimately, he or she can develop autonomy and independence from the coach. The coach's ultimate goal is to insure that coachees can effectively self-coach.

Maintenance is built into the entire coaching program. At this juncture, however, the coach takes specific steps to insure that what coachees have learned will be practiced and retained. One method behavioral coaches employ to do this is to carefully measure a coachee's progress and identify any factors that require immediate attention and adjustment. Hence, ongoing self-monitoring, as well as observation and feedback from others, begin immediately a coachee starts applying the skills in the workplace.

During this period, coachees learn to recognize triggers for both desired and undesired behaviors and ways to self-correct and self-regulate. As well as establishing a coachee's self-efficacy in these areas, the coach conducts a preliminary exploration of what might present obstacles to the coachee once the coaching relationship has ended. Together, the partners identify potential barriers and develop strategies to avoid or overcome these.

The seven-step coaching process

As noted earlier, the coaching process presented here follows a linear seven-step progression, with each step following the previous one in a logical order. These steps, however, represent a recommended framework only.

Step one: Education

Behavioral coaching offers individuals, teams and organizations information about behavior and techniques to alter and maintain behavioral change. Education, then, is the information platform from which any coaching program is launched. As noted, clients and coachees require significant amounts of knowledge regarding the nature of coaching, its benefits and how a coaching program is conducted and evaluated.

In Chapter 6 we look at the kinds of information presented to the client at various stages of the coach–client relationship, including the coaching needs analysis. Such information is critical not only to clarify what the coach is proposing, but also to dispel some of the persisting misconceptions about coaching. For instance, some clients believe that "manager as coach" means that the manager no longer performs management tasks in terms of getting things done, but spends all her or his time supporting and encouraging staff. Yet, managers have to insure that individuals reach certain performance levels; they have targets to reach and strategies and tactics to employ.

Coaching, as opposed to managing, involves focusing on an individual's development and enabling him or her to become more self-reliant and to solve problems and make decisions independently. Coach managers promote reflection and insight and help individuals to become more self-managing and self-generating. They have less need for control and are themselves open to feedback. This is not simply cheerleading, as some clients and coachees believe. Challenging and confronting entails examining weaknesses, defenses and blocks to progress, as well as providing support and encouragement.

Educating the client about the nature of change and the time and cost involved in truly effecting lasting behavioral change is a challenge to the coach. The coach as educator has to emphasize the importance of persistence, practice and repetition if new patterns of behavior and new thoughts and feelings are to replace old, unhelpful ones. Nevertheless, many clients are under pressure and want a quick fix. They expect the coach to have the solutions and a "model" that is all-encompassing and guaranteed to succeed, regardless of the coaching issue or coachees. Clients and coachees can become disillusioned when they realize the true demands of successful coaching. Education, then, involves the coach walking a tightrope between this potential disillusionment and conveying the genuine and lasting benefits coaching offers.

Another issue coaches have to educate clients about is the necessary autonomy of the coaching program. Coaching should not be subject to the control or caprice of any one individual, such as a manager. It is a collaborative process that will succeed only if the organization and individual coachees are aligned in an open and trusting commitment to achieving mutual objectives.

Coachees, too, require education about the coaching process. They need to understand the benefits as well as the demands and expectations of their role. The importance of self-awareness in relation to learning and taking action, and the need for practice, rehearsal and ongoing monitoring and evaluation also require discussion and exploration.

Written and verbal information play important roles in disseminating knowledge about coaching. The coach's behavior is also critical, however, as it is a model for how the coaching relationship is conducted; that is, the coach displays flexibility and adaptability, as well as a desire to learn more about the client's and coachees' perceptions and reality. Clarity, questions that generate reflection and new understanding, and authentic relating and trustworthiness serve to deepen relationships and model crucial aspects of the coaching collaboration.

Requisite coaching competencies at step one (education)

Knowledge of: research on coaching outcome studies; coaching as personal development; roles and responsibilities of participants; benefits of coaching; areas of coaching application; a structured coaching process; coaching methodologies; evaluation methods such as return on investment (ROI) and return on expectations (ROE), as discussed in step six; organizational dynamics, including values and how decisions are made; behavioral theories of learning and change; adult learning principles; organizational politics; resistance within organizations and how to manage this; cultural dynamics; content of targeted seminars and workshops on coaching; current business development issues; business processes and systems; management theory and practice.

Skills: strategic coordinating and project management; building rapport; generating trust and commitment; authentic relating; establishing credibility; aligning stakeholders with coaching objectives; active listening;

questioning; reflection; collaborative dialoguing; brainstorming; consensus building; pursuing helpful alliances; client liaison skills; diplomacy; social skills; managing relationships.

Step two: Data collection

Data collection is an essential step in the behavioral coaching process. For example, the information gathered by the coach during the coaching needs analysis phase (discussed later in this chapter and in Chapter 6) establishes the overall objectives of the entire coaching program.

Other reasons why data collection is critical to behavioral coaching include:

- It establishes the core areas for development around which the coach and coachee develop goals, action plans and strategies.
- It provides a baseline measure for behaviors that are targeted for change.
- It provides information that can be used as preintervention and postintervention measurements.
- The baseline and postcoaching data can be evaluated in relation to the coaching outcome (e.g., business and financial impact, ROI).
- The actual collection process aligns others in the coaching program and thus contributes to the probability that the learned skills will be maintained.
- It provides a multiperspective on the coachee's behaviors, strengths and weaknesses.
- The information gathered is a starting point for discussion between the coach and coachee.

Data gathering—phase 1

As noted, a considerable body of information is gathered during the coaching needs analysis. Depending on the scope of the coaching program, such as the number of coachees, number of sessions, the time frame and coachees' level in the organization, data is collected from various sources. These include key stakeholders, such as direct reports, the board of directors, peers, customers, suppliers and members of the executive or management team.

The initial data, as well as any later information, is collected anonymously, in written form, and compiled by the coach. The information is collated by the coach and presented directly to the coachee, with the coach deciding whether to disclose individual stakeholders' comments or ratings. One of the major reasons for collecting such data, after all, is to open up discussion around the coachee's strengths and areas for improvement. In response to the data, the coach establishes the key development areas and recommendations or suggestions for the coachee's future development. In addition, the coach develops a broad understanding of the coachee's strengths and weaknesses.

Prior to the commencement of the coaching sessions, the coachee can also meet with the parties who have been involved in the coaching needs analysis and data gathering. The purpose of these meetings is to gather further information and possible suggestions for the enhancement of performance and development. Of course, the likelihood of these meetings occurring depends on several factors, including the coachee's choice, the political situation and the various stakeholders' interest in and commitment to the coaching program.

Data gathering—phase 2

During the initial client–coach meetings, the coach and client agree on the evaluation methods to be employed. Once these have been established, the coach begins to collect data that will meet the evaluation parameters. A commonly agreed-upon method of evaluation is based on Kirkpatrick's four levels of evaluation. Although the focus in this section is on preintervention data gathering, for the purposes of economy we will discuss the four levels in relation to both precoaching and postcoaching evaluation.

Level one relates to the coachee's personal reaction to the coaching program. This includes questions about the degree of satisfaction with the program.

Level two measures the extent to which coaching has changed the coachee's beliefs, knowledge and skills. The major question at this level is whether the coachee has gained skills and knowledge she or he did not previously possess.

Level three is a measure of how the coachee's behavior has changed and how the new skills and knowledge have transferred to and been used in the workplace. This includes, for example, the degree to which coaching has affected work behaviors such as team performance and productivity.

Level four measures the business impact of the coaching program. For example, is there a financial pay-off for the company or organization? At this level, the organizational impact is measured in terms of the coachee's perceptions of the impact of coaching. This is separate from the ROI, which is discussed in evaluation, step six of the coaching process.

In addition to the above questionnaire, which is given at the beginning of the coaching program (precoaching evaluation) and at the end (post-coaching evaluation), several other forms of data collection are used by behavioral coaches. These include interviews, surveys, and focus groups.

Some of the information we discuss in this section may already have been gathered by the coach during the initial coaching needs analysis. In some situations, however, it is not collected until later in the coaching process. Regardless of the timing, the most common methods are interviews, focus groups, surveys, observation by the coach and others (participant observation) and analogue observation.

Interviews can be unstructured or structured, depending on the information required. They are conducted with stakeholders such as the client–sponsor, as discussed in Chapter 6. During these initial meetings, the coach collects data that relates to the company's or organization's vision, its business objectives and learning and development needs in order to place coaching as a relevant vehicle to help achieve these. The coach must develop a clear sense of the "gaps" that the coaching program is designed to bridge.

Table 5.2 Levels of pre-evaluation and postevaluation in coaching

Levels of evaluation	Precoaching evaluation	Postcoaching evaluation

Level one
The coachee's reactions to the coaching program
	Prior to coaching, my belief in the benefits of coaching is:
	   low moderate high
	   1 2 3 4 5 6 7
		After coaching, my belief in the benefits of coaching is:
		   low moderate high
		   1 2 3 4 5 6 7

Level two
The level of understanding and skill mastery
	Prior to coaching, my level of knowledge (or competency) about the skill(s) to be addressed in coaching (e.g., leadership skills, sales skills) is:
	   low moderate high
	   1 2 3 4 5 6 7
		After coaching, my level of knowledge (or competency) about the skill(s) to be addressed in coaching (e.g., leadership skills, sales skills) is:
		   low moderate high
		   1 2 3 4 5 6 7

Level three
The effectiveness and usefulness of the coaching program
	Prior to coaching, my ability to perform tasks (e.g., team leader, presentation, strategic planning) is:
	   low moderate high
	   1 2 3 4 5 6 7
		After coaching, my ability to perform the tasks (e.g., team leader, presentation, strategic planning) is:
		   low moderate high
		   1 2 3 4 5 6 7

Level four
The organizational impact as perceived by the coachee.
	Prior to coaching, my perception that it will impact on the organization (e.g., sales, team performance, customer service) is:
	   low moderate high
	   1 2 3 4 5 6 7
		After coaching, my perception that it will affect the organization (e.g., sales, team performance, customer service) is:
		   low moderate high
		   1 2 3 4 5 6 7

Coaches working with managers and leaders employ various methods to establish the general and specific competencies required for these roles. These can be based on research, on best practices or nominated by the company or organization. At times, the coachee is new to a position and the expected roles and responsibilities are not clear. Clarifying these is essential; the coach needs to conduct interviews to determine what they are, as well as which ones should be the initial focus of the coaching program.

Interviews are also conducted with other stakeholders such as the senior manager, the CEO, HR personnel and work colleagues. While such meetings can provide valuable information, they can also be time-consuming. One method to overcome this barrier is to conduct a focus group.

Focus groups extend the interview to a group of involved individuals, typically ranging from five to ten in number. Focus groups should be composed of a representative sample of the population. The major drawback of focus groups is that they are subject to domination by one or several individuals. Politics can also interfere, so the climate is not always one of openness and trust.

Surveys are another effective means of gaining information. If they are conducted methodically and efficiently, they can furnish the coach with helpful information that not only serves to guide goal setting and action planning, but can also be used in precoaching and postcoaching evaluation. Ideally, surveys are administered to a random sample that is representative of the relevant population. The survey format can include open-ended questions, checklists, yes/no answers, multiple choice questions and rating scales. Incomplete questionnaires or "outliers" (i.e., extremely high or low ratings) are usually excluded from the analysis.

The major drawback of using surveys is that the response rate generally is low. For instance, a 50 per cent response rate is considered good, while often surveys generate a response rate as low as 10 per cent. Keeping the survey questions brief and enlisting the support of the coaching program manager or senior manager can help increase the return rate.

Observation of the coachee in the workplace is an effective and reliable means of data collection and is usually conducted by someone who is not generally part of the work environment, such as a coach. Prior to the observation exercise, the coach and coachee agree on the following dimensions: the purpose of the observation; its relation to performance; what behaviors will be observed, including the individual's strengths and weaknesses; whether the data will be qualitative, quantitative or a combination; how the behavior(s) will be scored; how frequently the observations will be carried out; and how these will be reported and incorporated into the coaching program.

Naturalistic observation sessions provide information on behavioral frequencies, duration and intensity. They also offer the coach a unique opportunity to observe the social or interpersonal interactions between the coachee and his or her colleagues. Such data is particularly valuable when there is a marked discrepancy between the coachee's self-reports and others' reports. Finally, coaches have to be aware of "reactivity," or the process by which behavior is affected by its assessment; that is, the coachee may act differently than usual when under observation.

Participant monitoring is one way in which the effects of reactivity are minimized. It involves the use of observers who are a natural part of the work environment. These can include colleagues, managers, HR personnel and coaching program managers. They record selected behaviors, such as the number of times the coachee exhibits specific management skills such as giving positive feedback or enlisting suggestions from employees, rather than simply giving them instructions.

Participant monitoring, because it is conducted by observers who are naturally on site, is subject to less reactivity than infrequent observations by a coach. The observation periods are ongoing, so the coachee becomes accustomed to the observers and over time their presence has less effect on her or his typical behavior. The process depends on several conditions, namely that the participants employ accurate and reliable observation techniques and that the exercise is not too resource-intensive.

Regardless of the nature of observation or monitoring by others, research shows that judgment about a person's behavior may be influenced by aspects of the observer. These include the observer's knowledge of the target person, as well as his or her personal motivation to contribute reports. Other factors coaches need to take into account include how observable the behavior is, how evaluative it is, and the nature of the relationship between the observer and the coachee, such as the level of familiarity between them.

Finally, true and reliable measures of behavior mean that if two observers independently observe the same behavior, they should score their checklists exactly the same for 85 per cent of the time. Coaches, therefore, are encouraged to employ more than one observer where possible, and to compare the ratings in order to establish the reliability of the observation procedure.

Analogue observation, such as situational analogues, entails the coachee being assessed in an artificial scenario resembling a work situation. For example, the coach role-plays a difficult colleague while the coachee plays herself or himself in a typical work scene. The interaction is videotaped, then the coach observes the tape and assesses the coachee on the agreed-upon behaviors. Examples of behaviors observed in this scenario would include the number of times the coachee raises his or her voice, shows signs of frustration or anger, or interrupts the colleague/coach.

Requisite coaching competencies at step two (data collection)

Assessment

Before discussing assessment, it is useful to distinguish it from evaluation. Assessment in coaching involves measuring behavior and performance and documenting it in a way that highlights areas for growth and development. Evaluation, on the other hand, is a judgment or determination about the quality of a performance, process or product. We address evaluation in step six of the coaching process.

Although assessment is discussed separately, it clearly comes under the rubric of data collection. The scope for assessment in coaching is, in many respects, unlimited, and a detailed discussion of the topic is well beyond the scope of this book. Yet many experienced and novice coaches hold to the belief that there is an assessment methodology that incorporates all possible coaching situations. Unlike psychiatry's *Diagnostic and Statistical Manual of Mental Disorders* (DSM), however, no such diagnostic tool exists for coaching. Coaching is at an early stage in its development. A tremendous amount of research and years of professional practice are necessary before it will have a valid and reliable system of classification and assessment. Consequently, at this stage, it is necessary to speak in generalities about assessment and diagnosis.

Although we noted that a detailed discussion of assessment is not within the scope of this book, an in-depth understanding of the subject is critical for coaches. It is for this reason that the Behavioral Coaching Institute's coach training courses pay particular attention to assessment issues. In these courses participants review current assessment instruments, their reliability and validity, how they are used in coaching today and their advantages and disadvantages. Assessment case studies and relevant research are analyzed and assessment resources are evaluated.

Here, time allows us only to address the question of assessment from the three perspectives that have particular relevance to the behavioral coaching model. First, we outline some of the reasons why assessment is vital to the coaching process. We then situate assessment in the context of the coaching process steps. Finally, we discuss specific assessment instruments and techniques and their place in coaching.

Assessment in coaching—a rationale

The following is a summary of the role of assessment in coaching and the benefits associated with it. Assessment:

- provides data around which goal setting, personal development plans (PDPs) and action plans can be built
- establishes requisite competencies, the coachee's strengths and weaknesses in relation to these, and her or his untapped potential
- establishes what solutions have worked in the past
- helps coaches understand the motivational, cognitive and emotional factors that underpin the coachee's behavior
- establishes how ready the organization and the individual are for change
- establishes at what stage of change the individual is
- establishes the coachee's level of self-awareness
- isolates the individual's personal and professional subjective needs
- determines what beliefs and automatic thinking patterns are limiting growth and development
- clarifies the coachee's and the organization's stated and in-use values
- determines the coachee's level of self-efficacy and self-esteem as they affect performance
- offers insight into the coachee's world view, purpose and life meaning as these influence commitment and achievement
- establishes a history of any problems associated with current behavior patterns
- clarifies the coachee's knowledge of the disadvantages associated with current behavior
- provides precoaching and postcoaching information that, along with other data, can be used to justify costs and calculate the benefits of the coaching program.

Assessment and the coaching process steps

Assessment is carried out during all the steps of the coaching process. Here, we are considering assessment as it occurs at step two (data collection).

It is the coach's responsibility to source and select his or her own assessment instruments. While we mention several of the more commonly used instruments, each coach must choose those that are appropriate for the particular coaching program, the coachee's needs and the reliability and validity of the assessment tools.

There are four aspects to any assessment procedure. These are:

- *Setting up the assessment* The coach and coachee establish the purpose of the assessment.
- *Designing the assessment* The coach chooses which assessment instruments will provide the most valuable information and have the most direct bearing on the objectives of the coaching program.

- *Performing the assessment* The coach, or a third party, administers the selected assessment instruments and collects and analyzes the data. In addition, coachees self-assess (e.g., self-monitoring), often on an ongoing basis, and the results are analyzed and discussed in coaching sessions.
- *Reporting the assessment* The coach provides supportive, quality feedback on the assessment in relation to its impact on the coachee's objectives.

Assessment can be conducted in the following ways: on a continuous basis (formative); at the end of a set period (summative); in real time; by others, such as the coachee, peers or coaching program manager; and as a measure of individual and team performance.

Assessment instruments focus on three aspects in particular. First, they identify the individual or team's personality and behavioral strengths and weaknesses as they relate to requisite competencies. Second, they help identify areas for improvement and ways in which a coachee's strengths can be best leveraged. Third, insights gained from the assessment are the subject of collaborative dialogue, which sets the stage for transformational learning and change.

Research shows that top-performing companies, as well as being better at people management, are also better at measurement. The notion of precise and repeated measurement as advocated by behavioral coaching, however, is alien to some organizations. Therefore, prior to instituting methods of assessment and measurement, it is useful for a coach to estimate the types and degree of measurement that usually occur within the particular company or organization. Otherwise, she or he could meet with resistance to the process.

Some assessment methods

In this section we refer to various profiles and assessment tools developed by the authors. For the purpose of economy, we have chosen not to reproduce these here. Rather, we refer readers to *The Coaching at Work Toolkit* (Zeus and Skiffington 2002).

360-degree feedback or multirater assessment is a standard practice of many behavioral coaches working in organizations. This method of assessment is also used by consultants and HR personnel in change management, performance evaluation and performance development. It involves obtaining feedback from individuals that have contact with the coachee, including colleagues, managers, clients, direct reports and subordinates. Several well-known proprietary instruments are available (e.g., Benchmarks, Skillscope, Profilor, The Life Styles Inventory). Coaches frequently construct their own multirater assessment instruments, with questions relating directly to the coaching objectives in terms of competencies to be developed and enhanced, as well as strengths and weaknesses.

Behavioral coaches working in organizations and businesses often employ a shortened version of the multirater assessment. For example, we have developed a mini-360-degree questionnaire that includes asking colleagues, peers and managers to rate the coachee on five or six competencies on which the coaching is focused (e.g., five or six leadership competencies). It is important, here, that coaches consider whether 360-degree or other multirater peer data could have a negative impact on an individual's or team's ability to trust and work with each other.

Structured interviews are also conducted, with many coaches creating their own. These usually take the form of self-ratings on a variety of questions, including preferred leadership styles, motivators and values; handling stress; conflict management; assertiveness; team behaviors; strengths and weaknesses; and areas to develop. These interviews are typically conducted at the beginning of the coaching program and inform the content of the sessions. Some components of the interview are used for postcoaching measurement.

Profiles are questionnaires that can be used in open discussion during coaching sessions or completed in a coachee's own time. Some of the profiles we have developed include a leadership profile, a learning styles profile, a life balance profile, a values profile, a small business profile and a life/work balance profile. Profiles are particularly useful because they can be used to target and assess information that is directly related to the coaching curriculum, and many can also be used as precoaching and postcoaching outcome measures.

Some issues to consider in assessment

As we noted earlier, some interviews and behavioral observations are subject to distortion and bias. While formal, standardized psychometric testing can offset some of these problems, questions of validity and reliability remain central to the choice of any assessment instrument. Validity refers to what the instrument is actually measuring, that is, whether it measures what it purports to measure (face validity), as well as the accuracy of the measurement and whether the results have predictive ability. Reliability is a measure of the consistency of results. For example, if the assessment purports to measure personality traits or relatively permanent dispositions, then the same results should be obtained on a retest. Moreover, the results should be the same regardless of who administered the questionnaire.

Over the past decade or two, a large body of research has provided compelling evidence for a five-factor model of personality. These five factors are: extraversion/introversion which includes traits such as being assertive, social, expressive and gregarious; emotional stability, which includes traits such as being anxious, depressed, angry, insecure and emotional; agreeableness, which includes being courteous, flexible, cooperative, forgiving, tolerant and trusting; conscientiousness, which reflects dependability, being careful, thoroughness, achievement oriented and persevering; and openness to experience, about which there is less agreement, but which is associated with being curious, imaginative, open-minded, intelligent and sensitive.

Conscientiousness has been related to job performance across diverse populations and occupations, while extraversion is a valid predictor for sales performance. Agreeableness and emotional stability have been found to predict service performance. Various instruments build around these five factors. Two that have a growing empirical base include the Hogan Personality Inventory and the Neo Five Factor Inventory.

Certification is required to administer certain assessments. For example, some are restricted to psychologists and some to psychologists and HR personnel. Furthermore, the use of some instruments requires training. Understanding how to administer an instrument is obviously crucially important. However, assessments can be misused if the individual administering them does not debrief coachees adequately. Assessments can be threatening and coachees may focus on perceived negative aspects and feel vulnerable and defensive.

Finally, assessments are valuable only if they have direct relevance to the coaching focus. It is frequently more helpful to assess and discuss specific, relevant personality characteristics and competencies in detail rather than broader categories that may not bear on the coaching content. For example, a coach working with a leader or manager may have determined that being "opportunistic" is a requisite competency. The coach would then explore opportunism in further detail by assessing research-based facets of the construct. These include resourcefulness, practical know-how, risk propensity, creativity, entrepreneurial talents, situation appraisal skills, analytical skills, strategic skills, taking initiative and creating the future or visioning. The relevance and specificity of assessment instruments must always be considered along with validity and reliability issues.

Specific areas of assessment

Assessing aspects of the self

Changing behavior frequently entails changing aspects of the self. It is therefore important for both coach and coachee to have a clear understanding of the coachee's self-concept. In Chapter 2, we explored self-concept in relation to coaching as a form of personal development. We discussed the construct within the framework developed by Nancy Leonard and colleagues. According to their model, self-concept refers to four aspects of the self. These are the perceived self, the ideal self, social identity and self-esteem. The following guidelines, based on this model, provide a practical and comprehensive blueprint for assessing a coachee's self-concept.

The perceived self

- Assess traits informally through a structured interview of profile or through a formal assessment (e.g., The Big Five)
- Assess competencies and knowledge, skills and abilities
- Assess values (stated and in-use).

The ideal self

- Assess traits, competencies and values the coachee would like to have.
- What are the gaps between the perceived self and the ideal self?

- Are these gaps "realistic"?
- How are they affecting the coachee's life and work?

Social identity

- How does the coachee define his or her social self?
- What social categories does the coachee belong to?

Self-esteem

- *Chronic* What is the coachee's current level? Is it so low that therapy will be required?
- *Task specific* What are the feedback results from peers and others? What is the coachee's skills confidence level? What skills, training and coaching does the individual need?
- *Socially influenced* What are the expectations of others? What social feedback has been given regarding meeting these expectations? What gaps does the coachee wish to close?

Having assessed the coachee on these four elements of self-concept, the coach is in a position to understand what motivates the individual. Recognizing what motivates a coachee is critical in terms of setting appropriate goals and choosing meaningful reinforcement or rewards.

The primary aspect of motivation to consider is whether the coachee is inner-directed or outer-directed. For example, the individual's perceived and ideal self may be a function of a comparison with others and may be related to the expectations of others. If this is so, then the coachee can be said to be outer-directed. Her or his ideal self comes about through adopting the role expectations of reference groups (e.g., peers, the team). The individual is motivated to behave in order to gain the group's acceptance of his or her worth. Group status and having influence in the group are powerful motivators for outer-directed individuals.

On the other hand, an individual who is primarily inner-directed will be motivated by internal factors, such as wanting to achieve according to her or his own standards or "personal best." These individuals are driven not by the need for group acceptance and recognition, but rather by task achievement; that is, they require their efforts to be instrumental in achieving a task.

Assessing health

Behavioral coaching, although typically focused on business objectives, is essentially a holistic model. Not only does it include assessing aspects of the self, as described above, but it takes into account the individual's physical well-being. It is widely accepted that pressure, change and work overload can take their toll on a person's health. This, in turn, negatively affects work performance.

Two of the health areas most frequently explored in coaching are physical exercise and nutrition. The coach works with the coachee to develop a simple exercise plan, building it into the overall action plan for the program. If the coachee's needs are more complex, a qualified trainer may be enlisted. Similarly, the coach discusses the coachee's eating habits in relation to maintaining a well-balanced diet. If the coachee's habits are negatively affecting his or her health, the coach provides general information about healthy eating habits. Depending on the coach's level of knowledge, she or he can also help the coachee to develop a diet plan. If the coachee is excessively overweight or underweight and has obvious health problems, he or she is referred to a qualified nutritionist.

Assessing the shadow

As noted in Chapter 1 and elsewhere, unconscious forces shape our behavior, as well as that of teams and organizations. The unknown side of human nature is generally referred to as "the shadow side," which contains destructive and regressive forces but also our unknown strengths and potential.

Anger in organizations, whether between colleagues, between employer and employee or staff and customers is frequently triggered by unconscious factors. For instance, psychoanalytic theory attests to the pervasiveness of shame and feelings of unworthiness triggering anger and conflict in organizations. Similarly, feelings of loss can result in depression. In the current climate of corporate change and a perceived and real lack of corporate loyalty, individuals may be subjected to feelings of loss. They no longer experience the sense of collective safety and invulnerability that companies and organizations once provided. The structure of many organizations also mitigates against individual members developing a shared, affirming identity.

In order to cope with these and other unpleasant realities, we employ defense mechanisms, as discussed in Chapter 2 Defensive tactics can manifest on the emotional, cognitive and behavioral level. They are very powerful and, when challenged, cause the individual extreme anxiety. Coaches, for example, have to be aware of the unconscious impact that a performance appraisal or 360-degree feedback could be having on a coachee. We are not advocating that coaches who are not trained in psychotherapy or psychoanalysis attempt to analyze coachees. Nevertheless, coaches do need to be able to observe and explore emotional patterns if these are affecting a coachee's performance. They do this through heightening coachees' awareness of behavioral patterns and of those situations and people that make them uncomfortable, or even distressed.

The demand for change, even in a highly motivated and committed coachee, can engender anxiety, defensiveness and, sometimes, anger. Coaches have to be able to contain these feelings and allow coachees free expression within the bounds of the coaching sessions. Feelings can revolve around personal fears, life or personal problems or dissatisfaction because of unrecognized potential and talents in the workplace. The ability to successfully contain such feelings depends, in part, on the coach's awareness and understanding of these defense mechanisms. The coach's own self-knowledge and ability to cope with negative emotions in coachees and the feelings these may trigger in herself or himself allow for a shift or a transformation in the coachee's thoughts, feelings and behaviors.

Research and experience suggests that the first step in dealing with the shadow is to recognize when it may be at work. The second is to not take a coachee's behavior personally. Third, the coach has to clearly let the coachee know what he or she is observing. Such information has to be clearly and honestly stated and presented in a tone of inquiry that is not likely to induce further resistance or hostility. The coach's ability to deliver this information appropriately also serves as a model for the type of dialogue that successful coaching sessions are built around.

Organizations, too, have a shadow side, which can manifest in various ways. Frequently, it is seen in resistance to a proposed coaching program. Because the client or senior manager has secret fears about her or his role in the organization's problems or fears loss of control, she or he may unconsciously resist changes. Anxiety about destabilizing the political status quo can also trigger anxiety.

Clients can devalue the coaching profession, intellectualize about the methodology and processes, request endless information about the program or demand solutions. All of these behaviors are means of dealing with their anxieties and resistance to change. As with coachees, clients have to be faced with their behaviors. The coach has to reflect back what he or she is experiencing and engage the client in a non-emotional, non-judgmental, constructive dialogue about these "shadows."

Self-monitoring as self-assessment

In Chapter 3 we looked at self-monitoring, or the systematic observing of one's own behavior over time, in the context of behavioral techniques for managing the consequences of behavior. In this section, we explore self-monitoring in relation to self-assessment.

Self-monitoring in behavioral coaching frequently takes the form of a functional analysis, which, as noted earlier, is an assessment of the connections between a behavior, its antecedents and consequences. It helps to define the target behavior exactly and clearly, determine which antecedents function to produce the behavior and how the person's behavior functions to produce positive or negative consequences.

A functional analysis can be helpful in monitoring behavioral excesses (e.g., outbursts of anger) or deficits (e.g., wanting to give more positive feedback to team members). The data collected can vary in detail. Typically, the coachee keeps a log of the antecedents of behavior (A=activity, S=social, C=covert, E=emotions, P=physical, D=distant and O=other). The actual consequences and their type (either positive or negative) are recorded, as well as the coachee's comments.

The following table is an example of a standard behavioral A-B-C log. It was maintained by a senior accounts manager, J. H., who was receiving coaching for uncontrollable outbursts of anger. It was kept for several weeks to obtain a baseline measure of the outbursts. J. H. continued recording his behavior in this format throughout the coaching sessions.

Table 5.3 A functional analysis of "temper outbursts"

Antecedents	Type	Behavior	Data	Consequences	Type	Comments
Date/time	A, S, C, E, P, D, O		frequency, duration, intensity		+ve -ve	
Mon. 2 pm. J. H. working at desk. The general manager (GM) called him into office and told him a client had complained about his "badgering style"	A, S, E, C, P, D	J. H. raised his voice angrily. J. H. walked out of the office.	3 minutes	GM became more angry and vocal. J. H. was furious. J. H. failed to get critical data from GM.	-ve -ve -ve	Felt okay when working at desk. Felt I performed badly with GM.
Tues. 11 am. J.H. had a meeting with client/complainant. Called a meeting with GM	A, S, E, C, D	Tried to deal rationally with client's concerns. Apologized for outburst.	15 minutes 5 minutes	Client appeared placated. GM accepted same but reiterated his concerns about J. H.'s belligerent manner.	+ve +ve -ve	Felt more confident. Still concerned about temper displays.
Wed. 9.40 am. Spoke with client on telephone. Client unhappy with "proofs" for advertising campaign. J. H. felt defensive and anxious.	A, S, E, C, D	Assuaged client's concerns. Called in creative team and accused them of sloppy work.	15 minutes 6 minutes	Client agreed not to cancel contract. Team became angry and stormed out of office.	+ve -ve	Still frustrated but relieved about client. Angry with client and team. Disappointed and frustrated with self.

A = activity S = social C = covert E = emotions P = physical D = distant O = others

Although we are exploring self-monitoring at step two of the coaching process, it is equally valuable at the other steps. For example, as shown above, a coachee can employ self-monitoring to establish a baseline for behaviors. However, once the baseline has been established, goals set and action plans put in place (step three), the coachee continues to self-monitor in order to record changes in the targeted behavior that result from instituting behavioral change methods (step four). The monitoring can continue through steps five to seven to insure there is no relapse.

Self-assessment is a powerful means of insuring that coachees gain more control over their lives and become more independent and self-generating. Through self-assessment, coachees can also obtain information about their behavior compared with that of others. For example, a coachee observed and kept a record of the number of projects she or he submitted on time compared with colleagues. Another coachee kept track of the number of contributions he made at team meetings compared with other team members. Such information was then used as a baseline and as comparative data to set coaching objectives around.

Reflection is a crucial component of any learning experience and is built into all aspects of the coaching program and all steps of the process. During each coaching session, for example, time is allocated for the coachee or team to reflect on what has been learned and how the learning can be synthesized and transferred to the workplace. Assessments present coachees with feedback about their behavior patterns and performance. Reflecting on the data provides coachees with the opportunity to understand their emotional responses and to compare measured performance and behaviors with personal standards and aspirations.

Generating hypotheses about behavior

Coaching is about finding solutions. Before solutions are reached, however, coaches are frequently engaged in developing and testing hypotheses, often in relation to factors that appear to cause or influence a coachee's behavior. For example, based on a coachee's passive, non-assertive behavior in coaching sessions, a coach might hypothesize that the stated performance gaps may be a function of the coachee's personality style. In order to test this tentative explanation, the coach might conduct a 360-feedback appraisal or administer a particular personality profile. Another coachee might appear ambivalent about coaching designed to "groom" her or him for a more senior position. The coach might hypothesize that the ambivalence results from a values conflict or a knowledge deficit. In either case, the coach would test the hypothesis through questioning and data collection.

There are several hypotheses relating to coachees' behavior, and these have been categorized into three groups: individual factors, team conditions and organizational factors. Frequently, of course, the presenting behavior is a function of a combination of the three.

These possible causal factors are, of course, not all-encompassing. Rather, they are suggested as possible avenues for questioning, exploration, dialogue and assessment.

Individual factors:

- personality characteristics (e.g., need for control, assertiveness, self-esteem, self-efficacy)
- skill deficit
- unrecognized potential
- values conflict
- motivation
- psychopathology

Team factors:

- skill deficit
- performance goals not aligned with organization's vision and long-term plans
- role confusion
- conflict over limited resources
- personality conflicts
- team leadership issues

Organizational factors:

- no support from above
- politics
- resource allocation
- systems resisting change
- lack of career development opportunities

Single-, double- and triple-loop questioning

Behavioral coaches recognize the crucial role of questioning and "diagnosing" at various stages of the coaching process. Here, we discuss three types of questions that guide discovery and insight.

Single-loop questions are those that raise and explore issues on a superficial level. For instance, a sales team is not performing well, but the coach, client and coachee do not explore the reasons for this in any great depth. Consequently, potential solutions to the problem are not considered. Rather, solutions tend to focus on action, such as replacing the sales manager.

Double-loop questions provide the opportunity for greater insight. They go beyond the surface and question why certain situations have arisen and what factors have contributed to them. For instance, questions may be raised about whether the sales team's dysfunction is a product of inadequate resources or lack of follow-up training.

Finally, triple-loop questions provide an opportunity for the client and coachee to question their assumptions about the organization, its values and culture. These questions may invite reflection, for example, on the status of teams within the organizational hierarchy, the structure of the teams and how these things might be changed to improve performance.

Requisite coaching competencies at step two (data collection)

Knowledge of: reliable and valid methods of data collection and their advantages and disadvantages; establishing and facilitating focus groups; how to establish criteria of performance against which data is to be collected; how to systematically collect data and synthesize results into unique insights to target and enhance performance; conducting surveys; rationale for assessment; limitations associated with various assessment methodologies; 360-degree feedback or other multirater assessments; mini-360-degree assessments; structured interviews and profiles; performance measurements; knowledge, skills and abilities and gaps for development; functional analysis; self-monitoring and other forms of self-assessment; self-concept theory and assessment; models of personal development that relate coachees' issues to life stages and challenges, as discussed in Chapter 2; health issues around performance; strategies to deal with high-risk situations (e.g., avoidance, coping skills); shadow forces and ways to manage these.

Skills: respect and consideration for the individual being observed; collaboration with others involved in data gathering; strong observation skills, such as clearly articulating observation criteria, evaluating against the criteria and providing quality feedback; solid recording skills; non-judgmental, reliable and honest recording of observations; reflecting impartially and creatively on the data; role-playing in analogue situations; observation skills; recording skills; feedback and debriefing skills; introspection; reflection skills; generating hypotheses; insightfully linking assessment results to performance objectives; asking questions that generate insight.

Step three: Planning

In this section we discuss planning as it relates to targeting or selecting behaviors for change, setting goals and developing action plans.

Targeting specific, observable, measurable behaviors

Through the process of data collection (step two), the overall objectives of the coaching program are determined. For example, data gathered in interviews, surveys, multirater assessments and individual assessments may have indicated that a coachee needed to develop team leadership skills. While one of the competencies associated with high-performing team leaders was the ability to inspire team members, this broad category had to be converted or "pinpointed" into an observable, measurable and specific behavior. Discussion with the coachee and feedback from his peers showed that as a team leader he rarely engaged staff in discussion around their performance or the organization's strategic plans. Consequently, the behavior to be targeted was described as "not giving feedback to team members." Having identified the behavioral deficit, the coach and coachee worked on goals and behavioral change techniques to increase its occurrence. In another case study, an entrepreneur's objective was to grow her business.

Once she had engaged in the pinpointing process, it was obvious that she wasted too much time networking and socializing. The behavioral excess was then targeted for change.

Steps in targeting behaviors for change:

- Select measurable, specific, observable behavior(s).
- Identify the desired change (e.g., to communicate regularly to team members about strategic plans and performance issues).
- Identify the conditions that maintain the behavior (e.g., lack of knowledge about the organization's strategic plans; insufficient time).
- Collect baseline data about the behavior.
- Identify conditions that will generate new or desired behaviors (e.g., communication from the senior team about strategy; effective time management).
- Determine the reinforcers for the changed behaviors (e.g., improved self-confidence and "authority" with the team; less time in the office and more time with family).

Goal setting

Setting goals is another core component of the behavioral coaching model. Goals provide the focal point for the coach and coachee to determine strategies to move the coachee forward. They also provide a reference standard to assess performance task difficulty, self-efficacy, task performance and postcoaching performance. According to goal theory, setting goals (conscious intentions) can actually cause behavior because they direct our thoughts and actions. Goals are represented mentally, so they can be automatically activated by the environment.

Sports psychology, in particular, has generated a considerable body of research pertaining to goal setting. For example, it has been shown that individuals with high levels of self-efficacy set high personal goals, and that they perform well and achieve their goals. Other findings highlight the importance of relating short-term goals to longer term ones, as the latter provide meaning to the former. Achievement of short-term goals leads to a sense of self-mastery, success and increasing confidence, all of which increase the probability of achieving long-term success.

Some studies show that self-set goals are more desirable than assigned goals because they automatically engender higher commitment. However, in organizational coaching, even though the coachee is involved in structuring the goal hierarchy, the overall objectives and even specific goals are sometimes set by senior management. Recent findings indicate that individuals don't have to participate in work goal setting to demonstrate strong commitment. Nevertheless, certain conditions are necessary for this to occur and these revolve around the person assigning the goals. For example, the individual setting the goals should be a legitimate authority figure who inspires vision and provides a solid rationale for each goal. This person expects excellent performance from everyone, gives ownership, rewards success and provides corrective and positive feedback and suggestions. Coachees whose managers fit these criteria are clearly advantaged and are highly likely to achieve their goals. Where managers do not operate within this framework, the coach, either directly or through the coaching program manager, can attempt to enlist the manager in the coaching program. Otherwise, hard won gains dissipate when the coachee returns to an environment that does not support the changed behavior and growth.

Finally, many behavioral coaches employ a combination of goal setting and mind-mapping techniques in order to engage both left and right hemispheres of the brain. Research and anecdotal reports suggest that this combination leads to accelerated learning and enhanced performance and creativity.

Conditions for goal setting

Several conditions have to be met in order for goal setting to be an efficient and productive exercise. The behavioral coaching model nominates the following preconditions:

- The individual's or team's goals are aligned with the business objectives of the company or organization.
- Goals are based on clear choices and decisions.
- Environmental conditions are favorable for achieving the goals.
- Strategies to manage resistance and obstacles are put in place.
- Strategies to achieve the goals relate to specific behaviors in specific situations.
- The coachee has the requisite skills to perform the tasks.
- The coachee has knowledge of, and training in, specific behavioral change techniques such as stimulus control, self-regulation and management of the consequences of the specific behaviors.
- Goals are restricted to performance expectations over which the coachee has control.
- Goals involve self-competition and self-mastery.

How to set goals in six steps

There is a wealth of literature on methods of goal setting. The process behavioral coaches employ is based on research and includes the following steps.

Step one: Nominate performance gaps The coach and coachee, sometimes in concert with the senior manager or coaching program manager, analyze and nominate the gaps between current and desired performance. Gaps do not necessarily imply a deficit. For example, in executive coaching, the gaps are frequently between where the person is now and where he or she wishes to be, either personally or professionally.

Step two: Establish a history of goal achievement Obtaining a history of the coachee's past goal achievements and non-achievements provides the coach with a preview of potential obstacles to reaching current goals. It informs the coach of strategies that helped and did not help. In addition, the period of reflection allows the coachee to consider past and current patterns of behavior that may affect goal achievement. Importantly, this dialogue highlights the coachee's strengths, which can then be leveraged to enhance the probability of goal attainment.

Step three: Clarify and record overall objectives Although the words "goal" and "objective" are frequently used interchangeably, we refer to an objective as the individual's, team's or organization's ultimate destination or target. For example, a team leader's objective was for his team to make the most sales in the company. His goals, or the steps by which the objectives were to be met, included developing a program of team and individual coaching as a follow-through on sales training and to recruit two top-performing salespeople.

Step four: Nominate all possible goals All goals that relate to the stated objective(s) are drawn up, preferably with the aid of mind mapping. These goals are then rated according to their level of achievement possibility.

Step five: Goal selection Each goal is evaluated in relation to the SMART model; that is, each goal should be specific, measurable, achievable, realistic and time-limited. The goals are then prioritized in terms of immediate relevance and urgency, as discussed above. Some coachees experience choice conflict, making it difficult for them to prioritize goals. In these situations, the coach determines whether the coachee would benefit from training in problem solving or whether it would be more helpful to simply explore all alternatives in terms of their risks, consequences and obstacles and prioritize accordingly.

Step six: Goal formulation The selected goals are formulated into items and their attendant behaviors, and the coachee builds these into a development plan. The behaviors are under the coachee's control and have an optimal probability of achievement and agreed-upon outcome measures. The coach and coachee explore all possible obstacles to goal achievement and develop preventative and coping strategies to deal with these.

Action planning

Action planning involves documenting the steps or actions coachees will take to achieve their goals. There are two types of action plans. The first, referred to as a personal development plan (PDP), is a record of a coachee's overall plans for development. Constructing a PDP, on which both the coach and coachee sign off, provides a valuable opportunity for the coach and coachee to reflect on and dialogue about the key skills to be developed and the requisite critical success factors. It provides a structure around which the coach and coachee can systematically develop strategies to facilitate goal achievement.

The PDP is also a record of achievement that can, with the coachee's consent, be shared with management, the coaching program manager or HR personnel. Furthermore, it is a document that can attest to the effectiveness of the coaching program.

A personal development plan: Coaching for team leadership skills

Ways to apply strengths as identified in assessments and profiles:

- Inspire and align team members to the company's vision.
- Develop and mentor two junior managers.

Ways to close the identified skills gaps:

- Identify requisite competencies for my position.
- Coaching for team leadership skills.
- Develop a mentoring relationship with T. U., a senior executive.

Benefits of developing these skills:

- Personally: increased confidence in abilities, more effective relations with team, more recognition from senior management.
- For the organization: increased productivity, improved working environment, "grooming" and development of individuals with high potential.

Which skills are most important for myself and the organization to develop?

- Leadership skills; creating vision and aligning team; coaching skills; interpersonal skills, especially conflict resolution.

What resources do I need to close the skills gap?

- Coaching sessions over a period of six months to develop skills, advanced leadership training, conflict resolution training

What is the measure of success for each of these skills?

- Leadership: to obtain higher scores on postcoaching multirater assessments of leadership qualities compared with precoaching

- Creating vision and aligning team: increased team focus and decreased delivery time on major projects

- Coaching skills: each team member will have an individualized development plan and meet with me on a weekly basis

- Interpersonal skills, especially conflict resolution: less, ideally no, avoidance of conflict situations by self, decrease in number of destructive conflict struggles between team members and more open, constructive dissent in the team.

An action plan is used to document a coachee's goals and achievements between sessions. It contains the "homework" or tasks the coachee has agreed to perform, and is discussed at the following session in terms of achievements and obstacles. Maintaining a weekly log such as an action plan provides both coach and coachee with an easily accessible means of evaluating progress. It keeps the partners focused and accountable.

Several factors have to be taken into consideration when constructing an action plan. These include whether the coachee has the knowledge, skills and abilities to perform the action; how much time the action will take; what the individual and organizational constraints are; and what impact the actions will have on others in the workplace.

Table 5.4 A weekly action plan

Action steps	Expected results	Date to achieve	Achieved? Yes/No	Coachee's comments
1. Practice relaxation exercise twice daily.	Lowered anxiety level.	Daily	Yes	Felt calmer, thinking was clearer, less apprehensive.
2. Make appointment with manager to discuss recent performance appraisal and job description.	Clarify roles and expectations of the job. Gain additional resources and support from management.	Monday 22nd	Yes Yes	Felt more self-confident about my competencies when the manager agreed to certain changes in my job description and offered further training.
3. Discuss any changes to role with team members.	To align and gain support from team.	Friday 26th	No	Felt too apprehensive about facing the team in light of the negative feedback they had given me. Delayed arranging a meeting with them until it was too late in the week. Felt even more anxious.

Requisite coaching competencies at step three (planning)

Knowledge of: behavioral analysis; operationalizing behaviors; obtaining baseline measures; reinforcement; goal theory; a comprehensive goal-setting model; behavioral contracting; personal development plans; action planning criteria; hypotheses generation.

Skills: identifying behaviors; maintaining momentum; problem solving; exploring obstacles; modeling desired behaviors; balancing the organization's and individual's objectives and goals.

Step four: Behavioral change

Having established the coachee's goals and an action plan, the coach and coachee focus on changing the targeted behaviors through established behavioral change techniques. In Chapter 3 we detailed and gave examples of numerous behavioral techniques that behavioral coaches employ at this stage of the coaching process. These included conducting a behavioral analysis, as well as techniques to manage antecedents, behaviors and consequences.

Techniques to manage antecedents included modeling, prompting, self-instructions, stimulus and self-regulation. Some of the suggested techniques to manage behaviors included shaping, using alternative responses, relaxation, coping statements, practice and reframing. Finally, we discussed validated techniques to manage the consequences of behavior. In this category, we examined reinforcement, extinction, self-monitoring, promoting generalization and environmental support, to name a few.

During this fourth step of the coaching process the coach conducts "skills coaching" and "rehearsal coaching," as discussed earlier in this chapter. Regardless of the coaching focus, every coachee undergoes some type of skills acquisition. This can be team sales skills; interpersonal skills, including assertiveness and giving feedback to staff; or hard skills, such as strategic planning. These skills have to be learned and rehearsed prior to the coachee actually performing them in the workplace.

Skills coaching and rehearsal coaching frequently necessitate the use of other coaching techniques. For instance, coaches may also work with an individual's or team's belief systems as they affect goal achievement. Additionally, they may help coachees to manage their emotions more effectively (self-regulation) and encourage self-awareness and reflection on performance and achievement.

Requisite coaching competencies at step four (behavioral change)

Knowledge of: a variety of behavioral change techniques; learning theory; reinforcement; self-monitoring strategies; strategic planning; business planning; leadership development; team building; performance models, such as sales; conflict resolution theory and practice; assertion models and techniques; cross-cultural factors.

Skills: team coaching; skills coaching; rehearsal coaching; questioning, challenging, and disputing self-limiting beliefs; exploring obstacles and blocks; managing emotions; managing fluctuations in behavior.

Step five: Measurement

At this step in the process, the coachee is at the action stage of change and the coach is employing performance coaching. As noted earlier in this chapter and in Chapter 1, performance coaching involves working with coachees as they apply the learned skills in the workplace. These skills are measured on an ongoing basis in order to track progress.

Self-monitoring is invaluable at this step in the process. For example, the coach and coachee could agree that the coachee will measure a specified behavior (e.g., temper outbursts). The coachee would maintain a log and record the frequency, duration and intensity of the outbursts, and these would be measured against the baseline.

Coachees typically rate these dimensions on a Likert-type scale, a scale from 0 to 100, or by using simple yes/no responses. For instance, a coach working with a coachee's temper outbursts asked her to record the following two types of measurement information on a daily and weekly basis for three weeks:

Self-monitoring exercises

1   On a scale of 0 to 100, rate yourself on the following questions *on a daily basis* for three weeks:
    a   How frequently are you experiencing temper outbursts? ( )
    b   How intense are these outbursts? ( )
    c   How long do the temper outbursts last? ( )
2   On a scale of 1 to 7, where 1 is "very rarely" and 7 is "very often," please rate yourself on the following questions at the end of each week:
    a   Are you experiencing temper outbursts less frequently than before? (Y/N)
    b   Are you experiencing the temper outbursts less intensely than previously? (Y/N)
    c   Do the temper outbursts last for shorter periods? (Y/N).

The coachee's peers or manager can also be enlisted to rate the coachee's behavior on a scale of 0 to 100. The data is then collected and the coach and coachee are able to measure progress in managing the angry behavior. If the data indicates that the coachee is not performing as expected, then the coach employs alternative strategies, or further rehearsal of the anger-regulation skills.

Finally, the coach plays a significant role in measuring the coachee's performance. The coach observes or shadows the coachee as she or he executes the newly acquired skills. Feedback is given as soon after the event as possible and behavioral adjustments are made. Toward the end of the measurement phase, a 360-degree feedback assessment can be conducted and precoaching and postcoaching ratings compared.

Requisite coaching competencies at step five (measurement)

Knowledge of: behavioral analysis; measurement techniques and data collection; data analysis and interpretation methods; self-regulation skills.

Skills: align coachee and other participants in the measurement process; adaptability; flexibility; supporting; challenging; problem solving; measuring progress against objectives; managing fluctuations in progress.

Step six: Evaluation

Coaching is based on results and is linked to specific business objectives. Measurement and evaluation are therefore necessary to establish this linkage. Evaluation allows coaches to ask whether they are achieving the objectives of the coaching project. It can show organizational and individual growth, track expenditure in relation to ROI, and, importantly, contribute to the growth of the coaching profession. It is only through evaluation that coaching programs can be changed and enhanced.

Importantly, coaching is only one of several programs an organization can employ to further learning and development. It therefore has to be systematically evaluated in order to justify its use. Furthermore, as we are all aware, coaching and training and other development programs are usually the first to be cut in times of economic unease or downturn. In such periods, it is critical that coaches can provide a financial justification for their services. Being able to provide ROI data, for example, even if it is not specifically requested, gives a coach a competitive edge. Data from the evaluation process can also contribute to research into coaching outcomes.

The overall purpose of any evaluation is to show how the individual and the organization have changed as a result of coaching. To do this, the coach has to use all available data to determine the outcome of the program. Behavioral coaches require an evaluation strategy that includes timely, cost-effective and efficient methods that are of most value to the business or organization. As we noted previously, methods of evaluation have to be agreed-upon in collaboration with the client and other key stakeholders. Some of the questions that come under discussion during meetings and interviews with stakeholders include the following, which can be used by the coach as a checklist.

- The purpose of the evaluation strategy
- The value of the strategy to the business or organization
- Methods of evaluation that have proved valuable in the past
- At what levels should data be collected? (e.g., according to Kirkpatrick's four levels)
- What methods are most effective? (e.g., client surveys, coachee reports, surveys of focus groups, 360-degree feedback, peer reviews)
- Is an ROI required?
- Will there be a pilot or initial phase to test the evaluation methods, which can then be further refined and developed?
- What are the time frames and deadlines for evaluation data to be submitted?
- What are the responsibilities of the client, the coachee and other stakeholders?
- What are the necessary resources?
- What factors could affect the evaluation method? (e.g., changes in business structure, products and personnel)
- What intangibles will be measured and will these be assigned a monetary value?

When is ROI appropriate?

In discussions with key stakeholders it should be determined whether the coach will employ ROI methods, conduct a return on expectations (ROE), or a combination of both. These decisions are based on the scope of the coaching program, its cost, time frame and the client's overall objectives.

Importantly, the focus of a coaching program determines, to a great extent, which evaluation method is most appropriate. The critical point is whether the coaching contract is short term or long term. For example, if the contract for sales coaching is for three to six months, then an ROI could be calculated at the end of this period. However, if the coaching focus is more on soft skills such as interpersonal or assertiveness skills, the true benefits will not always be apparent at the end of the program. When the focus is on intangibles, ROI is not usually appropriate; ROE is generally the superior method of evaluation in this case.

Evaluating intangibles

Soft skills can be evaluated in relation to their effects on employee morale, absenteeism and work satisfaction. However, in order to rule out the impact of extraneous variables, it is necessary to compare these factors with those of a control group that has not received coaching. We will discuss the use of control groups in more detail later in this chapter.

Some of the intangibles coaches measure include changes in job satisfaction, changes in leadership and management style and changes in teamwork. Unlike consulting, for instance, coaching typically focuses on soft skills. If an ROI is too difficult to calculate, the coach can show how changes in the coachee's behavior affect the bottom line without putting a monetary value on this.

Figure 5.1, for example, shows a flow chart of the benefits of coaching for a soft skill, namely, team leadership.

Figure 5.1 The impact of coaching "soft skills"

A framework for evaluation

Figure 5.2 is a summary of the steps behavioral coaches follow to conduct a reliable and efficient evaluation of their coaching services.

Conducting an ROE

Many coaching and consulting practitioners suggest that a formal ROI is not necessary. They claim it is not cost-effective and is an unnecessary burden on the coach and the organization. As well, many claim that it is virtually impossible to isolate the effects of the numerous variables that

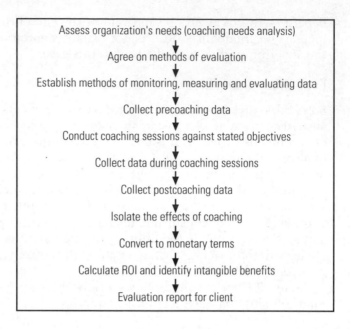

Assess organization's needs (coaching needs analysis)
↓
Agree on methods of evaluation
↓
Establish methods of monitoring, measuring and evaluating data
↓
Collect precoaching data
↓
Conduct coaching sessions against stated objectives
↓
Collect data during coaching sessions
↓
Collect postcoaching data
↓
Isolate the effects of coaching
↓
Convert to monetary terms
↓
Calculate ROI and identify intangible benefits
↓
Evaluation report for client

Figure 5.2 Steps in the evaluation process

affect coaching outcomes. Moreover, coaching individuals for development, for example to enter management, may not have any true business impact until that person assumes the new responsibilities.

As a result, many coaches and clients choose to conduct an ROE to evaluate coaching outcomes. An ROE essentially involves setting out the plans of the coaching program, gaining consensus on the objectives and then tracking the program to insure that the objectives and goals have been met. The underlying assumption of conducting an ROE is that as long as the coaching program focuses on the organization's business objectives and results in positive changes, then it will be valued by the organization. Coaches have to establish the goals of the organization and those of individual coachees, the changes that have to be made to meet these goals, the degree of learning that has to occur to effect these changes and how they will be measured. Finally, the evaluation plan must include how the learning will be applied on the job, as well as the overall business impact, although not in monetary terms. Among the many things an ROE can encompass and measure are productivity, organizational strength, customer service, reduced customer complaints, level of conflict and job satisfaction.

Conducting an ROI

Behavioral coaches follow several established guiding principles when conducting an ROI. The methodologies should be as simple as possible, while being credible and based on accepted practices. They should be economical, time-effective and able to account for multiple factors. The method should be flexible and applicable to both hard data (e.g., the percentage increase in sales) and soft data (e.g., improvement in morale). These intangibles can be presented as supportive qualitative data.

An ROI can present, measure and evaluate the financial returns of a coaching program. It can also quantify reaction to and satisfaction with the project, the amount of learning, application and implementation (e.g., according to Kirkpatrick's four levels). In addition, an ROI evaluates business impact, actual financial returns and data on intangible benefits.

A common model for calculating ROI is:

$$\text{ROI} = \frac{\text{net coaching benefits}}{\text{coaching costs}} \times 100$$

Depending on the scope and time frame of the coaching program, an ROI can be calculated at three months and six months, and a postcoaching evaluation can be undertaken at nine months.

Measuring benefits

The following is a selection of coaching benefits that can be included in an ROI:

- bottom-line profitability
- sales figures
- retaining executives who receive coaching
- cost reductions
- quality of products and service
- overall productivity.

Some of the "soft" data that can be calculated includes:

- leadership skills
- management skills
- conflict resolution skills
- working relationships with employees
- job satisfaction
- time management
- organizational commitment
- client relationships.

Measuring costs

Some of the costs to be measured for an ROI include:

- direct costs of implementing the coaching program (e.g., research and development costs, sessional fees, travel expenses, accommodation, assessment)
- time, including any follow-up contact via telephone, email and video conferencing
- cost in productivity to the organization while coachees are in session
- cost of time to the organization in overseeing and administering the program.

Use of control groups in evaluation

In any outcome study, it is critically important to establish the extent to which the results of the invention are due to the intervention itself, rather than other, extraneous variables. One method to isolate the impact of a coaching program is to employ a control group. Essentially, this is a group of randomly selected individuals, as identical as possible to the coaching group, which doesn't receive coaching.

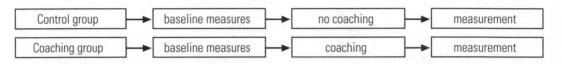

Figure 5.3 Use of a control group in behavioral coaching

The baseline measures are taken in relation to the specific behaviors targeted for change in the coaching program. At the end of the coaching sessions, the changes in the control group are compared with those in the coaching group. The differences can then be attributed to the coaching program. It is important that the groups do not work together or communicate during the coaching program. Otherwise, the results might be "contaminated." Obviously, in the work environment, meeting these conditions can be difficult for logistical reasons.

Trend line analysis

Another useful technique for obtaining at least an approximate measure of the impact of coaching is trend line analysis. This involves drawing a line to predict the future using previous performance as a base. The difference is calculated as the actual average minus the predicted average. Any improve-

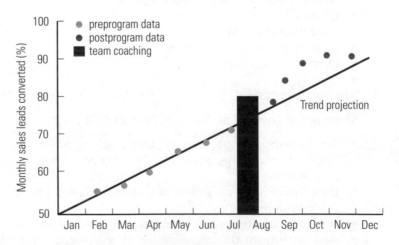

Figure 5.4 Trend Line Analysis (adapted from Phillips, 2000)

ments over the levels predicted by the trend line can be attributed to the coaching program. This method is not as reliable as using control groups, however, because it does not control for fluctuations in situational events.

Other more complex forms of evaluation include forecasting, which is a mathematical interpretation of the trend line that allows for the impact of other variables. Describing such methods is well beyond the scope of this book, however. We suggest that coaches become familiar with and competent in applying the evaluation method that is appropriate to their coaching services.

Reporting to the client

On the previously agreed date or dates, the coach reports to the client. The frequency of these reports depends on the time frame of the coaching program and the client's expectations as set forth in the contract. For example, a six-month program usually necessitates both a midterm report and a final one. The content of these reports should match the items in the proposal.

The final report typically includes the following:

- background to the coaching program
- the overall objectives of the program
- how the coaching program was implemented, the scope of the program and who was involved
- the methodology for collecting data, such as surveys, focus groups, questionnaires, behavioral observations and assessments
- a summary of the evaluation process, emphasizing its reliability and validity
- the objectives and goals of individual coachees and/or teams and how these have been achieved
- what the organization has learned
- any additional learning or benefits of the coaching program
- how changes will be maintained
- any changes in organizational culture
- how confidentiality was maintained
- methods of converting data to monetary value
- methods of evaluating intangible benefits
- costs of the program
- ROI figures
- overall business impact, including intangible benefits
- follow-up plans in place to insure maintenance of learning
- recommendations for future coaching assignments

Requisite competencies at step six (evaluation)

Knowledge of: evaluation methods such as ROI and ROE; alternative methods of evaluation; data analysis and presentation.

Skills: provide supporting data with feedback; non-collusive, honest reporting; manage own anxieties; accept accountability.

Step seven: Maintenance

Maintenance, or making sure that the gains made in coaching are not lost, is the final step in any learning or change process. Coachees are now able to self-coach to a considerable degree; that is, the role of the coach is becoming increasingly redundant. The coaching program has moved coachees toward self-reliance, self-mastery and self-leadership and they are equipped to use the knowledge, skills and abilities gained in coaching to self-manage.

To insure that there is no regression to earlier behaviors, a coach has to be aware of the conditions that facilitate maintenance. For instance, within organizations, research shows that the critical success factors for maintaining change include a culture that encourages learning and development; an environment that rewards risk taking; access to resources; active support from key stakeholders; ongoing dialogue with participants and stakeholders; and ongoing measurement.

Insuring that individual coachees are able to self-coach and thereby solve problems, self-correct and develop their own development strategies entails two sets of actions on the part of the coach. First, the coach must insure that coachees have thoroughly learned and practiced the new behaviors, particularly under demanding conditions. Self-monitoring, and self-reports, as well as observations and reports from managers and peers, establish the stability of these changes. Second, coachees have to be prepared to manage potentially difficult situations without the assistance of the coach. During the coaching sessions, the coach and coachees engage in ongoing dialogue about those aspects of the action plan and strategies that are most helpful and those that don't work. Together, they take the necessary corrective action. Yet when the coach is no longer available, coachees must continue with their long-term development plans. Self-correction and self-regulation skills are vital if coachees are to maintain commitment and motivation.

In order to help coachees continue on the development path, the coaching partners need to establish those situations that are most likely to cause regression or relapse. Experienced coaches find the following framework useful for increasing the probability of successful self-coaching:

- Isolate any concerns or fears coachees have regarding the prospect of self-coaching.
- Link these fears with specific beliefs that can be challenged.
- Link these concerns with specific knowledge, skills and abilities and put a plan in place to bridge these gaps.
- Link these concerns with specific situations and develop cognitive or behavioral techniques to manage these if and when they arise.
- If a coaching program manager has been involved in the program, meet with that person to discuss the maintenance techniques that you and the coachees have put in place. Enlist the coaching program manager's assistance, ideally in the form of regular, brief "check-in" meetings, which would decrease in frequency as coachees' competency and confidence in self-coaching grows.
- Arrange a time for follow-up, either face-to-face or by telephone or email, within six weeks of the end of the program.

- Agree on a period of postcoaching measurements, usually through interview-based assessment over a period of a year. This not only provides support to coachees so that they don't feel "abandoned," but the coach can obtain data on the ongoing benefits of the coaching program.

Requisite competencies at step seven (maintenance)

Knowledge of: principles of self-coaching; methods for challenging self-limiting beliefs; strategies for self-regulating emotion; maintenance strategies; regressive forces; potential high-risk situations; ongoing evaluation methods.

Skills: flexibility; liaison skills; foster independence; ability to let go; commitment to coachee.

Core coaching competencies

There is no significant body of evidence to indicate how much coaching knowledge and which types of skills and abilities are related to successful coaching outcomes. Nevertheless, there is a consensus that superior knowledge and experience are required in coaches working at high levels of coaching, such as working with CEOs and senior executives. Hard skills such as strategic planning and increasing business, as well as political maneuvering and the ability to align board members, demand considerable experience and expertise.

Regardless of the level at which a coach is working, to be a successful practitioner requires specialist coach training. It was in response to the demand from organizations for coaches with specialist skills and competencies that The Behavioral Coaching Institute's training courses were developed. These courses were designed to meet the explicit need for certified internal and external behavioral coaches and applied management coaching programs.

The Behavioral Coaching Institute's tailor-made, "hands-on" coach training and certification courses, facilitated by the authors of this book (see About the Authors), focus on developing core competencies within the practical framework of the behavioral coaching model as it applies to a participant's own workplace. There are, then, several core coaching competencies that span all stages of the coaching process and all types of coaching programs. In Chapter 1, we nominated seven specific roles of the coach today. These were increasing self-awareness, modeling desired behaviors, getting to the core of an issue, giving instructions, targeting behaviors for change, giving feedback, and keeping coachees focused and on track. In this chapter we explored various requisite competencies at each stage of the coaching process.

Here, we discuss several higher-order categories of coaching competencies that subsume the seven mentioned above. These are interpersonal relating, managing emotions, cognitive skills, decision-making skills, planning and intuition.

Interpersonal relating is the foundation of any successful coaching relationship. A great deal has been written about this topic and the competencies and micro-processes involved. These include building rapport, generating trust, listening, asking questions and challenging. Underlying these competencies or skills is the coach's philosophical stance or way of being with and relating to clients and coachees.

As we mentioned in Chapter 1, behavioral coaching is informed by postmodernism, which views knowledge as social and relational rather than situated within a dichotomy of expert (coach) and non-expert (client or coachee). Within the framework of generating and exchanging knowledge, coaching dialogue requires openness and curiosity about and connection with the other person. The coach and coachee view themselves as collaborative, equal partners engaged in a mutual endeavor.

It is this shared dialogue that generates new ideas, shifts and transformations in the client, coachee and coach. Although, by necessity, coaching requires a structure such as we present in this chapter, within this there is a continuous process of conversation that is dynamic and generative. It is through this style of conversation that the coach and coachee learn about each other's perceptions, world views, values and meaning. Finally, it is through relatedness that new ways of thinking, behaving, problem solving and feeling come into being.

Managing emotions. In Chapter 3 we explored strategies to regulate emotion and in Chapter 7 we discuss the areas of coaching to which these are especially relevant. Here, we focus on coaches' ability to manage their responses to coachees' emotions. As well as containing a coachee's emotions, it is helpful for coaches to be able to recognize and manage what is known as "emotional contagion."

The phenomenon of "emotion contagion" is well documented. Briefly, it refers to the tendency to automatically mimic and synchronize facial expressions, vocalizations, postures and movements with those of another person. Consequently, emotional convergence, which is for the most part outside of conscious awareness, occurs. While such "matching" is known to facilitate rapport, it also has its drawbacks. Emotion contagion, particularly of negative emotions, can occur in the coaching dyad between the client and coachee, among teams and at an organizational level. Anger and depressive moods tend to be the most "contagious," and individuals who are highly emotionally expressive cause greater contagion. Coaches need to be able to deal with this phenomenon, which, clearly, can have a negative impact on the coaching relationship or on a team's performance.

Strategies coaches can employ to reduce their susceptibility to "contagion" include heightened self-awareness and monitoring of subjective emotional responses as they occur. As well as recognizing his or her own emotional state, a coach can convey this to the coachee, client or team. Emotional honesty demands that a coach is aware of her or his internal experiences and is willing, when appropriate, to communicate these emotional states to others. Rather than generating avoidance or other forms of emotional collusion, this opens up dialogue, especially when the emotion is a reflection of the other's state.

Cognitive skills are called upon at every step of the coaching process. For example, at step one coaches employ situational analysis, diagnosing or narrowing down a considerable amount of data to core issues. Information-processing skills, analytical abilities and forming and testing hypotheses occur at every step. Targeting or selecting behaviors for change demands pattern recognition skills, as well as insight into individual and organizational behavior.

Many executives and others in business and organizations process information rapidly and a coach has to be able to match this rate, otherwise he or she will lose credibility. Closely related to this skill is that of lateral thinking, which facilitates problem solving and creative solution generation. Behavioral coaches are always looking for new strategies and procedures to effect change.

Metacognition, or awareness of one's own thinking processes, is another critical skill for behavioral coaches. They need to be able to track and process what is occurring in a conversation or situation. There is not usually a great deal of "time out" to engage in metacognition, however, as coaches also have to be present and engaged in what is happening.

Decision making is a coaching competency that spans the entire coaching program. At all steps in the process, coaches apply heuristic methods or rules for making choices that allow them to take into account the organization's and coachees' needs and the greatest range of possible solutions. Decisions at the education stage include how best to obtain the coaching contract and how to design a program that will balance the organization's goals with those of potential coachees. During the coaching needs analysis, the information gathered must truly reflect the organization's objectives, values and learning and development needs.

At the data collection phase, the coach decides which assessment instruments to use, and which data collection methods, within any existing constraints, will yield the most valuable information. The coach then decides which behaviors to target and how to operationalize these. Although the coach and coachees work together to establish goals and subsequent action-planning strategies, ultimately it is the coach who decides whether these goals meet certain criteria and whether they are likely to be achieved. Furthermore, many coachees are unfamiliar with behavioral change techniques, and it is the coach's responsibility to decide which techniques will be employed and how they will be measured.

At the evaluation step, the coach decides which questionnaires, surveys and other measurements will be employed to capture the results of the coaching program. Some of these broad decisions will have already been made in agreement with the client (e.g., if or how an ROI will be calculated), but there are numerous decisions involved in collecting, collating and presenting the results of a coaching program.

Finally, at the maintenance phase, the coach decides which behaviors are more likely to be subject to relapse or regression and which techniques will best prevent this from happening. Decisions have to be made about the most effective methods for long-term follow-through and how these figure in recommendations to the client.

Planning is another requisite coaching competency that is critical across the seven steps of the coaching process if a program is to be conducted systematically. Having made certain decisions, as discussed above, a coach must determine which plans will insure that these are acted upon. Planning begins with a comprehensive method of presenting information to clients. It includes contingency planning to meet various questions and resistances from the client.

Coaches also have to plan the overall coaching program. There are two major aspects to this. The first includes planning methods of data collection, as well as how to target behaviors for change, obtain baseline measures, set goals and develop performance and action plans. The second includes planning each session, including the behavioral techniques that will be most appropriate and effective. The coach also plans monitoring and measurement techniques, methods of evaluation and how these will be reported to the client, as well as strategies to maintain behavioral changes.

Finally, coaching is a dynamic experience that is affected by various personal, economic and environmental fluctuations. For example, although coaching sessions are planned, they are subject to shifting interpersonal dynamics between the coach and coachees, as well as between coachees and the organization. These disruptions and diversions demand flexibility and contingency planning in order to manage and balance changes to the original plan.

Intuition. In the Preface we refer to behavioral coaching as an art in relation to the coach's unique signature and use of methodologies and techniques. Even though there are structured steps to follow in the use of behavioral techniques, for example, these are never applied in the same manner by every coach or even between one coach and different coachees. These variations, which are a function of the coach's personality, experience and creativity constitute the art of coaching. We also described behavioral coaching as a montage, or fusion of different forms.

Another way of approaching coaching as art is in the context of intuition. Experienced coaches rely heavily on intuition even within a structured, scientific model. Intuition, as we use the term, refers to hunches or unconscious decision-making processes founded on knowledge and experience. Intuition is difficult to quantify, yet it is a valuable competency for a successful coach.

Summary

In summary, the model of coaching presented here is a matrix underpinned by Prochaska's change methodology, as adapted for coaching. At the different stages of change (reflective, preparation, action and maintenance), a coach employs distinct forms of coaching. These are coaching education, skills coaching, rehearsal coaching, performance coaching and self-coaching. Both the stages of change and the five forms of coaching are interrelated with a seven-step coaching process. The steps are education, data collection, planning, behavioral change, measurement, evaluation and maintenance.

The behavioral coaching model is applicable to all coaching programs. Nevertheless, within it, coaches have the flexibility to employ a variety of coaching styles, interpersonal behaviors and cognitive models. That is, the model allows for individual differences and the uniqueness of the coach, coachees and organization or business. It is a fluid, dynamic working model that is subject to refinement and revision.

Finally, in order to encapsulate the key components of the behavioral coaching model in a practical checklist for coaches, we have deconstructed it in the following way:

Table 5.5 A deconstruction of the behavioral coaching model (Skiffington & Zeus 2001)

The coaching process steps	Change tasks for the coach at each stage	Y/N
1. Education	Are you familiar with Prochaska's change methodology?	
	Is the client fully aware of the nature, process, applications and benefits of coaching?	
	Have you conducted a coaching needs analysis or agreed to conduct one before the coaching sessions commence?	
	Are the organization's business objectives clear?	
	Are you familiar with the organization's culture and values?	
	Do you understand the organization's leadership and management styles?	
	Do you recognize potential allies? Are the forces or resistance (the shadow) clear to you?	
	Is the coachee aware of the process, the coach's role and accountability and his or her responsibilities?	
	Do both the client and coachee understand the fundamentals of behavioral change?	
	Have you contracted for your specific services, including the broad objectives of the program?	
	Is there agreement on the methods of evaluation you will use and the reporting procedures?	
	Have you modeled the behaviors that will facilitate a truly open, collaborative coaching partnership?	
2. Data collection	Have you obtained all information from all key stakeholders?	
	Are you clear about the key competencies to address from the organization's and coachee's view?	
	Have you conducted a precoaching "levels of evaluation" assessment?	
	Has the coachee been observed by you in her or his workplace?	
	Are managers or others involved in observation and reporting?	
	Are you certain they are trained to observe and collect accurate and reliable data?	
	Are you competent at administering and debriefing the assessments you employ?	
	Do you have a range of assessment tools?	
	Have the assessment instruments given you specific data relevant to the coachee's needs and objectives?	
	Have you explored the coachee's self-concept?	
	Do you understand the coachee's motivation? Is the coachee's health a factor in his or her performance?	
	Do you recognize the coachee's shadow side?	
	Are you confident about working with it?	
	Do you have a system to manage the data?	

Table 5.5 (continued) A deconstruction of the behavioral coaching model (Skiffington & Zeus 2001)

The coaching process steps	Change tasks for the coach at each stage	Y/N
3. Planning	Have you selected specific behaviors for change?	
	Does the coachee know how to conduct a functional analysis of her or his behavior?	
	Are there baseline measures of the targeted behaviors?	
	Are the antecedents and consequences of the behavior(s) clear?	
	Do the set goals meet standard goal-setting criteria?	
	Does the coachee have a documented personal development plan?	
	Is there an agreed-upon process for the coachee to maintain a weekly log of action steps?	
4. Behavioral change	Do you have a clear idea of skills coaching and rehearsal coaching at this step?	
	Are you competent to coach for a variety of skills?	
	Are you confident about your knowledge and ability to implement coaching behavior change methods and techniques?	
	Have you explored the coachee's limiting beliefs?	
	Does the coachee have techniques to manage her or his thoughts, emotions and behavior?	
	Do you have a referral system for individuals who require training, therapy, etc.?	
5. Measurement	Are you sure about what performance coaching entails?	
	Have you established reliable and valid measurement procedures?	
	Are others (peers, managers, coaching program manager) aligned and skilled in the measurement and reporting procedures?	
	Can you interpret the data in relation to the coachee's goals and need for further skills coaching?	
	Will the measurement data make a valid contribution to your final evaluation?	
6. Evaluation	Are the initially agreed-upon evaluation methods still relevant?	
	Will you conduct a return on investment?	
	Are you confident about doing this?	
	Do you have an agreed-upon method to measure and evaluate "intangibles"?	
	Did you use control groups?	
	Did you employ a variety of evaluation methods (e.g., trend analysis)?	
	Are the results documented in an acceptable and agreed-upon report format?	
	Are you confident about communicating the report to the client and key stakeholders?	
7. Maintenance	Is the coachee aware of the major challenges regarding sustaining momentum and maintaining gains?	
	Are you confident about using maintenance strategies?	
	Are there specific procedures in place to insure the coachee doesn't revert to earlier behaviors?	
	Are the others enlisted in these procedures?	
	Are there contingencies in place if the coachee does regress?	
	Is the coachee able to manage without you?	
	Can the coachee self-correct and self-regulate her or his thoughts, feelings and behavior without you?	
	Have you established follow-through plans?	

6

Client-Centered Management for Coaches

An introduction to client-centered management

In Chapter 5 we outlined and discussed a behavioral coaching model, its principles and applications. Our intent in this chapter is to explore and offer established guidelines for the coach's rules of engagement with the client, as well as rules of practice for both internal and external coaches.

When we refer to client-centered management, we nominate the client as the sponsor or the person to whom the coach is reporting and who assumes responsibility for the coaching program. The coaching program may involve one-on-one executive coaching, coaching managers to coach, or group or team coaching, or be an extensive organizational coaching intervention. The client, then, is typically distinct from the actual coachee, although on occasion the sponsor may also be a coaching candidate. The client is the person or persons who hold authority for the continuation of the coach's services.

Behavioral coaching's client-centered approach derives many of its guiding principles from the work of Carl Rogers (1902–87). As most of us are aware, Rogers developed the person-centered approach in humanistic psychology. Typically, his approach is utilized in psychotherapy, counseling and education. While many coaches employ Rogers's principles in their work with individual coachees, his framework also offers a valuable and practical blueprint for dealing with clients.

It may seem unusual to apply these guidelines in the context of a client relationship. Much of the coaching literature resonates with the importance of empathy, respect and positive regard for coachees. Rarely, however, do clients receive similar attention and care. Interestingly, Rogers himself noted the limits of his ability to change the overall structure of the organizations in which he worked. Indeed, there is evidence to suggest that he was frustrated at his lack of effectiveness when dealing with levels of administration above his own.

It may be, as some authors have proposed, that Rogers's therapeutic language and assumptions about the nature of individuals were too "soft" and too closely related with nurturance, rather than discipline. Nevertheless, Rogers believed that the therapeutic relationship was only one instance of a "lawful" interpersonal dynamic, and that the same lawfulness should govern all such relations. Behavioral coaching, then, applies these principles to the relationship between the coach and the client.

Rogers's views of human nature are implicit, although rarely acknowledged, in coaching theory and practice. For instance, Rogers believed that:

- individuals are essentially trustworthy
- people have a natural desire to grow and develop
- we all have vast resources for self-understanding and self-help.

Essentially, he claimed that three characteristics of a helper or teacher promoted growth and understanding. These are:

1 Congruence or genuineness
2 Unconditional positive regard
3 Accurate, empathic understanding.

It is worth noting here that Rogers submitted his theories to empirical testing. Research has established, for example, that when teachers develop relationships with their students based on these principles, students become self-initiated learners, more original, more self-disciplined, less anxious and less other-directed. Behavioral coaches report that coach–client relationships based on Rogers's criteria result in more effective, more satisfying and more productive coaching engagements. We will now discuss these three elements as they underpin and play out in the coach–client relationship.

Congruence

Congruence, which exists on a continuum, refers to a state of being in which the individual is integrated and authentic, spontaneous and self-disclosing. The individual is real and genuine. Her or his thoughts, feelings and behaviors are integrated and there is no facade or role-playing. While it is generally agreed that coaches should aim for such congruence in their relationships with coachees, little attention is paid to the incongruence a client may initially experience.

Organizations and businesses do not necessarily promote authenticity. The corporate or organizational culture dictates behaviors and formalizes roles. Indeed, how well an individual fits with the workplace culture is frequently a predictor of success and advancement. The client, then, presents first of all as a representative of the organization or business. His or her genuine "self" is submerged in the role. What may appear as spontaneity is frequently a cultivated eccentricity that serves only to reinforce the person's position of power and unnerve the coach. The client may be cynical or distrustful. Certainly, and understandably, she or he is often unwilling to self-disclose, or expose the real problems, weaknesses or issues the organization is facing.

In such situations, it is tempting for a coach to retreat or hide behind his or her technical knowledge or credentials. Experience and anecdotal reports suggest that coaches can become trapped in a cycle of defensiveness and role-playing, which puts their congruence and authenticity at risk. It is only through being open to genuine encounters and understanding their own values, reactions and triggers that coaches can model the congruence necessary for meaningful relationships that will engender change and learning.

In order to exhibit genuineness, coaches need to be aware of their feelings and be willing to express them in words and behavior. There are always risks involved in being genuine and authentic. These include rejection and being taken advantage of by the other. Nevertheless, the repercussions of not being genuine affect not only the coach's sense of "self" and "self-worth," but the future of the relationship with the client. It is true that coaches are hired for the knowledge, experience and content they bring to the coaching engagement. They are also engaged because they present as being real, honest and "at one" with who they are and what they are doing.

In summary, congruence implies that the coach:

- is genuine and does not hide behind facades or roles
- expresses her or his true feelings in words and behavior
- is willing to risk being open and honest
- models authentic behavior to the client.

Unconditioned positive regard

- To behave toward all individuals with unconditional positive regard at all times is virtually impossible. It is something coaches strive to do, with varying degrees of success. Essentially, it means that while the coach cares about the client, this caring is not conditional on how the other behaves. Ideally, it is a non-possessive kind of caring, which does not demand personal gratification. Rogers used the word "acceptance" to describe how caring for another person allows him or her to be a "separate" entity, with his or her own feelings, experiences and meaning.

- Accepting the client does not necessarily imply approval. It does, however, demand that the coach be non-judgmental. Many coaches report that once they have started working with a client, they tend to be less judgmental. Probably this is because by then they have a deeper understanding of the client's reality and world view, and her or his behaviors can be put in context and understood, even if they are not "approved" of. It is in the earlier stages of the coach–client relationship that acceptance is critical, and this stage tends to be more demanding on the coach.

- Preconceptions about an individual or a situation constitute one of the major barriers to acceptance. Coaches may harbor stereotypic or fixed ideas about the type of industry the client works in, or about the behaviors displayed by individuals in particular positions within organizations. One or two negative experiences with an HR professional or a CEO in a particular industry, for example, could lead a coach to generalize this experience across all HR personnel or CEOs. Such generalizations and preconceptions preclude any genuine encounter. While it is true that we all adopt certain professional roles, each individual plays out this role in a unique fashion. It is this uniqueness that coaches have to encounter if truly client-centered relationships are to develop.

- Non-verbal communication or body language is discussed widely in self-help books, management books and pop psychology. While most of us have our own personal interpretations of the signals people give out, however, our reading of these may be incorrect and lead to conclusions that lessen acceptance of others. For example, research, especially that conducted by Paul Ekman, challenges the veracity of many of our interpretations of body language.

- Two areas of particular relevance to our discussion are the "myths" about fast-talking individuals and "smiling." Fast-talking people are frequently considered to be unreliable. Clients who talk rapidly and at length are often perceived by coaches as wanting to bamboozle, impress or even mislead. Research has shown, however, that long and frequent pauses, particularly in response to a question, are actually more likely to signal an intention to deceive. Similarly, smiling is usually considered a signal that the client is pleased with what he or she is hearing and that the encounter is proceeding according to plan. But while smiling may certainly indicate pleasure, it can also signify contempt, helplessness or fear. Relying too much on body language, then, can jeopardize a coach's ability to relate to a client; a coach should not allow her or his idea of the person to interfere with the relationship.

- Acceptance of the client is frequently taken for granted as something we all do as professionals. Indifference, and even cynicism, however, can be disguised as acceptance. To accept an individual in the client-centered sense is challenging. Coaches have to be aware of their previous experiences and how these may be affecting the current encounter. Moreover, it is only through acknowledging the preconceptions and stereotypes we bring to an interaction that we are able to see beyond these to an acceptance of the uniqueness of the present client.

In summary, unconditional positive regard implies that the coach:

- cares about but does not necessarily approve of the client
- does not judge the client
- is aware of the preconceptions and stereotyped thinking he or she brings to any encounter with the client
- recognizes and appreciates the uniqueness of each and every client.

Empathy

In the literature and everyday coaching language, unconditional positive regard and empathy are often used interchangeably. However, behavioral coaching recognizes these as being two separate but related constructs.

Unconditional positive regard precedes empathy. It is something the coach brings to any encounter with the client. From this, empathy is experienced and acknowledged.

In *The Coaching at Work Toolkit* we explored empathy as an aspect of the coach's personality. We discussed it in the context of the coach adopting a tutorial or learning approach in order to understand the other. Empathy was also acknowledged as a social competence and a function of a coach's self-awareness. In the present context, we address empathy as a critical component of client management. It involves developing an accurate understanding of the client's world as seen from the inside. There are two aspects to empathy: understanding the client, and acknowledging this understanding. One without the other cannot engender a client-centered relationship.

A coach exhibits empathy by questioning and listening to the client. The coach's questioning and general behavior, however, should never seem intrusive or threatening. Empathic questioning allows the coach to understand the client's situation. For instance, experience shows that there is always something at stake for the client. There is something to win and something to lose, be it a reputation, a promotion or a personal investment of time and energy. Coaching programs are never initiated in a vacuum. The coach's objective is to clearly establish the context of the coaching engagement and what demands this is placing on the client.

Clients frequently experience some anxiety around the introduction of a new project. The project might balloon out of control, resources may run out and the program may fizzle. By acknowledging the client's anxiety and fears and offering reassurance in the form of commitment and expertise, the coach not only alleviates concerns but cements the relationship with the client even further. Importantly, the coach has to allow the client to freely express any concerns, while containing her or his own anxieties about the project. On the other hand, if the coach offers reassurance too soon and too effusively, rather than listening carefully, the client may feel that he or she has not been heard and the relationship will be damaged.

How effectively a coach is able to empathize with the client's situation is a function of her or his skill in "perspective-taking," which is an awareness of the other's situational and individual circumstances. The ability to take another's perspective is a well-documented aspect of the developmental process, and ranges from egocentrism to being other-centered. Individuals are able to see the other's point of view to varying degrees. While therapists may be trained in this skill, coaches are frequently left to rely on their own devices or natural capability. Coaches, however, are sometimes in a state of unconscious incompetence, and so do not know they are lacking in this area. Behavioral coaches appreciate the critical importance of supervision, role-playing with peers and ongoing self-assessment to develop and master this aspect of client relations.

Research shows that significant learning occurs more readily in relation to situations that are perceived as problems. As mentioned, a client may be defensive about perceived shortcomings in himself or herself or in the larger organization or business. Nevertheless, a coach can set the stage for the client to freely discuss issues or problems through carefully directed empathic questioning and listening. Appreciating and acknowledging the issues a client is facing, as well as the strengths to leverage is essential for the ongoing development of trust.

Empathic questioning and listening also allow a client to discuss the constraints or resistances the coaching program may face. It is only when both coach and client recognize the obstacles they may come up against that solutions can be found. While this is clearly vital at the beginning of the relationship, it is also crucial at various stages of the coaching project. As we are all aware, many coaching programs either do not get off the ground or grind to a halt long before any objectives have been met.

One of the major contributing factors to such outcomes is that there was never a forum for open and honest discussions about the obstacles or resistances that might be encountered or about the accountability of program participants. If the coach becomes defensive in the face of feedback or tends to minimize or avoid difficulties and conflict, others engaged in the coaching endeavor will do likewise. It is the coach's role to establish a climate that generates ongoing, frank discussion and to model accountability and responsibility.

Empathy involves an appreciation and acknowledgment of the client's expectations. Whether or not these are realistic, at the beginning of the relationship it is more important to allow the client to clearly articulate his or her needs and expectations. It is only when these have been voiced that the coach can generate dialogue around whether or not these expectations can be met and how the coach and client can work together to achieve desired outcomes. Coaches, too, have expectations, and these also have to be stated clearly and honestly at the beginning of the relationship. In this way, the coach and client put in place a blueprint for ongoing discussions and feedback about mutual expectations and their fulfillment.

In summary, empathy implies that the coach:

- questions and listens to understand the client's situation from her or his perspective
- acknowledges this understanding
- encourages and generates an open and trusting discussion around the client's anxieties
- encourages, accepts and gives honest feedback
- establishes a pattern of ongoing frank dialogue about expectations and outcomes.

Coaching, then, is as much an interpersonal exchange between the coach and client as it is between the coach and coachee. A truly client-centered approach to coaching demands that the coach displays congruence in a context of unconditional positive regard and empathy for the client. If this does not happen, the client will have only minimal confidence and trust in the coach. Furthermore, as research and anecdotal reports show, unless this regard and empathy are present, clients are unlikely to engage in a working relationship with the coach, despite the coach's credentials and experience.

Best practice in client-centered management

The purpose of this section is to describe the stages of client-centered management and associated best practices. Although there are clearly variations in procedures for internal and external behavioral coaches, especially in terms of attracting clients, the fundamental principles and practices for excellent client management do not differ significantly.

Client management in behavioral coaching is grounded in quality improvement and outcome management practices. Although we nominate and discuss "best practices," we are aware of the dangers of copying practices and models that are not appropriate and will not meet a client's needs. While standard, best practices are critical for the further maturity and development of the coaching profession, the best practices discussed here are neither mandatory nor exhaustive. Flexibility and adaptability are as important in client management as they are in the actual coaching relationship.

Nevertheless, behavioral coaching has established the following critical success factors for any coaching program.

- Coaching programs must be linked to specific organizational or business visions, strategic plans and goals.
- There must be consensus among all stakeholders on the expectations and objectives of the coaching program.
- The scope of the coaching objectives has to be realistic within the nominated time frame.
- The coaching objectives must be specific.
- The coaching objectives must be measurable.
- There must be agreement on the suitability of the coaching methodologies that will be employed.
- There has to be a consensus on what will be evaluated, at what levels and how frequently.
- A detailed coaching needs analysis has to be conducted.
- Nominated coachees have to be educated about, and be receptive to, coaching.
- Data-collection processes have to be established before the commencement of the program.
- The organizational culture must promote and support coaching.
- The client has to agree to provide the necessary resources.
- There has to be ongoing monitoring and evaluation of the results of the program.
- The program must be time-limited.

Steps in client-centered management

As Figure 6.1 shows, behavioral coaching nominates eight stages of client-centered management. There are two critical dimensions the coach must consider at each of these stages: the education of the client and developing the client relationship. We will address the coach's goals and objectives within these two dimensions at each of the eight stages of client management. First, however, it is necessary to discuss the centrality of client education in coaching.

Client education

In general, the coaching literature focuses more on client management than on client education. Yet client education is critical for the introduction, endurance and ultimate success of any coaching program. For instance, unless a client is knowledgable about what coaching can and cannot achieve, he or she may demand a coaching program that is not suitable or even feasible. The client, through education, has to reach a position from which she or he is able, in discussion with the coach, to agree on and contract for *specific* objectives. If the client's objectives are non-specific (e.g., "I want my people to be better managers"), the coach is in a no-win situation. Regardless of the results, there will always be areas of "better management" that the coach did not, or could not, address. Dissatisfaction will ensue and the coach's reputation and that of the coaching profession will be damaged.

Such agreement is generally not reached after one or even two meetings. Again, depending on the scope of the coaching program, the coach may need to interview or brief other stakeholders so that they too are involved in clearly defining the objectives, goals and outcome measures of the program. Various stakeholders may have different objectives. It is only through free, open discussions and negotiation that a consensus can be reached. Unless stakeholders are cognizant of the parameters of coaching, its benefits and limitations, and the process of implementation and measurement, it is difficult to obtain "buy-in," and the seeds of dissatisfaction are already sown.

Clients require education about the measurement and evaluation methods the coach will employ. While a busy client may want to "leave that to the coach," best practices show that it is imperative that the client is informed of and agrees to the measurement and evaluation methods that will be used before the commencement of coaching. The initial contract should be followed by a specific contract that outlines a personal development plan and includes observable behaviors that will attest to change and progress, and how these will affect business growth.

Finally, there has to be agreement on how the coaching program will be conducted. Program management in behavioral coaching, as detailed in Chapter 5, involves three stages: design, implementation and management. As we have already discussed the logistics of program design, implementation and measurement, our emphasis here will be on client management and the coach–client relationship from the inception of a program to its completion.

For the sake of clarity we will now address best practices at each of the eight stages by examining the coach's goals and objectives within two dimensions: educating the client and the client relationship. We employ the term education in its broadest sense; that is, giving information in such a way that learning about multifaceted aspects of coaching will ensue.

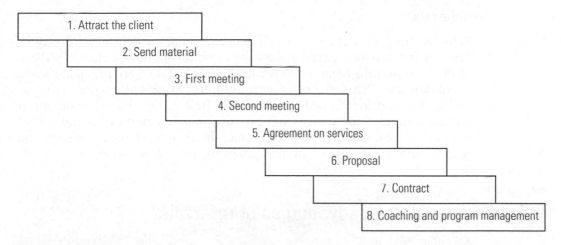

Figure 6.1 Eight steps of client-centered management

Step one: Attracting the client—gaining entry

Attracting clients is obviously a critical first step in setting up an external coaching business. However, an understanding of best practices in attracting clients and marketing is essential for any successful coaching practice, internal or external. Best practices suggest the following six "entry points" to be the most typical and effective means of "getting a foot in the door." Referrals and cold calling are obviously more applicable to external coaches. The other four methods (repeat business, seminars and workshops, networking and articles/books) are relevant to both internal and external coaches.

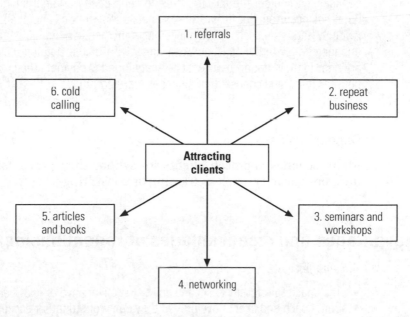

Figure 6.2 "Entry points" for attracting clients

Referrals

Being referred to a client is, of course, the most straightforward way of "getting in the door." Executive coaches who do not have a client database or contacts within organizations they wish to sell to are at a significant disadvantage. Prior places of employment, past colleagues, current colleagues, and friends and family should first be considered as potential referral sources. Such sources may produce an actual name of an individual in a key position in an organization or may simply refer the coach to someone who "could be interested" in implementing a coaching program.

Advantages and disadvantages of referrals

Advantages

- Some level of credibility and professionalism is already established.
- The referred individual may already have a knowledge and interest in coaching.
- It is assumed that the coach has some knowledge of the organization or business, its challenges and potential coaching needs.

Disadvantages

- Organizational politics, of which the coach could not be aware, may be at play.

For example, coaches report that they frequently speak with someone in an organization who shows a keen interest in coaching. This person, in turn, refers them to another individual, usually lower in the hierarchy although critical to the implementation of any program, who "blocks" any further discussion about coaching services. Of course, the coach is free to contact the original source and discuss what has occurred, but the warning signals about politics and agendas are clearly evident. Rarely do such circumstances lend themselves to a satisfactory coaching engagement. Internal coaches, who are aware of the political power plays and agendas in their organization, are better equipped to navigate their way through the political maze and choose their alliances more carefully.

Repeat business

Many coaches approach clients for whom they previously worked in a different capacity, such as training or consulting.

Advantages and disadvantages of repeat business

Advantages

- The coach's professionalism and ability to deliver have already been established.
- Both coach and client have proved they can work together successfully.

Disadvantages

- Unless the coach is able to provide evidence of coach training and coaching experience, credibility is an issue. The coach may be seen as "jumping on the band wagon" of the latest trend for trainers and consultants.

Seminars and workshops

In-house

In *The Coaching at Work Toolkit* we discussed and provided guidelines for conducting an introductory seminar on coaching. Best practices suggest that such seminars and workshops should be educative, be limited to one to two hours and be attended by key stakeholders, and that coaching benefits should be tied to the perceived needs of the organization. If the client has approached the coach to conduct the seminar, the coach is in a position to nominate a fee. Otherwise, the seminar is free and part of the education process.

Advantages and disadvantages of seminars and workshops

Advantages

- When key stakeholders are present, the coach can address each of their concerns, thereby increasing the probability of "buy-in" and hastening the decision-making process.
- Workshops present an opportunity for the coach to use experiential and interactive techniques that allow the audience to actually experience what coaching entails.

Disadvantages

- Most businesses and organizations are accustomed to a particular format for presentations and seminars. The coach has to be cognizant of this format, and perhaps even attend a presentation by another vendor, to insure that expected standards are met. Standing up and giving an informal, chatty discourse on coaching can fail miserably if Powerpoint productions, hand-outs and a formal question and answer period are the norm.
- Although there are generic points the coach can cover in any presentation on coaching, she or he has to consult with the prospective client or nominated liaison person to determine how to tailor the seminar or workshop to the needs of the organization. Doing so can be time-consuming for both the coach and the client.

Three simple guidelines for a coach to bear in mind when preparing a seminar or workshop and when deciding on the structure of the presentation itself are:

- *Why am I here?* What are my objectives and the objectives and expectations of the audience?
- *What am I talking about?* What topics am I covering, in what depth and in what format?
- *Where to from here?* In order to expedite the decision-making process, it is critical to briefly nominate the steps that will take place as a lead-in to the commencement of the program. Outline, as simply as possible, the next steps the client and you need to take. Providing this information shows that you are in control and that you have a process that works. It also makes it easier for the client to say "yes" to your services.

Public seminars and workshops

Seminars and workshops on coaching directed to the public are usually only successful if the coach is a specialist in a particular niche area (e.g., coaching in small businesses or work/life balance issues). The potential audience has to be carefully targeted, costs have to be kept to a minimum, and the coach must have carefully thought out strategies to "hook" the audience.

Networking

Depending on the coach's skills and existing channels, networking can generate clients. Not everyone enjoys networking, however. Introverts, for example, may shy away from the idea or force themselves to participate, with minimal results.

Advantages and disadvantages of networking

Advantages

- Networking with other coaches allows the coach to develop potential alliances and partnerships.
- Staying current with best practices and benchmarking one's efforts, successes and failures against those of other coaches reduces feelings of isolation and generates new or alternative methods of solving problems.
- Networking with targeted prospective clients within their own industry can open the door to a "first meeting."
- Networking with other professionals (non-coaches) presents opportunities for cross-referrals.

Disadvantages

- The existing networking channels among coaches vary in their usefulness. Many are purely card-swapping exercises, with little intellectual input or exchange of

information. They can simply be a waste of time, and, worse, demoralizing. It is possible, however, for the enterprising coach to form his or her own smaller networking group from chosen attendees.
- Networking within specific industry groups yields better results when the coach has a forum to speak about her or his services. Once the coach has researched upcoming industry conferences, training days or weekends, she or he can approach the initial networking event with a tangible plan in mind.

Articles and books

As we are all aware, the printed word can be a powerful means of establishing credibility and expertise. Best practices suggest that writing an article for an in-house newsletter, for an industry-specific newsletter or for general consumption, through a local or national newspaper for example, can be an effective means of attracting clients. With the proliferation of general articles on coaching, coaches are more likely to generate interest if their writing is targeted to particular populations and is specialist in nature. In this way, the coach is offering something unique. Articles that are most likely to appeal to prospective clients are not overly theoretical and contain examples of the coach's experience and expertise.

Advantages and disadvantages of using print media to attract clients

Advantages

- The article or book can establish expertise and credibility.
- The specific coaching needs of a targeted population or industry can be addressed.

Disadvantages

- Writing, especially a book, can be time-consuming and should not be relied on as the sole source of marketing.
- Targeting the reading population and reaching that population are critical. An excellent, original article on a coach's web site is recommended, but traffic to the site has to be built and managed. This, too, can be time-consuming and expensive.

Cold calling

Many coaches shudder at the mere thought of cold calling prospective clients. Best practices for successful cold calling include:

- carefully targeting potential coaching clients
- determining that the communication is with a decision maker and not a "gatekeeper"

- having a reasonable working knowledge of the current reality of the targeted organization
- following "a selling model" that has been practiced or employed beforehand
- where possible, offering evidence of experience similar to the potential buyer's needs
- carefully scripting the call, but being confident enough to be able to adapt to meet the prospective client's particular style and needs.

Some coaches waste their time and probably also alienate a prospective client by attempting to sell their services on the first call. Others send a proposal or material without obtaining the prospective client's consent. Sending a proposal at this stage is extremely unhelpful. It is useful to ask the potential client if he or she would like to receive some material. Only forward such material when the answer is "yes." The purpose of the cold call is to set up a meeting with the client.

Advantages and disadvantages of cold calling

Advantages

- If the coach is skilled at cold calling, comes from a sales background or has had some training in selling, cold calling can be a time-efficient means of introducing coaching and specific coaching services.

Disadvantages

- Coaches who are not skilled in cold calling are at risk not only of failing to obtain a meeting with the potential buyer, but also of negatively affecting their reputation in the field. Although a good salesperson is not necessarily a good coach, mediocre coaches who can market their services well maintain an advantage over superior coaches who lack selling skills. Coaches who are not skilled at or are apprehensive about cold calling can do well to nominate someone else to do the calling. This way, they can focus on the actual coaching and/or the management of the coaching program.

Regardless of which "entry points" a coach chooses, the goals and objectives in terms of client education and the client relationship fall under the headings shown in Figure 6.3. These goals and objectives apply equally to internal and external coaches.

Step two: Sending material

As mentioned, coaches should send material to a prospective client only if that person has agreed to receive and review it prior to the first meeting. Otherwise, the prospective client should receive the material at the first meeting. Figure 6.4 outlines the coach's goals and objectives when forwarding material.

CLIENT EDUCATION

Your unique selling proposition
- why you have contacted the buyer
- the specific, potential business/organizational applications of your specialty coaching services
- your track record as relevant to the buyer.

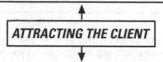

ATTRACTING THE CLIENT

CLIENT RELATIONSHIP
- engender curiosity
- establish initial credibility
- obtain a meeting (30 minutes) with key stakeholders and decision-maker(s).

Figure 6.3 Step one: Attracting the client—goals and objectives

---

CLIENT EDUCATION

Your coaching capability statement
Background information on the coaching process
Evidence to support the effectiveness of coaching
- professional, academic and coaching credentials of the coach
- the coach's philosophy and approach
- why your coaching methods work
- the benefits of your coaching—general and specific
- stages in the coaching process (e.g., a coach–client protocol)
- what is involved
- information on coaching research/coaching outcome studies relevant to the prospect's industry or stated issues.

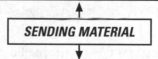

SENDING MATERIAL

CLIENT RELATIONSHIP
- further establish credibility and capability
- develop a shared understanding of the nature and benefits of coaching
- sow the seeds of a potential working collaboration.

Figure 6.4 Step two: Sending material—goals and objectives

Step three: First meeting with the prospective client

Prior to the first contact or meeting with a prospective client, experienced coaches typically research the organization or business they are attempting to engage. Furthermore, they carefully prepare and write down their answers to the following questions:

- Why am I here?
- What is my measure of a successful meeting?
- What does the client expect from me at this meeting?

The following figure lists the coach's major goals and objectives at the first client meeting.

CLIENT EDUCATION
Information on how your services will meet the buyer's needs.
Assurances and evidence that you are able to meet the stated needs.
- your broad measures of success (e.g., learning, accountability)
- your coaching resources (e.g., partners)
- your coaching model—a brief outline
- potential costs of the program
- what you require (e.g., meeting(s) with other stakeholders and decision-makers, access to interviews, surveys and performance appraisals)
- what the second meeting will involve.

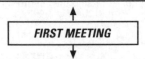

FIRST MEETING

CLIENT RELATIONSHIP
- clearly outline your position and rules on confidentiality
- display positive, unconditional regard
- use empathic questioning and listening to establish key issues, catalysts for change, prospect's expectations
- match, pace, summarize and acknowledge your understanding of the stated needs
- engender trust through honest, open discussion around the buyer's needs
- decide whether you wish to work with the potential client
- commit to documenting the meeting.

Figure 6.5 Step three: First meeting—goals and objectives

A great deal has been written about dealing with "different personality types" and how to best match their styles. A useful, validated typology that behavioral coaches employ as a guide to relating to both clients and coachees is the social styles profile. Based on the two dimensions of responsiveness and assertiveness, the social styles profile consists of four distinct interactive styles. These are drivers, analyticals, amiables and expressives. These styles do not provide a definitive characterization of an individual. Rather, they reflect the tendency to act in certain ways in certain situations. Behavioral coaches work within this framework as a means of understanding interpersonal dynamics, not in order to undertake personality profiling.

The four styles can be briefly described as follows.

Drivers like to be in control of themselves, their work environment and any client interactions. They usually focus on results, are competitive and thrive under pressure. Such individuals process information rapidly and expect the same from others. Drivers tend to change their minds abruptly without supplying reasons and become impatient when others don't agree with their conclusions.

Analyticals are likely to prolong any decision-making process while they gather all the available data. They are questioning, sometimes challenging, and are task-oriented rather than person-focused. Many analyticals have perfectionist tendencies and expect high standards from themselves and others. Generally, analytical types are formal and businesslike and do not offer or request much personal information. Business is usually conducted in an unemotional, logical and rational fashion.

Amiables emphasize relationships and cooperation. They are sensitive to the feelings of others, tentative and don't appear to want to impose their views. Rather, they question extensively in order to establish the ideas and concerns of others. Although methodical, they are not great planners or goal setters. Amiables rely on relationships to achieve results and prefer personal interactions to telephone or emails. Such individuals, despite being quite self-disclosing at times, don't necessary reveal their true thoughts and feelings, especially negative emotions.

Expressives are extroverted, energetic, enthusiastic and highly persuasive. They prefer working with others, networking and having a wide circle of varied companions. Expressives tend to be visionary and impulsive and can lack patience with details. Moreover, they may initially be enthusiastic about a project, but they don't always follow through on its implementation because they lose interest.

Understanding and matching an individual's style can help the coach to develop rapport more easily. It also allows the coach to meet the client's expectations in terms of conducting the business relationship.

Step four: Second meeting with the prospective client

As noted previously, depending on the scope of the coaching program, the urgency of the coaching needs and the size or bureaucratic complexity of the organization or business, one meeting with the prospective client may be sufficient. Typically, however, sizable coaching programs require at least two meetings before an agreement on services is reached.

Coaching readiness

In *The Coaching at Work Toolkit* we detailed guidelines for conducting a coaching readiness survey. Some of the things the coach explores at this stage are the history of change in the organization, available resources and commitment, knowledge and beliefs about coaching and whether data that is relevant to the coaching program can be accessed. These questions can be discussed informally, or a formal survey can be undertaken.

Figure 6.6 summarizes the goals and objectives of the second meeting.

CLIENT EDUCATION

Specific information on how your coaching program will meet the discussed needs

Briefing on your role and how your program will unfold

An outline of your process for calculating a return on investment or return on expectations at the end of the program

A process to ensure coaching readiness and alignment

- establish the proposed next steps (e.g., meeting/focus groups/brainstorming sessions with other stakeholders; assessment protocols; surveys; 360-degree feedback; interviews with coachees, team members)
- discuss how the program will be evaluated
- outline a time frame for coaching assignment and general program management strategies to roll out the program, if desired.

SECOND MEETING

CLIENT RELATIONSHIP

- building on trust and rapport
- enhancing confidence in your commitment and capabilities
- open a free, empathic and honest discussion about the restraints or resistances the coaching program will face and possible strategies to weaken these
- learn about different perspectives and objectives within the environment
- build a solid consensus on what the changes will look like.

Figure 6.6 Step four: Second meeting—goals and objectives

Step five: Reaching an agreement

The stage at which an agreement on services is reached depends on the scope of the program and whether the client initially contacted the coach, or vice versa.

Generally, after discussion, the agreement is translated into a written proposal.

Coaching needs analysis

In our previous books we addressed the importance of, and provided guidelines for, coaches to conduct a coaching needs analysis. In our second book, *The Coaching at Work Toolkit*, we provided questions coaches should ask and information they should gather at both the organizational level and the individual coachee's level. Rather than repeating this information here, we refer our readers to the relevant sections in our two previous books.

It is, however, worth reiterating the benefits of conducting a needs analysis. Such an analysis identifies individual and team coaching needs, enables coaches to focus their programs on identified areas in order to achieve specific results, provides coaches with insights into the performance of individuals and teams, and provides objective data on the issues and concerns nominated by the client.

A coaching needs analysis can be carried out as a separate service prior to the commencement of a coaching program. For a fee, the coach conducts interviews and surveys and establishes focus groups in order to gather data relevant to the organization's learning and development needs. The needs analysis is then presented to the client, who decides whether or not to proceed with the coaching program. Alternatively, the coach conducts the coaching needs analysis as part of the coaching program. In this case, it is built into the proposal and the coach begins to collect information immediately after the contract has been signed.

CLIENT EDUCATION
Specific information on what you will provide
Specific details of what resources you will need
- a definite time frame for the coaching program
- the total costs of the program
- how you will conduct a coaching needs analysis
- what data collection system you will use
- the specific monitoring processes you will use
- what assessment instruments you will use and the feedback process
- what specific organizational objectives and outcomes you will be measuring and how frequently you will measure these
- how you will guarantee ongoing learning and transfer of skills
- what reporting procedures you will use—to whom and how frequently
- when a final review will be completed
- what follow-up procedures you intend to put into place.

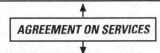

AGREEMENT ON SERVICES

CLIENT RELATIONSHIP
- clarify the client's exact expectations and priorities
- further reassure the client that you are committed and capable of meeting these expectations
- reassure the client that you are in control of the proposed project
- specify the exact time frame when a written proposal will be delivered to the client and follow-up as promised to further engender trust and confidence.

Figure 6.7 Step five: Reaching an agreement—goals and objectives

Step six: The proposal

A proposal is the written documentation of the verbal agreement of services between the client and the coach. Rather than discuss the proposal in terms of client education and the client relationship as we have done with the other stages of client management, here we have chosen to detail the critical elements of a successful proposal. Best practices show that proposals should be no longer than two or three pages.

A proposal

1 *Define the background and the current situation* For example: Company X has recently undergone a major restructuring program. As a result, the executive team lost one of its long-standing members, who was replaced by two inexperienced team members. Since then, the executive team has not functioned at its full potential. Second, the changes in the organization have had a particularly destabilizing influence on Business Unit Y. Middle managers in Unit Y report increasing problems with staff morale, absenteeism and retention. Company X is seeking to build a strong, top-performing executive team to support management in Unit Y in order to improve performance and productivity.

2 *Objectives or identified needs* For example, the objectives of the coaching program are to:

- develop the leadership competencies of the two new team members
- build a high-performing executive team
- improve morale in Unit Y
- improve retention in Unit Y.

3 *Outcome measures or success factors* For example:

- The leadership competencies of all team members will be documented.
- A 360-degree feedback will show significant levels of improvement in the nominated competencies of the two new team members.
- New, streamlined processes will be put in place within the next two months to enable the executive team to reach consensus and initiate and complete projects more quickly.
- A climate survey on morale will show improvement on current levels within three months.
- The retention rate over the next six months will improve from the current level.

4 *Accountabilities* This section of the proposal details what the coach will provide, as well as the client's responsibilities. For example:

The coach's role is to:

- undertake a thorough coaching needs assessment
- conduct staff interviews
- conduct agreed-upon seminars and focus groups with stakeholders to enhance buy-in and obtain ongoing support for the coaching program
- provide one-to-one executive coaching sessions, team coaching sessions, evaluation of the program and progress reports to the client.

The client's role is to:

- advertise the coaching program
- discuss the objectives and expectations of the coaching program with the targeted coachees before the commencement of the program

- insure that coachees attend the program
- provide the coach with any necessary data, such as key performance indicators, performance appraisals and staff surveys.

5   *Reporting procedures*   It is important to establish reporting procedures before a coaching program commences. Of course, this does not preclude any other discussions or meetings between the client and coach. Coaching programs, especially those that take place over a considerable period of time, are subject to "shifting objectives." The coach must be flexible and able to manage the stated objectives, as well as any other issues that arise during the course of the project.

For example, for a six-month program, a coach may commit to:

- A written report to all stakeholders detailing the results of the coaching needs analysis, including assessment and coachees' individual objectives. The report should be submitted within four weeks of the program's commencement.
- A meeting with stakeholders to obtain feedback on the report and to insure ongoing support for the program.
- A written report tracking progress on the stated objectives three months into the program.
- A meeting with stakeholders for feedback on the report.
- A final written report or final review submitted at the end of the program detailing the program's objectives and successes, as well as any recommendations for future coaching engagements.

6   *Methodologies*   This section should briefly document the types of coaching services that will be provided. For example:

- Twelve, ninety-minute, one-to-one sessions with the two new team members. These will be conducted on a weekly basis and will focus on the three leadership competencies identified in the 360-degree appraisal.
- Four, two-hour coaching sessions with the executive team will be conducted every three weeks.
- Four individual, one-to-one coaching sessions will be conducted with executive team members, excluding the two new recruits.
- A climate survey on morale will be followed by three workshops for all staff in Unit Y on identified issues.
- Six workshops for managers in Unit Y will be conducted to identify major issues around morale and staff retention, develop strategies to deal with these issues and enhance management skills around staff development in order to improve retention rates.

7   *Time frame*   Here, the coach has to nominate the dates on which the coaching program will commence and conclude.

8   *Terms and conditions*   The coach should nominate the costs of the coaching program and the terms of payment. For example:

The total cost of the coaching program = $XX

- The cost of twelve individual coaching sessions for two executive team members =
- The cost of four team coaching sessions =
- The cost of four individual coaching sessions for the executive team =
- The cost of three workshops for Unit Y staff =
- The cost of six workshops for managers of Unit Y =

Terms of payment. For example:

- One half of the total amount of the program ($XX) is due upon acceptance of this proposal. The remaining $XX is due ninety days after the initial payment.
- Once the proposal is accepted, payment is to be made. The fees are usually non-refundable, although you may reschedule the commencement of the coaching program to a future, mutually agreeable time.

9 *Acceptance of the proposal* The proposal can replace the need for a separate contract. Two copies should be made of any proposal. Both copies, signed by the coach, should be forwarded to the client, who also signs both copies, and returns one to the coach.

The format for the terms of acceptance is standard in the consulting and coaching world. It should indicate that once the client has signed off on the proposal, she or he has agreed to the terms and conditions therein and has given approval for the program to commence on the stated date.

Step seven: The contract

As mentioned above, a thorough proposal, on which both the client and coach have signed off, can bypass the need for a separate contract. However, as noted, experienced behavioral coaches also emphasize the importance of contracting with the coachee around the development or action plan. For example:

1 *Objectives:* The coach (name) and coachee (name) agree on the following two objectives for their coaching sessions:

- to improve working relations with team members
- to delegate more effectively to team members.

2 *Measurements:* The coach and coachee agree on the following behavioral measures to support this action plan.

Work relations:

- Angry or emotional outbursts with team members, by the end of the coaching sessions, will be at least 75 per cent less frequent.
- A process whereby the coachee, as team leader, meets with each team member for a half-hour review/discussion each week, will be in place by the end of the third coaching session.

Delegating:

- The coachee will nominate three "pieces of work" to delegate. The first work project will be delegated by the end of the fourth coaching session, and the second and third project by the end of the sixth coaching session.

The coachee agrees to seek feedback from the team member to whom the work was delegated, and to nominate delegation skills that can be practiced and enhanced in the following coaching sessions.

Step eight: Coaching and program management

In Chapter 5 we discussed the design and implementation of a behavioral coaching program, as well as the measurement and management of such a program. The management of the coaching program was discussed from a "technical" or procedural point of view. Here, in keeping with our emphasis on best practice client-centered management, we will examine the interpersonal relationship between the client (sponsor and/or decision makers) and the coach during the coaching project.

As behavioral coaches we nominate four areas of a client relationship that are critical to the success of a program. These are ongoing trust; truthfulness; giving credit to others; and patience and sensitivity. We will briefly discuss each of these elements as they affect the coach–client partnership.

Trust as an ongoing process

Trust is not something that can be established easily or quickly. It develops over time and may be betrayed by either party. A client's trust develops as a function of what the coach does, as well as what she or he says. Making clear commitments and promises and keeping them in the specified time frame are key factors in developing a trusting relationship. Importantly, a coach should never make promises that he or she cannot fulfill.

A coach can further develop trust by continuing to draw out from the client her or his expectations. Trust in the coach's capabilities is engendered when the coach listens carefully and acknowledges that he or she understands the client and the current business realities.

Clients' trust in a coach deepens when they are assured that the coach is there for "the long haul." They need to know that the coach will not come into the business or organization, introduce changes that may or may not work, then leave. The coach's commitment to the coaching program, from inception to completion, must be established. Follow-up processes to insure that the learning and changes have been maintained should be built into any agreement.

Certainly, as noted by Flores, trust is not a one-way or a simple process. Coaches also have to develop trust in their clients. It is helpful for coaches to be aware of their own attitudes toward trusting others. We may have had less-than-satisfactory experiences around trust and these can affect future relationships. Coaches need to examine what causes them to trust or mistrust others. Some people are too trusting, while others are prematurely mistrustful. An awareness of our relationship to "trusting" can alert us to seek objective evidence for our feelings, rather than assuming they are always a true reflection of the current relationship.

Truthfulness

Research shows that senior managers believe truthful, straightforward communication to be the most important factor in successful coaching. We believe that this applies equally to the coach–client relationship. The coach has to be truthful about the progress of the coaching program. To sugar-coat the situation in the hope, or even belief, that it will improve does everyone a disservice. It both undermines the client's trust in the coach and precludes the possibility of discussing and solving any problems.

It is critical, then, that coaches establish a climate of truthful communication so that any blocks or barriers to a program can be reviewed. A coach, for example, may be experiencing a lack of support from certain key stakeholders, or coachees may not be adhering to their coaching contracts. Coaches require the confidence and skills to manage such conflicts in an open, productive manner, and this can only be done if truthfulness is encouraged and rewarded.

Giving credit to others

Another crucial aspect of coach–client management is the coach's ability to overcome her or his own need for ego-gratification and give credit or kudos to others. If the coach is not overly invested in the outcome of the program, he or she is more likely to recognize and acknowledge the contributions of others. Reinforcing and rewarding the efforts of others increases morale, commitment and self-responsibility. Furthermore, understanding what the client and others involved in the program recognize as their own strengths and acknowledging these can further enhance the relationship with all participants.

Patience and sensitivity

As we are all aware, change, let alone transformation, takes time. Clients frequently become anxious or concerned about the rate of change and may express doubts about a program's effectiveness. The coach not only has to contain her or his own impatience and anxieties, but reassure the client.

Educating the client about the expected peaks and plateaus associated with any new change program can offset some of his or her impatience and apprehension. The coach has to maintain and express optimism, charting and informing the client of progress while remaining sensitive to the client's needs and concerns.

In summary, there are eight phases to client-centered management in behavioral coaching. These are attracting the client; sending material; first meeting; second meeting; agreement on services; proposal; contracting; and coaching and managing the program. We have discussed stages one to five in relation to the goals and objectives of the coach. For stages six and seven, we provided examples of a proposal and contract that illustrate many of the principles, objectives and best practices of behavioral coaching.

Developing a coaching philosophy

Behavioral coaching is not confined to assessing, monitoring, analyzing and measuring the behavior of coachees. It also recognizes the importance of examining and evaluating coaches' own behavior. If coaches are genuine students of behavior, then their behavior demands equal scrutiny and ongoing growth and development should be undertaken. Coaching, after all, is an interpersonal phenomenon and the interpersonal exchange is partly a function of the coach's value systems and beliefs.

Because a coach's philosophical position underpins her or his coaching practice, it is critical to examine this. Therefore, in this section, we explore the coach's philosophy and how this affects his or her coaching style, objectives and management of clients and coachees. It is important that coaches are conscious of their world view and how it informs their coaching practice. We use the term philosophy in its broadest, popular sense; that is, it refers to a coach's attitude toward life. This of course can include her or his metaphysical stance, ethics, aesthetics and systematized principles.

A coach's view of the cosmos is a significant aspect of his or her philosophical outlook. When talking about a cosmic viewpoint, we are referring, in a fairly broad sense, to the individual's beliefs about how the universe is ordered or structured. For example, some of us believe that we live in a random, uncaring universe, while others have faith in some cosmic order, perhaps a higher order or an interventionist god, gods or deities.

Some of the major philosophical underpinnings of coaching include humanism, existentialism, eastern influences and constructionism. Here, rather than examine each of these in depth, we have chosen to explore key elements of the coach's world view and how these manifest in the practice of coaching. While such concerns may seem far removed from the practicalities of coaching, they nonetheless influence coaching practice in numerous ways. These include:

- the model or style of coaching we employ
- our coaching objectives
- the clients we choose
- how we position accountability.

Our coaching "models" and style

Coaching in a random universe

Coaches who hold the view that the universe is uncaring and random tend to favor models of competency, achievement and self-responsibility. They highlight the importance of coachees having an internal locus of control and sometimes display impatience, even mild contempt, for coachees whose locus of control is external.

Life is viewed as a series of challenges and the underlying premise of the coaching engagement is that coachees need to face up to these challenges and conquer them through action and self-overcoming. Suffering and difficulties are not necessarily seen as leading to understanding and insight; rather, they should be vanquished. Coachees are encouraged to create their own paths and values and to strive for self-reliance.

A "softer" approach adopted by some coaches who hold similar beliefs about the universe derives from eastern philosophy, as discussed in *The Coaching at Work Toolkit*. The universe may be random and uncaring, but the coach encourages coachees to accept and "live life as life lives itself." In this coaching contract, there is less emphasis on achievement and mastery. Life may be a challenge, but it is not necessarily a battle. Life and/or the organization does not owe us anything, and the coaching sessions provide a safe haven for coachees to reflect on and explore their sense of entitlement, otherwise they cannot be in the present and "at one" with what they are doing.

Such an approach is not as passive as it may appear. Of course, the coach and coachees agree on strategies to put in place and actions to take. What is different is that the coach is not giving coachees anything. In fact, the coach's role is to help coachees do away with what is stopping them from living a more harmonious and joyful life. For example, work competencies may be established and the ultimate goal may be for the coachee to enhance her or his performance of these. The way to improvement is to help the coachee take away the thoughts, ideas, expectations and fears that prevent her or him from "just doing what she or he is doing."

Coaching in an ordered universe

Coaches who practice within an ordered or meaningful universe also tend to adopt certain models of coaching. For instance, they are more likely to employ models of nurturance, holistic models or spiritually based approaches. A coachee is supported in search for his or her path, which may even be predetermined. The critical point here is that there is agreement between the coach and coachee that there is a path for each individual, and their joint task is to find the coachee's path rather than create one out of chaos.

Even when a coachee has an external locus of control, she or he is not considered a "poor coaching candidate." The coach is able to integrate this outlook with the coachee's own, self-determined path. Coachees are more likely to be guided and supported to find, rather than to create, meaning and value, both personal and professional. Mastery and achievement, while important, are not the focus of the coaching sessions. Indeed, sometimes professional or "earthly" achievements are only significant if they reflect the individual's spiritual growth and development.

As coaches, we are the first to underscore the centrality of self-knowledge in coachees. In fact, it is an implicit, and sometimes explicit, criterion for "a good coaching candidate." In all fairness, we have to apply the same stringent criteria to ourselves. With this in mind, we have developed the following questions to enhance coaches' conscious recognition of their personal philosophical outlook.

1   Do I believe there is order in the universe or is it random?
2   If there is order, what shape or form does it take?
3   How do my answers to the above two questions affect the way I lead my life?
4   How do these answers affect my coaching practice?
5   How do these answers affect the types of clients and coachees I prefer to work with?
6   How do my views affect my coaching relationship with non-preferred clients and coachees?
7   On a scale of one (not at all) to seven (very much), how willing am I to alter my philosophical approach to match those of clients and coachees?

The coach's philosophy and coaching objectives

In our previous books we examined coaching objectives in several different contexts, for example, in one-to-one executive coaching and establishing coaching programs in organizations. Here, we are focusing on two of a coach's main, broad objectives and how these are affected by his or her philosophical position. These two objectives are facilitating personal and professional growth and financial gain.

Facilitating personal and professional growth

A great deal of the coaching literature and many coaching web sites and brochures nominate the core objective of coaching as facilitating personal and professional growth. These two areas typically are positioned as though they are interchangeable. While there is certainly an overlap between these two aspects of growth, a coach's philosophy tends to determine which one will be the central focus of a coaching intervention.

Coaches who believe that their mandate is to enhance professional skills and competencies tend to focus more on organizational goals than those of individual coachees. They are more committed to performance or changes in external behavior than to internal change. Conversely, coaches for whom personal growth is paramount sometimes emphasize coachees' goals and values to the detriment of their professional development. The focus in the coaching sessions is on internal change, which may not manifest sufficiently or early enough for organizational goals to appear to be being met.

It is helpful for coaches to understand where their major interests and competencies lie. While professional development and personal growth are related constructs, as are internal and external change, a coach's emphasis will affect the objectives of a coaching program and the choice of outcome measures. Ideally, coaches can work in situations where there is no conflict between organizational and individual objectives.

The following questions are designed to help coaches clarify whether they prefer to focus on coachees' professional or personal development.

1   Do I believe that personal and professional growth always go together?
2   Do I prefer to focus on personal growth issues, even within an organizational context, or on professional competencies?

3 Do I believe that internal change always has to accompany, or even precede, external change?
4 Am I more committed to fostering changes in performance or changes within the individual?
5 How comfortable am I dealing with internal changes?
6 In what coaching situations might I focus too narrowly on either external or internal changes?
7 Do I have a mandate or obligation to help improve a coachee's general quality of life?

Financial gain

Another major objective of running a coaching practice, as with most businesses, is to reap financial gain. To some degree, all coaches are subject to economic imperatives. Our attitudes toward money and the significance it holds for us form part of our philosophy and affect how we conduct our coaching practice. For example, coaches for whom financial gain is an overriding objective tend to target coachees at high levels in large corporations. Others work with entrepreneurs or businesses on a profit share or incentive basis. Profit is the bottom line for corporations and most businesses, and any coach wishing to work successfully in these areas has to recognize that profit is an overarching and guiding principle. Other coaches, however, are uncomfortable in the corporate world. The notion that the fundamental aim of coaching is to enhance performance, and therefore profit, is not in line with their philosophy and values. Some options these coaches choose include working for the public sector or for non-profit organizations.

Clearly, both positions are tenable and we are not suggesting that either one is ethically superior. Nevertheless, it is important that coaches clarify their objectives regarding financial gain. Objectives and goals affect the types of clients coaches choose, the services they provide and how willing they are to tolerate clients they dislike or whose philosophy is at odds with their own.

The following questions will help coaches clarify their true, in-use principles around financial gain.

1 On a scale of one (not very) to seven (extremely so), how important is financial gain to me?
2 On a scale of one (not at all) to seven (very), how willing am I to work with clients and coachees purely for the money?
3 If money were not a major issue, would this change who I coach and how I coach?
4 If financial gain is not my main objective in coaching, what is?

The coach's philosophy and choice of clients

A coach's attitude to life determines, to a certain extent, the type of client and coachee she or he chooses, or at least prefers to work with. For example, coaches who hold the view that life is a striving to overcome challenges and to continually succeed in the face of adversity are attracted to a particular coachee profile. Coachees who are top performers, high achievers, competitive, ambitious and action-oriented "fit" with this philosophy. Coaching high-performing individuals for development and career advancement, especially around performance skills, attracts coaches in this category. The coach can champion and challenge these individuals to even greater heights of success.

Alternatively, coaches who believe that life is something of a "battle" frequently choose to work with individuals who are "struggling" with work or life issues. Such coaches adopt a more nurturing, supportive role. They also tend to experience and acknowledge greater empathy for coachees' difficulties.

Coaches for whom professional achievement is only one, and not necessarily the most important, facet of an individual's life are more likely to work with clients on "remedial" or performance issues at a lower level in an organization. Even when coaching for development, the emphasis in the coaching sessions tends to be as much on values and life goals as on work competencies.

The coach's philosophy and accountability

The extent to which coaches hold clients and coachees accountable is largely a function of their belief in free will. Some coaches adopt the philosophical position that we create ourselves, our person and our values through an act of free will. Consequently, coachees always have a choice in any situation. Coaches who maintain this outlook hold themselves, clients and coachees accountable to a far greater extent than coaches with a different existential position. They are also likely to encourage coachees to set difficult, demanding goals and to be unsympathetic if these are not met. Coaches who emphasize accountability can be seen as cold, uncaring and unsupportive. The refrain "It's your choice" can seem simplistic, if not cruel, particularly to coachees who genuinely do not see that they have choices either in a specific situation or in life more generally.

Increased accountability and the accompanying self-responsibility are desirable outcomes of any coaching interaction. However, coaches who do not explicitly explain their philosophy to the client and coachees prior to the commencement of a coaching program do themselves and their client a great disservice. The client and coachees either accept the coach's viewpoint or they don't. If they don't, the coach can choose to educate them or to not work with them. Alternatively, coaches who believe that we are shaped mainly by our genetics, childhood experiences and environment are less likely to hold clients or coachees to such rigorous standards of accountability. Coaches from a therapy or counseling background, for example, tend to give the coachees "the benefit of the doubt," and will explore in depth the reasons why a coachee may not be adhering to agreements. These coaches tend to be more supportive and patient, whether or not they employ a "pathology model." Here, the notion of choice is raised after an issue has been explored, rather than before.

Closely related to a coach's approach to accountability and choice is how he or she views change. Many coaches believe that individuals react in certain ways simply because they lack the knowledge to behave differently and the coach's task, therefore, is to provide this knowledge. Even though the information provided may be accurate and timely, however, it may not be appropriate in the eyes of the coachee. Exploring change must include extensive input from the coachee about her or his life and work situation and expectations. Change shouldn't be delivered as a prescription.

Coaches also need to review their feelings about change. Do we sincerely embrace change in our coaching practice or do we cling to our methodologies, regardless of the coaching outcomes? We educate others about change, so should be willing to adopt new tools and techniques and incorporate ongoing research findings into our work. Likewise, we may expect coachees to follow a prescribed behavioral change program but respond emotionally when there is resistance or regression. How do we as coaches view our own attempts to change? When we fail in our efforts, do we blame ourselves or our lack of commitment or do we accept that change is difficult, incremental and subject to lapses? Change is complex and fraught with many obstacles and setbacks. It is no different for coaches than it is for coachees.

In summary, a coach's philosophical position affects all aspects of his or her coaching practice. In particular, behavioral coaching stresses the need for coaches to be aware of how their attitude to life influences their coaching models or style, their coaching objectives, how they choose clients and what accountability demands they place on their clients and coachees.

Learning from successful coaches

In this section, we summarize twelve critical success factors nominated by practicing behavioral coaches in the life, executive and business arenas. These lessons have been gleaned from our experience, from research and from anecdotal reports from colleagues and successful coaches, both internal and external. Of course, these twelve lessons do not constitute an exhaustive list. For the purpose of economy, we have chosen those practices most frequently reported by coaches as contributing to successful coaching outcomes. The lessons relate to coachee and client management.

Lesson one: Recognizing "red flags"

Coaches, particularly those who do not have psychological training, frequently ask us for "red flags" that may signal that coaching is either not appropriate or is likely to have poor results. Following is a list of some of the major warning signs that successful coaches recognize as useful and valid predictors of unwanted coaching outcomes.

• When a coachee continually "moves the goal post," that is, does not follow through on assignments from session to session and presents a new, usually unrelated, area or issue to address in each session

- When the coach feels overly involved and overly invested in a coachee's well-being and in the outcome of the coaching sessions
- When the coach feels that she or he is doing most of the work in the sessions
- When the coachee regularly misses or cancels sessions
- When the coachee is unable or unwilling to receive feedback, regardless of how diplomatic or tentative the coach may be
- When the coachee adopts a "victim role," always blaming others and is unwilling to accept responsibility for his or her part in any situation
- When the coachee displays extreme emotional states, such as distress or anger, within the sessions and the coach is unable to move the action beyond this emotionality
- When the coachee continues to request help and strategies to change, but does not act on any of the preferred solutions or guidelines
- When the coachee has an issue with substance abuse that is affecting her or his work performance and ability to learn or change within the coaching process
- When the coachee presents with such high levels of pervasive anxiety that he or she is unable to concentrate or learn during the sessions
- When the coachee presents with signs and symptoms of depression that are clearly affecting her or his life and work performance
- When the coachee appears overly dependent on the coach. Such dependence may manifest as an unwillingness to act without the coach's explicit consent, seeking approval from the coach or implying that the coaching relationship is "special."

There is a general consensus among successful coaches that being faced with any of the above situations is challenging and likely to induce stress. All underscore the importance of having a personal coach, a peer supervisor or a mentor with whom they can discuss such issues. A referral system to a competent, licensed therapist is considered mandatory for all coaches.

Lesson two: Contracting with the coachee

Both internal and external coaches emphasize the importance of contracting with coachees at the beginning of any coaching program, after objectives have been established. Typically, contracts or agreements focus on two areas: the rules of engagement for the coaching sessions, and the development or action plan.

The rules of engagement Effective contracts or agreements, such as those discussed in our second book, *The Coaching at Work Toolkit*, specify the logistics involved in the program, including protocols for scheduling and cancellation of sessions. Such an agreement also nominates the expectations of the coach and coachees and the commitments the coach and coachees make to each other.

Contracting for the development or action plan Research and experience indicates the necessity of contracting for the actions the coach and coachee have agreed on. Following the initial assessment and goal setting, both parties generally agree on two or three objectives and measurable behaviors that support the action plan. The goals must be clarified and there has to be agreement that both coach and coachee are committed to achieving these objectives. The objectives, measurable behaviors and a time frame are then set down in writing in a personal development plan that both parties sign off on.

The contract or agreement can be drawn on if a coachee's commitment wavers and agreed-upon objectives are not being met within the designated time frame. However, experience shows that many coaches, especially those internal to an organization, rely too much on contracts as a means of regaining a coachee's focus or commitment. Indeed, contracts are sometimes used in a way that makes a coachee feel like a "disobedient or disappointing child," with the coach adopting the role of the punitive parent. Contracts are best used to explore, identify and discuss changes in levels of commitment. If they are used to induce compliance rather than true commitment, genuine change is unlikely to occur and objectives will not be met.

Lesson three: Maintaining confidentiality

Coaches, particularly those internal to an organization, emphasize the centrality of clearly defining and maintaining strict rules of confidentiality between coach and coachee. Most of the coaching literature addresses issues of confidentiality, so rather than repeat those guidelines, we have chosen to nominate several practices that coaches report as being conducive to truly maintaining confidentiality. Prior to the commencement of the coaching sessions, the client, coach and coachee should agree to and sign off on what information will be shared, in what detail and with whom.

Some coaches insist that information be shared only when both the coach and coachee are present. All test scores, results of personality profiles and any other personal data should be accessible only to the coach and coachee. Finally, if the coach belongs to the HR department or is an internal consultant, information gathered from the coaching sessions cannot be revealed in interviews or discussions concerning promotion or career development. Trust betrayed, even if inadvertently, is difficult to regain and can seriously impair the coaching partnership and negatively affect the coaching outcome.

Lesson four: Role confusion

Closely related to confidentiality issues that internal coaches, in particular, may face is the risk of role confusion. Experienced and long-time practicing coaches, both internal and external, emphasize that internal coaches who also function as HR personnel or consultants have to be clear about the boundaries between coaching and managing roles. They are more likely than external coaches to be aware of a coachee's need for improvement and the consequences if such improvement does not occur.

The coach's role, however, is not to address the need for improvement. That is the job of management, whose responsibility it is also to spell out the consequences, either positive or negative, of a coachee's behavior. If a coach falls into the trap of trying to hammer home the need for improvement and the consequences if this does not occur, he or she is at risk of not addressing what the coachee actually needs to enhance performance. The coach will also fail to explore any blocks or obstacles that may be preventing forward movement.

Lesson five: Diagnosing the "real" issue

As many experienced coaches acknowledge, the presenting issue in coaching is not always the most critical or even the "real" issue that needs to be addressed. For example, executives who present as workaholic, lacking balance and approaching burn-out may appear to be good candidates for coaching for time management and delegation skills, or even career coaching. The real, underlying issue, however, is frequently a psychological one. Fear of intimacy or poor interpersonal skills may be the root cause of workaholism.

In other instances, an individual's behavior may appear to be the cause of a problem, but on closer questioning and investigation it may be found that issues to do with the team or management are contributing equally to the situation. Adopting a healthy skepticism and testing hypotheses about the true nature of a "problem" from a systems perspective serve to isolate "real" issues that lend themselves to a coaching intervention.

Lesson six: Self-awareness

In our previous books we discussed several aspects of coaches' self-awareness that we believe contribute to successful coaching outcomes. Here, we will discuss self-awareness from two slightly different perspectives: awareness, mindfulness and being present to coachees; and a coach's awareness of her or his own reactions to specific situations.

1 *Awareness of the coachee* Virtually all successful coaches underscore the importance of the coach possessing an above-average capacity for heightened awareness within the coaching interaction. There is a consensus that effective coaching demands that the coach be attuned to:

- *The coachee's level of engagement* Is the coachee focused or distracted? What signs does the coachee exhibit when he or she is experiencing either of these states? Successful coaches are highly intuitive and immediately recognize when a coachee is distracted, and are able to quickly refocus attention and interest.

- *The coachee's emotional state* Experienced coaches highlight the importance of being able to track a coachee's emotional shifts. Recognizing when a coachee is displaying emotions such as joy, optimism and enthusiasm and being able to leverage these states to intensify learning and growth is conducive to change and transformation. Alternatively, if a coachee is expressing anxiety or deflation, the successful coach uses this material to immediately explore, discuss and manage what may be impediments to progress.

- *The coachee's language* It is critical to an effective coaching interaction that the coach is cognizant not only of what is being said but *how* it is being said. Many coaches also emphasize the importance of "making the unsaid said" and the skills involved in doing this. For instance, asking questions such as "What are you thinking but not saying?" or "Would it be helpful for you to say what you are thinking at this moment?" generates openness and paves the way for discussions that may otherwise not surface.

- *What is most helpful to the coachee right now?* Again, there is a consensus among many coaches that allowing this question to inform coaching sessions is an invaluable technique. It focuses the coach's awareness on the needs of the coachee rather than on her or his own needs or agenda. Coaches are more alert to signals from the coachee for when to listen, question, offer support, challenge or make suggestions.

2 *Self-awareness of the coach* Much of the coaching literature, including our previous two books, underscores the centrality of coaches being highly aware of their reactions to coachees and coaching issues. Self-awareness is a complex and multifaceted construct. In this chapter, we have chosen to discuss five aspects of self-awareness that practicing coaches deem essential to a powerful coaching relationship.

- *Avoiding being caught in a defensive cycle* Argument and debate are integral to many coaching interactions. Experienced coaches learn not to take this personally and to recognize that it may be the coachee's style of processing information and relating. For example, many individuals adopt the position of devil's advocate, and an unsuspecting coach can find herself or himself responding in a defensive, argumentative fashion. Understanding what triggers our emotions and how we process them is critical for our own personal development and for the healthiness of the coaching partnership.

  We have to learn to recognize our own self-limiting beliefs, as well as the preferences that we translate into demands. Completing a coaching self-assessment profile (see *The Coaching at Work Toolkit* for examples), particularly after a difficult session, can help a coach to process what has happened. Successful coaches also advocate the use of self-assessments as a learning tool and as a way to solve problems.

- *Understanding the need "to tell"* A coach's need to tell and advise may spring from a genuine wish to impart information and solutions that will benefit the coachee. Coaches from a consulting background typically struggle with this issue. The need to tell, however, can also have its roots in the coach's uncertainty, impatience or the desire to be seen as an expert.

  Experienced coaches are cognizant of the risks involved in offering premature solutions or telling a coachee what path to take. They recognize how telling can preclude a coachee's acceptance and ownership of strategies or solutions. Furthermore, they warn that offering solutions inappropriately can signal to the coachee that the coach is not listening or is attempting to apply generic solutions. Successful coaches understand when to deliver as much as what to deliver.

- *Understanding how the coach personally deals with conflict* Although coaches commonly work with coachees on conflict management, this does not necessarily mean that coaches are aware of how they themselves deal with conflict. Successful coaches are in agreement that a coach has to recognize whether or not he or she has a typical style of managing conflict, and, if so, what this is.

  For example, we need to understand our tendency to avoid, force, accommodate or collaborate and how our style may affect the coaching partnership. Does it result in minimizing or maximizing conflict between the coachee and her or his colleagues or the organization or even between the coachee and coach? Case discussions with peers or a coach or mentor can help bring to light a coach's conflict style and methods to deal with conflict more effectively.

- *Recognizing the coach's response to authority* There is a growing appreciation within the coaching profession that a coach's attitude to authority can derail a coaching program. If the coach identifies more closely with authority as embodied by the organization, he or she may not fully support the coachee and not take the individual's personal developmental needs sufficiently into account. On the other hand, if the coach's attitude to authority is subversive or ambivalent, she or he may collude with the coachee and undermine the importance of the organization's goals and objectives.

  Everyone has "blind spots," or aspects that are known to others but not to oneself. Our attitude to authority, which is deep-seated and grounded in early life experiences, is often more evident to others. Hence, as most successful coaches recognize, peer supervision and case discussions with other experienced coaches are critical if coaches wish to enhance their awareness in this area.

- *Recognizing a coachee's dependency needs* Coaches can unintentionally foster dependency in their clients. One of the agreed-upon methods to offset this possibility is to set strict time limits around the coaching program and put a cessation plan, including follow-up, in place. The ultimate aim of successful coaching is to enable coachees to be self-reliant. Through teaching and encouraging the ongoing practice of skills, techniques and strategies, coaches insure that coachees can transfer their learning to other life and work situations long after coaching has ended.

Lesson seven: Goals and "personal best"

Some research suggests that the most successful athletes are goal-focused rather than competitive; that is, they set goals that will better their own performance rather than measuring themselves against others. Similarly, individuals experience a greater sense of control and mastery when measuring themselves against their own efforts than those imposed by the organization. Of course, this is not to say that organizational goals and objectives can be ignored. However, coaching outcomes are more likely to be successful if organizational goals are framed within the individual's own measures of his or her efforts and success.

Lesson eight: Previewing outcomes

Many coaches report that testing the action plan or proposed strategy before it is put into action is critical to successful coaching. It allows the coach, client and coachee to pre-empt, explore and devise solutions or ways to deal with potential obstacles. Previewing outcomes allows hidden barriers, self-limiting beliefs and environmental obstacles to surface. These can then be explored, which accelerates learning and moves the action forward at a faster pace.

Lesson nine: Self-monitoring

Self-monitoring in behavioral coaching can range from keeping a brief record of a specific behavior to maintaining a journal. Successful coaches attest to the importance of asking coachees to self-monitor in order to provide assessment data about a particular behavior. This also functions as an intervention because, as mentioned previously, observing one's own behavior tends to bring about change in the desired direction. However, there is the question of how accurately an individual can note and record her or his own actions. In order to obtain more reliable data, coaches look for corroborating evidence to determine the accuracy of the coachee's judgments.

Writing about an upsetting event or "a critical incident" in a journal helps the coach and coachee gain insight into the coachee's beliefs and expectations about the event. It paves the way for the coachee to become more aware of his or her role in a particular situation, as well as how others may have perceived his or her actions. When the coachee shares the journal with the coach, together they can recognize and explore the coachee's strengths and successes as well as her or his defensive patterns such as withdrawing, avoidance or blaming. Both self-monitoring and keeping a journal serve to increase the coachee's self-awareness and self-responsibility.

Lesson ten: Visualization or mental rehearsal

Mental rehearsal (or covert imagery rehearsal) is a standard technique employed in sports coaching. While its use and benefits do not figure significantly in the executive and business coaching literature, experience and research show that visualization techniques can yield valuable results in various areas of coaching. These include making presentations, preparing for a job interview, meeting a new client, cold calling, dealing with an unwanted response such as anger, delivering unwelcome news and discussing career development with an unreceptive boss.

There is a general agreement that visualization works best when it is preceded by relaxation. The individual should be guided to picture the actual situation where the event (e.g., the client presentation) will take place. Generally, the technique has proved more effective when the coachee engages all the senses and can visualize and feel his or her movements and actions within the correct time frame. Importantly, the coachee has to practice the skill and mentally perfect it prior to the event so that it becomes automatic and effortless.

Lesson eleven: Role-playing and videotaping

Videotaping role-plays is a recognized and common technique employed by many trainers, but seems to be underutilized in coaching. Videotaping offers the opportunity for coachees to practice new behaviors in a safe environment and receive genuinely objective feedback. It allows us to see ourselves as others do and to receive immediate feedback on how we look, speak and sound to others. The coach can model the desired behavior, then together the coach and coachee can critique the coach's performance. The coachee then has the opportunity to practice the newly acquired behavior and the cycle of critiquing and practice continues until the coachee has mastered the behavior.

As well as videotaping, many coaches employ audiotaping. Areas that lend themselves to audiotaping include making sales calls, rehearsing how to speak to a difficult client or colleague and practicing interview skills.

Lesson twelve: Self-care for the coach

Like most professions, coaching can be stressful. While individual coaches face unique challenges, there is agreement that certain aspects of being a coach can present difficulties for all practitioners. For instance, marketing coaching services in an increasingly competitive environment can be particularly stressful, especially for coaches working in isolation who are unable to benchmark their services and strategies and are uncertain about how to move forward. Second, coaching frequently involves travel, which we all know can take its toll on our health and personal relationships.

Finally, enduring coaches stress the importance of regular exercise, a healthy diet and non-negotiable free time. Coaches have to learn to say no to clients, family and friends without feeling guilty, or feeling guilty but still saying no. Again, having a colleague, coach or mentor with whom to debrief, and, importantly, who can offer positive reinforcement for efforts and successes, is critical for the longevity and efficacy of any coach.

In summary, behavioral coaching approaches client management from a client-centered stance. Experience shows that centering on the client's needs, expectations and concerns as much as those of coachees is critical to the success of any coaching program. Coaching is a collaborative enterprise between the coach, the client and the coachee.

7

Behavioral Coaching Today

During our years of conducting coach training and certification courses, we have tracked the ongoing development of behavioral coaching and found that increasing numbers of coaches are employing the approach we have described throughout this book. Some of the major areas where it is being used include executive coaching (CEOs), transformational leadership coaching, coaching female executives, coaching in education, business coaching, cross-cultural coaching, sales coaching, coaching in the health-care industry and personal coaching.

Executive coaching

It is generally agreed that today CEOs and senior executives come under tremendous pressure to perform, although often without the necessary support and guidance. CEOs and executive teams are also subject to increasing scrutiny from shareholders and boards, who are demanding better results faster. At the same time, mistrust of the corporate world has escalated. Perhaps it should not come as a surprise, then, to learn that the failure rate of costly new hires is very high. Research indicates that from 30 per cent to 40 per cent of these people resign, are fired or "underperform" within a year or two of being hired. CEOs are expected to operate at peak capacity within six months of taking up the job, despite studies suggesting that twelve to eighteen months is a more appropriate time period.

Many corporations do little to assist CEOs in the initial but critical leadership transition phase. Sometimes an outgoing CEO will provide informal "transition coaching," but often there is a staggering loss of corporate intelligence as one person leaves and another takes up the reins. Furthermore, corporations frequently fail to enhance a new CEO's credibility, make public her or his expertise or set up meetings with key stakeholders. As a result, new CEOs frequently have to build important relationships from scratch and look for their own sponsors and champions.

Although CEOs are frequently hired to initiate major changes in an organization, without an in-depth knowledge of the business and the prevailing culture, they often come up against resistance or "forces of regression" they are ill-equipped to manage. Their leadership competencies are often not sufficiently developed to cope with the multitude of demands placed upon them.

Coaching for leadership development is undertaken with selected executives, senior managers and teams, or as part of a company-wide coaching initiative. Coaches, both internal and external, are also contracted to work within specific business units or with individual referrals. Some areas of leadership coaching include leaders in transition, new hires, individuals being "groomed" for promotion, individuals in new positions, management competencies to complement technical expertise, developing and communicating a strategic vision, strategic planning, culture change, ambassadorship, leading executive teams, overcoming isolation, and interpersonal skills such as communication and dealing effectively with colleagues and with power.

When working to enhance and develop leadership at the top levels of an organization, behavioral coaches are guided by research indicating that derailment is generally a function of three major factors: failure to build partnerships and teamwork with the executive team and subordinates, confusion about roles and expectations and lack of political savvy or insight.

EXECUTIVE COACHING FOR LEADERSHIP 1

S. N. is a recently appointed CEO whose predecessor has been fired after only nine months on the job because of "irreconcilable differences with the board." S. N. has received no succession or transition coaching, so the company has agreed to hire an executive coach for her. S. N. is clearly uncertain about her roles and the expectations of the board of directors and the shareholders. The coach first conducted surveys with board members and the senior executive team to establish their expectations. Then, S. N. and the coach drew up a list of leadership competencies that would best meet these expectations. They prioritized these, and using behavioral assessment, examined S. N.'s strengths and weaknesses within each area. Together, they targeted one specific, measurable behavior for each competency and obtained a baseline measure for it. Some of the behaviors targeted for change included identifying and enlisting the support of two individuals who would champion her and help develop good working relationships with the currently alienated executive team and employees; initiating dialogue with all stakeholders within six weeks and scheduling ongoing meetings with them at three-month intervals; and holding weekly strategy meetings with the executive team and second-weekly individual development meetings with each team member. A follow-up mini-360-degree feedback at nine months established that S. N.'s team was functioning more cohesively and felt better supported and more motivated, that her leadership style was rated highly and that her credibility and influence within the company was considerable.

EXECUTIVE COACHING FOR LEADERSHIP 2

In his prior CEO role, R. C.'s leadership style was autocratic. The company had been in crisis and strategic changes had to be enforced to save the business. While his style had been appropriate and successful at the time, R. C. is now facing major challenges in his current position. Feedback, mostly informal, has suggested that his style is alienating both employees and the board. As a consequence, R. C. has hired an experienced executive coach who himself had worked as a CEO. The coach conducted a mini-360-degree feedback with the board members and the executive team. It indicated that R. C.'s domineering, demanding style did not "fit" with the culture of the new organization. The second issue was that R. C. felt unsupported by the board, which despite an unequal distribution of power and underlying friction presented consensus on important decisions. Having assessed R. C.'s leadership style and the expectations of the team and board, two broad objectives for coaching were set. These were to develop a more participatory, collaborative leadership style, and to establish better working relations with board members. The behaviors to be changed included obtaining information and feedback from employees about a major strategic initiative to merge three business units in preparation for a new product launch; enrolling the coach and the HR department to conduct a survey and establish focus groups to provide education about the rationale for the planned changes; providing regular, honest reports to the board; and formally acknowledging his need for support from the board, as well as the need for open discussion and dissent among members. For the first time in the company's history, the board was subject to performance appraisals and peer reviews. After ten months, the planned initiative had been successfully accomplished. Ongoing feedback from R. C.'s team and direct reports showed that his style of leadership was now more inclusive and collaborative. Although friction was still present among board members and power plays sometimes erupted, performance reviews indicated that the board was functioning more as a team.

Transformational leadership

As well as leading and influencing others such as staff, colleagues, board members and shareholders, leaders need to understand themselves and develop a sense of self-leadership or personal mastery. As we have noted throughout this book, understanding one's personal life meaning, vision and values is important for everyone, but it is critical for leaders. Those at the top of an organization have to understand why and how they behave as they do and how their behavior is perceived by others and affects the larger organization or business.

Some leaders, and indeed coaches, dismiss self-awareness or self-knowledge as a "soft skill" that is neither appropriate nor necessary at very senior levels. On the contrary, research suggests that understanding one's own strengths, weaknesses and behavior patterns, as well as how one manages frustration and adversity, are crucial for excellent leadership. A lack of awareness in these areas has been associated with executive derailment and is often at the core of the irreconcilable differences that result in the executive and the company parting ways.

Coaching leaders for transformational change involves changing the very way they think, improving their ability to deal with ambiguity and enhancing their creativity. This increases the individual's capacity to step back and reflect on assumptions about such things as culture, values, organizational objectives and vision that were previously taken for granted.

One key aspect of development and transformation is moving away from a "subjective" point of view, which includes the unquestioned parts of the self, as well as theories and behavioral patterns that we accept as given and do not reflect upon. Leaders need to be able to assume a more "objective" viewpoint from which such assumptions can be questioned and changed. In coaching for transformational leadership coachees are encouraged to allow their assumptions to surface so they can be examined. Assumptions are often at the core of behaviors; changing assumptions can therefore open up opportunities to use behavioral change techniques to adopt more effective behaviors.

As well as working with leaders to transform their view of themselves, others and the world, behavioral coaches operate within a framework of leadership based on results. Rather than focusing on the personal attributes of successful leaders, they work with coachees to achieve results for employees, the organization, its customers and its shareholders. Some of the skills addressed include establishing and focusing on specific business outcomes, communicating these to the team or group, accepting responsibility and ongoing measurement of results and regularly reviewing business practices. Goals and action plans are all set around desired outcomes.

Finally, some documented benefits of leadership coaching include an enhanced ability to develop and foster trust; increased accountability within the organization; the development and maintenance of more satisfactory relationships with the board, shareholders and employees; enhanced credibility and influence as an ambassador; increased ability to align others to the company's vision and mission; successful change management projects; enhanced managerial competencies; increased self-responsibility; an increase in others' responsibility; and the creation of a culture that truly values learning and development.

Throughout the book we have discussed Prochaska's methodology and its place in the behavioral coaching model. The following case study illustrates the stages of change as applied to coaching for leadership. It also highlights the importance of self-awareness in leaders and the critical role played by feedback and behavioral change methods in the coaching process.

COACHING AND CHANGE STAGES

W. Z. was promoted six months ago to assistant chief financial officer and leader of a six-member executive team in a large, public sector finance company. His role as assistant CFO has recently come under scrutiny because of a perceived lack of cohesion that could affect the team's ability to make critical decisions. Initially W. Z. was at the reflective stage (phase one) of change, where he defensively attributed the team's weaknesses to cut-backs in resources and poor leadership on the part of his predecessor. The behavioral coach worked to change W. Z.'s attributions and gained his permission to conduct an informal survey among senior management and his colleagues. The feedback, which W. Z. reluctantly accepted, did propel him to the reflective stage (phase two). He accepted the need for change, but was uncertain about which leadership competencies and skills to develop. During the preparation stage, W. Z. attended a two-day intensive workshop on leadership development and wrote down his impressions and the behaviors he believed he needed to change. Following this, the coach and W. Z. established several behaviors to target and W. Z. self-monitored and obtained a baseline measure of these as well as a measure of the team's performance. Throughout the action stage, W. Z. employed behavioral change techniques such as stimulus control, alternative responses, self-reinforcement and on-going monitoring and evaluation. Over a period of seven months, in order to reinforce the new learning and behaviors (maintenance stage), the coach gathered regular feedback from management and the team. Any reversion to earlier behaviors was monitored, and W. Z. learned to self-correct. At the end of twelve months post-intervention measures of the team's performance were taken, the positive results of which also served to reinforce W. Z.'s new leadership style.

Coaching executive women

Women executives face not only those issues common to all leaders, as discussed above, but other challenges to do with misconceptions about women in leadership, for example. Some of the challenges they face are a function of internalized beliefs, while others are external.

Personality and communication are often considered to be at the core of the challenges facing women in executive roles. To a great degree, however, this is a question of perception. For example, males who demand their rights are considered assertive, whereas females who do the same are more often considered aggressive. Likewise, it is acceptable for males to demand and tell, whereas women are expected to ask or suggest. Sometimes women in top positions internalize male standards and values, but this usually comes at a cost to their self-esteem and sense of being true to themselves.

Research suggests that competencies for successful women executives include being decisive, tough and demanding, and prepared to take career risks. At the same time, however, most women are socialized to be accommodating, nurturing and collaborative, and to keep the peace. In fact, a recent study conducted at a London university college found that women who behave according to feminine stereotypes are more likely to succeed in job interviews. Interviewers looked for "modest," non-verbal behaviors in women and expected them to take responsibility for their failures and play down their successes. Men, on the other hand, were more likely to be employed if they were assertive, dominant and took credit for their past successes. Balancing these conflicting demands is difficult, yet, fortunately, women are more likely to seek help from coaches than men.

Because of the increasing number of women in the workforce and in executive positions, there is a greater demand for women to be coached. Some of the most common coaching issues that surface include life balance and the expectations of peers and family, political maneuvering and relationship building with key stakeholders, being assertive, delegating and managing dissent and conflict.

AN EXECUTIVE WOMAN AND COACHING

Part of the reason M. P. was hired as a senior executive was to contribute to changing the culture of the organization. After five months in the position, however, she feels marginalized and unsupported by other members of the executive team. Management has suggested a coach for M. P., who agreed to coaching on the condition that the coach also work with the team. M. P. initially blamed the problems on the other male team members, whom she thought were hostile toward her because she was a woman. Nevertheless, she agreed to a 360-degree feedback process, which showed that her colleagues resented her domineering and controlling style. The coach also gave M. P. feedback that she felt M. P. was not truly listening to her, that she interrupted and that she appeared impatient with the coaching process. The coach and M. P. assessed her personal strengths and weaknesses, her style of managing conflict and her typical style of dealing with her colleagues. Importantly, the coach explored some of M. P.'s beliefs such as "No one listens to me because I'm female" and "If I ask for help, I'll be seen as incompetent and weak." Some of the behaviors targeted for change included asking colleagues for their opinions rather than "telling" them what she thought, not interrupting, and controlling her impatience. Over three weeks, M. P. monitored these behaviors for a baseline. Various behavioral change techniques were then instituted. These included learning and practicing a simple relaxation technique on a daily basis, challenging her limiting beliefs, using self-statements, and employing alternative responses such as asking rather than telling, listening rather than talking and taking several deep breaths instead of venting her impatience. In time, M. P. successfully changed her behavior. A six-month feedback session and informal comments from the team showed that M. P. was working more collectively and that her communication style had altered significantly, being more inclusive and less dominating. M. P. continued to struggle with her impatience, which she viewed as a "character flaw" and something she would always have to monitor and manage.

The manager as coach

In our first book, *The Complete Guide to Coaching at Work*, we devoted an entire chapter to "the manager as coach." It covered aspects such as the role of the manager as coach and requisite coaching skills and provided an outline for a coaching workshop for managers. Certain misconceptions about managers and coaching persist, however.

As mentioned earlier, coaching is sometimes presented as an alternative to managing. Managers, though, have deadlines to meet and projects to complete. They may therefore be reluctant to adopt a coaching role for fear that doing so will hinder them in their management duties.

Coaching involves managers aligning their team and employees to the organization's objectives and vision, and fostering independent and creative problem solving. Managers are also expected to develop their staff. There is, after all, a consistent body of research that shows a direct link between human capital management and superior shareholder returns. Coaching offers managers a methodology for enhancing the individual's or team's current skills. They thereby develop employees who are committed and can be trusted to use their discretion and judgment to act in ways that are congruent with organizational objectives and goals. Managers have to manage and coaching is simply a vehicle for them to enhance their management skills.

Behavioral coaches working with managers to be coaches emphasize the differences between managing and coaching. Prior to teaching and rehearsing coaching skills, such as providing constructive feedback, establishing personal development plans and managing workplace conflict, coaches have to educate managers about what coaching is and what it is not. Unless current misconceptions about managing and coaching are dispelled, managers may only pay lip service to coaching, but will not be committed to its adoption in the workplace.

COACHING THE MANAGER

B. W. is a senior manager undertaking coaching as part of an organizational initiative. Although her business results are exemplary, a recent 360-degree feedback has indicated that her staff feel excluded from decision making and that her style is too "directive." B. W. was initially reluctant to develop a more participatory style of managing because she feared it might negatively affect productivity. She was also in line for promotion, however, and realized that she would have to begin to show more leadership qualities if she was to move ahead. The first area she and the coach focused on was delegation. B. W. committed to developing one of the team so that he could adopt the team-leading role that she now performed. The function of the team was also expanded, so that members played an active role in decision making about changes that involved their participation. Over the following four months, as the replacement team leader assumed more responsibility, B. W. found she had more time to attend to business matters. The team became more self-managing and she continued to work with the coach on her communication style.

Behavioral coaching in education

One of the expanding areas of behavioral coaching is in the field of education. Behavioral coaches work with individuals, groups, teachers, students and administrative personnel on a wide variety of coaching interventions. They train senior teachers to coach new and inexperienced teachers and students, and establish and monitor peer coaching programs. Coaches also work with students on life skills, study skills and social skills, as well as career choice and preparation.

Coaching the teacher

Behavioral coaching is not simply another term for traditional mentoring or peer supervision between teachers. Instead, coaching focuses on assessment of a teacher's strengths and weaknesses, developing a personalized action plan and working to the coachee's agenda rather than that of the governing educational body. The coach's role, then, is distinct from that of supervisor and is unrelated to performance evaluation. Of course, if the coachee wishes to set objectives around performance evaluation, the coach acts in a strictly confidential role to support, guide and provide feedback.

Coaches are usually experienced teachers, so to a certain extent their role may be seen as that of mentor. Experienced teachers do mentor junior or inexperienced teachers. In this role, they are responsible for conveying and upholding the standards and values of the teaching profession. However, coaching, unlike mentoring, focuses on the individual teacher's values, standards and objectives. Whether coaches are senior teachers or ex-teachers employed as external coaches, they are trained in behavioral coaching methodologies, including behavioral change techniques, ongoing training and follow-through. The coach and new teacher usually meet on a weekly or second-weekly basis for six months or a year. Telephone and email coaching are used as adjuncts to face-to-face meetings.

Two of the major coaching areas for new or inexperienced teachers are curriculum instruction and classroom management. The former involves the coach sharing resources and materials with the coachee, and together the coach and coachee develop goals and strategies to deliver creative and effective lesson plans. Coaching for classroom management includes logistical strategies such as classroom arrangements, interactive techniques, discipline and rewards.

Behavioral coaches help teachers with their personal as well as their professional growth. For example, many coaches explore self-esteem within the framework we set out in Chapter 5. Assertiveness, self-limiting beliefs and means of regulating emotions such as frustration and anxiety are also addressed. In fact, some research indicates that support in these areas is the key benefit of coaching for many teachers. Other reported benefits include increased confidence and self-efficacy in managing students' behavior, trying out new ideas and activities and more effective teaching through the provision of more interactive, participatory lessons.

Coaching teachers often occurs within a framework of what is known as linguistic coaching, which is a system of conversational analysis and communication based on the work of Flores and colleagues. One of the premises of this approach is that we cannot communicate effectively unless we are skillful at distinguishing between fact and interpretation. This is a form of cognitive challenging, as the following case study demonstrates.

COACHING TEACHERS

J. M. is a 40-year-old school principal who was assigned a new school at the beginning of the academic year. She has become increasingly anxious about attending parent–teacher events and is dreading the upcoming annual student evaluation meetings with parents. During dialogue with the coach, it became evident that J. M. believed that the sometimes angry and "demanding" parents were "out to get her." The coach challenged J. M.'s assertions. Through the process of examining factual data rather than her interpretations, J. M. was able to recognize that the parents were motivated more by their concern for their children's welfare and academic success than by any ill feeling toward her. She redefined her concept of "demanding." As a consequence, J. M. developed the skill of translating complaints into goals. She felt more in control and eventually was able to rid herself of her "victim" mentality.

Peer coaching

Experienced teachers also derive significant benefits from coaching, especially in relation to enhancing their skills and general professional development as educators. The aim of peer coaching is to refine present teaching skills, and this has proved particularly effective with senior teachers.

Peer coaching allows teachers to share a professional dialogue about the science and art of teaching. It involves teachers receiving support, assistance and feedback from fellow teachers. At times, visiting master teachers or resource teachers teach alongside coachee teachers rather than simply observing their performance. The coach and coachee plan and evaluate lessons as partners.

Typically, all teachers involved in a peer coaching program are trained in the fundamentals of behavioral coaching, including goal setting, action planning and interpersonal and helping skills. Peer coaching allows teachers to gain feedback not only from the peer coach, but from other colleagues. The exchange of knowledge helps teachers feel less isolated and more supported. The sharing of knowledge is especially critical today, when information technology dictates that teachers absorb increasing amounts of information and be able to facilitate their students' ability to manage it.

In what is sometimes called "challenge coaching," teams, including teachers, administrative staff and librarians, for instance, work together to resolve problems such as service design and delivery. Team coaching, in the education context, is a variation on peer coaching and team teaching.

Some of the documented benefits of peer coaching are that it fosters a sense of companionship, friendship and belonging; feedback allows teachers to recognize their strengths and weaknesses and develop strategies to work with these; it helps teachers transfer skills learned in a workshop or training setting to the specific needs of their students; it furthers professional development; and it helps maintain enthusiasm and accountability. Finally, it fosters a school climate of inquiry, observation and non-evaluative feedback.

Teachers usually voluntarily pair up, matching subject expertise wherever possible. Each develops a personalized development plan and the pair meets on a regular basis to discuss and provide feedback and mutual support around their plans or a current teaching situation. Classroom observation features in some coaching relationships. The coach and coachee agree on what will be observed and how this will be measured (e.g., checklists, ratings, anecdotal observations). Importantly, any feedback given is strictly confidential and the coaching climate is one of trust, collaboration and non-judgment.

Coaching students

Teachers increasingly strive to create classroom environments that foster and support self-control and self-discipline. Growing suicide and crime rates among adolescents, and a lack of social skills and self-regulation in some students, present enormous challenges for teachers. Often teachers have to deal with students who are oppositional, unmotivated, distracted and even aggressive.

Teachers, of course, have to teach; they don't have the time or the resources to individually coach all students. Nevertheless, two types of coaching, namely cognitive coaching and coaching for children with attention deficit disorder (ADD), have been translated to the classroom. Briefly, cognitive coaching is a method of instruction based on the under-standing that metacognition (or being aware of one's own thinking processes) fosters independent learning by providing insights into one's thinking. Coaching for ADD and attention deficit disorder with hyper-activity (ADD-H) includes helping students to understand how attention problems affect their behavior. It also encourages motivation and active involvement in changing behavior. Very specific short-term goals, goal completion, skill building, and planning and developing strategies for time management are critical features of successful coaching for these students.

Teachers also employ behavioral coaching techniques in group settings. The group may be composed of students who have a common problem to address or the coaching may be part of a life skills curriculum. Indeed, a study of socially rejected fifth graders found that coaching improved their social skills and thus their ability to form relationships with peers.

Group coaching is employed with students to enhance self-esteem, improve social skills, develop accountability and responsibility, inculcate goal setting and planning habits, manage emotions more effectively and improve communication and interpersonal skills. Teachers working in this area require training in behavioral change techniques, problem solving, advanced communication skills, empathic listening, conflict resolution and building self-esteem.

Finally, as the following case study illustrates, the stages of change methodology discussed throughout the book lend themselves readily to coaching students.

STUDENTS AND COACHING

A. S. is a school psychologist/counselor who is also trained in behavioral coaching. She has been asked by the principal to coach a group of five, 15-year-old students who consistently fail to complete their homework assignments and do not participate in school lessons. Previous attempts, some punitive, to alter these behaviors have proven unsuccessful. Recognizing that the students were in the first phase of the reflective stage, A. S. provided a free, interactive and open forum for discussion about values, future hopes and possible career directions. Despite their gradual acceptance of the long-term negative repercussions of poor school performance, several of the students were ambivalent about giving up their current behaviors. They cited potential losses such as leisure time and their identity as members of a "tough" gang, which earned them respect from some of their peers. A. S. built in a reinforcement system, whereby each time one of the students completed an assignment to an acceptable standard, he or she was rewarded with a shorter coaching session. During the preparation stage, A. S. also provided the students with some basic skills training and information about completing assignments. As part of the preparation stage, the coach asked teachers to publicly acknowledge the students' efforts. After several partially successful endeavors and half-completed assignments (action stage), each group member finally produced an acceptable assignment. Two months later, A. S. was still coaching the students to sustain their behavioral changes (maintenance stage) and to work toward increased class participation.

Coaching for academic success

Because few high schools, colleges or universities have the resources to offer students individualized attention, more students are employing behavioral coaches to work with them on both personal and academic issues. Some of the categories of students who benefit from behavioral coaching include high-performing, highly motivated individuals who want to enhance their performance, students with poor organization and study skills, and students with attention deficit problems. Behavioral coaches work with students on skills such as note taking, mind mapping and time management, as well as relaxation techniques and self-statements to manage test anxiety. Coaching sessions also focus on career guidance and choice.

ACADEMIC SUCCESS AND COACHING

D. T. is a final year high school student who works weekends in a hospital to help pay her tuition fees. Although extremely smart, she is struggling to make her grades and is at risk of failing the final exams. A fellow student has recommended an academic coach. D. T. is highly motivated and enthusiastic about changing her study habits. Through an extensive assessment process, the coach first established that D. T. was not depressed, anxious or ambivalent about her life or prospective career as an oncologist. Her personal life was satisfactory and she had a fulfilling relationship with a fellow student. The

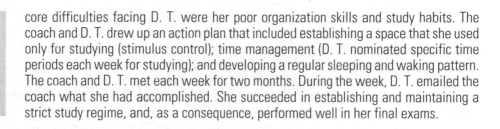

core difficulties facing D. T. were her poor organization skills and study habits. The coach and D. T. drew up an action plan that included establishing a space that she used only for studying (stimulus control); time management (D. T. nominated specific time periods each week for studying); and developing a regular sleeping and waking pattern. The coach and D. T. met each week for two months. During the week, D. T. emailed the coach what she had accomplished. She succeeded in establishing and maintaining a strict study regime, and, as a consequence, performed well in her final exams.

Career coaching

Globalization, changes in business structures and economic fluctuations have resulted in significant, probably irreversible, changes to the career structure in the past two decades. A major impact of these forces is that individuals are now responsible for their own career development. Coaching for careers and career transitions offers individuals support, resources and guidance during what are often stressful times. Many organizations recognize the importance of career development as a means of retaining staff, and therefore offer internal career coaching programs, although these are often conducted by external coaches.

In *The Complete Guide to Coaching at Work* we nominated some of the specific areas on which career coaching focuses. These include starting a career, burn-out, executive career development, re-entering the workforce, impression management and pre-retirement and retirement coaching. We outlined the coach's role in working with newly appointed executives and explored career coaching by managers.

Increasingly, behavioral coaches work with executives to prepare them for a career move or to assist them in a new position. The coach may be hired by the organization or privately by the individual. In both situations, coaches typically explore and work on potential derailment factors and on leveraging the executive's strengths and achievements to prevent failure.

Despite an abundance of research and literature on executive derailment, many organizations still fail to provide new hires or individuals promoted to a more responsible position with sufficient support and guidance. However, three of the major reasons for executive derailment can be successfully addressed by behavioral coaching. These are: an inability to build partnerships with peers and subordinates and treating others in an arrogant manner; lacking internal politically savvy, particularly in relation to understanding and managing key stakeholder relationships; and a lack of clarity about roles and expectations, especially when transitioning to an unknown area.

EXECUTIVE CAREER COACHING

B. G. was recently promoted to a senior executive position and was made leader of an executive team. In his previous role as deputy CIO, B. G.'s boss had encouraged him to be confronting and controlling and to micro-manage. While these behaviors earned B. G. a promotion, they no longer serve him well; in fact, they work against him. Furthermore, his roles and responsibilities are not clear and B. G. has dealt with this uncertainty by being even more confronting and defensive. A behavioral coach, hired by the organization, interviewed B. G. and other stakeholders, including the executive team, on the requisite competencies for his position. Feedback suggested that B. G.'s controlling style was a major concern and that the team lacked clear priorities and strategies. Together, the coach and B. G. established a development plan, the first phase of which was to enhance his communication and interpersonal style. In videotaped role-plays, the coach modeled appropriate behaviors, which B. G. then practiced and critiqued. Having learned new "relating" skills, B. G. then approached the team to set up a series of inclusive strategic planning meetings. After several months of weekly coaching, a 360-degree feedback established that B. G. had made significant changes in his interpersonal style and that the team was more purposeful, had clearer directives and was more aligned with the organization's vision and objectives.

Career coaching also falls under the umbrella of personal coaching. Coaches work with individuals on examining their values and career aspirations and on setting goals and action plans around achieving these.

PERSONAL CAREER COACHING

R. M. has completed her final year of high school and is under considerable pressure from her parents to study law. Although she has been accepted into a university of her parents' choice, R. M. is unhappy and unmotivated. On the recommendation of a teacher, she has enlisted a behavioral coach to guide her on her career choice. Discussions with R. M. revealed that she wanted to study visual arts and psychology at a different university and do a postgraduate course in art therapy. Furthermore, she wanted to take a year off from study before she began university. R. M. was defensive and hostile toward her parents, whom she considered "controlling and conservative." Further dialogue with the coach revealed that R. M. had never discussed her aspirations with her parents in an "adult" manner. Whenever the subject was broached, she would become angry and accusatory and her parents would retreat into disapproving silence. Together, R. M. and her coach devised an action plan, which included finding a job that would support her during her year off from study; scripting and practicing a non-emotive, assertive conversation with her parents about what she wanted; and, as a compromise, attending the university her parents chose, which was closer to the family home, but to study visual arts rather than law. R. M. found employment within several weeks. The dialogue between her and her parents was successful in that R. M. kept to the script and did not regress to her previous, unhelpful communication style. Although her parents were unhappy about her career choice, they were also willing to compromise. They agreed that the final decision belonged to R. M., although they continued to regale her with stories about successful lawyers and the difficulties of "making money" as an art therapist.

Business coaching

As noted, business coaches often work with small-to-medium enterprises to develop and grow their business. Coaching for entrepreneurs, start-ups, mergers and developing a business in order to sell it are some of the more common areas of business coaching. Within these broad categories, behavioral coaches, who usually have a background in small business, coach for business or strategic planning, developing and growing a market, staff relations, networking, life balance, time management and partnership conflicts.

Coaching entrepreneurs is a particularly challenging but exciting occupation. Coaches have to understand the business itself, including its financial situation, position in the marketplace and operating systems. Otherwise, they will lack credibility and fail to gain respect. Research has identified several capabilities of a successful entrepreneur, including business acumen, being commercially oriented, innovation, customer knowledge, self-responsibility and accountability, being focused on results and persevering through adversity. Behavioral coaches work with entrepreneurs to develop these competencies.

It is also well established that the qualities that cause entrepreneurs to be successful can also work against them, especially when business growth and development are at stake. Ambitious, hard-driving and independent individuals find it difficult to accept the necessity for change, particularly in relation to their own behavior and business practices. Behavioral coaches may need to focus on planning, for example, which is often haphazard and subject to impulsive changes and a lack of follow-through. Some entrepreneurs are afraid of losing control and refuse to delegate. They may also fail to recognize the importance of developing their employees, even though employer attitudes have been shown to drive both customer satisfaction and revenue.

COACHING ENTREPRENEURS

T. N. is an entrepreneur who had owned, operated and sold several small businesses. His current business, several boutique clothes manufacturing companies, is in difficulties, so T. N. has employed a business coach. The coach explored the above-mentioned competencies and assessed T. N.'s strengths and weaknesses in relation to these. It became clear that T. N.'s knowledge about the needs of his consumers was significantly less than his customer knowledge in his previous businesses. He wasn't especially interested in the fashion business, and as a consequence failed to anticipate consumer needs and trends. Together, the coach and T. N. devised an action plan, which included T. N. hiring an assistant to research the industry, and attending the weekly staff meetings with his management team. The assistant was also instructed to conduct staff surveys regarding customers' requests and complaints. T. N. himself revisited his initial vision and mission statements and established goals and strategies in areas he felt he had neglected, such as being innovative and creating value for his customers.

COACHING AND PARTNERSHIPS

P. K. and T. H. own a multimillion-dollar retail company. Initially friends, they have become increasingly alienated from each other, mistrustful and constantly in conflict over the company's day-to-day management, as well as long-term strategic plans. P. K. wants to merge with a larger competitor, while T. H. is totally opposed to the idea. The coach met separately with each owner, assessing his values, needs, strengths and weaknesses, future vision and plans. While P. K. was excited about the prospect of a merger and growing the business, T. H.'s emphasis was on lifestyle and spending less, rather than more, time on the business. Because of their divergent goals and aspirations, conflict had escalated to the stage where these critical differences had become lost in day-to-day disagreements about the management of the business. The business coach facilitated several meetings between the two partners, whereby they could openly and non-emotionally discuss their plans. Eventually, T. H. agreed to sell his share of the business to P. K., who continued with the merger. The coach continued working with P. K. during this period, focusing on integration, forming a collective vision and clarifying strategic plans.

Cross-cultural coaching

Long-term successful business relationships require a thorough knowledge of other parties' cultural values and behavioral and management styles. As we noted in Chapter 1, coaching individuals and teams in cross-cultural settings is a rapidly expanding niche for behavioral coaches. Such coaches are specialists who know about and can guide and support others through the complex process of cultural adaptation.

This type of coaching is not confined to individuals who are relocating. Corporations and businesses increasingly recognize that all employees require an understanding of cultural differences. Whether the individuals are involved in a cross-national merger, are members of an international team, or are simply on a brief assignment in another country, knowledge of the cultures involved is essential. Indeed, it is generally agreed that if organizations are to succeed in a cross-cultural setting, they must implement policies and procedures that are truly global and that genuinely reflect cultural diversity and uniqueness. The risks and failures associated with attempts to "transplant" one culture to another have been well documented.

We mentioned several variables behavioral coaches take into account in this coaching role. These included verbal and non-verbal signals, what is not said, preferred learning styles, the "respect" or authority afforded the coach and the significance of collectivism in a culture. The willingness to discuss personal, private matters also varies significantly across cultures. Furthermore, "silence" can have different connotations in different cultural settings. For example, it can signify respect, reflection or that the individual is offended or ashamed.

Importantly, how feedback is received across cultures has a significant bearing on how coaching programs are devised. Coaching, after all, is founded on feedback. The personal and professional boundaries dictated by a culture, as well as the "authority" of the coach, determine how, when and to whom feedback is given at both an individual and team level.

How learning and skill acquisition occurs within a culture also affects how coaching is delivered. Some research, for instance, suggests that in most Asian cultures, common rather than individual values and goals are given priority. Leaders, too, are less likely to share information and help others adapt to change. Clearly, these variables have to be taken into account when either coaching within these cultures or coaching others to succeed in business and organizations within these settings.

Every culture is different and unique. Not all individuals uphold the predominant values and beliefs of their own culture, and there are often major regional diversities in language and behavior. Behavioral coaches recognize the importance not only of understanding the national culture, but of appreciating how organizational and individual differences interact with it.

When coaching individuals to adapt to a different culture, some coaches work within a stage framework of the honeymoon stage, culture shock, initial adjustment, isolation, acceptance and integration. In a cross-cultural business or organizational setting, individuals have to learn to negotiate in step with the cultural norms, understand the importance of relationship building, communicate effectively and deal appropriately with conflict. Importantly, how others view trust and their expectations around the boundaries of personal and professional relationships have to be clarified and managed. Coaching assists in developing and maintaining these critical skills.

Behavioral coaches prepare executives, managers and their families not only to move to other countries. Frequently, when these individuals return to the home country, they experience culture shock and a loss of friends and colleagues. They may even undergo a period of mourning. Coaching supports individuals through this transition period, examining the personal and professional changes they have undergone and changes in values, as well as general feelings of alienation and restlessness.

Finally, behavioral coaches also work with individuals who are in the service industry, as well as consultants, trainers and educators with a range of corporate clients who work in different regional and territorial markets. Understanding a culture's "rules of politeness," its work ethic, how "time" is perceived and to what extent the customer is valued are critical to long-term successful business relationships and outcomes.

COACHING FOR CROSS-CULTURAL EXPANSION

H. J. is one of three partners in a small boutique consulting firm that has established a niche market in leadership development workshops. The clientele has expanded and H. J. is training globally. The first two international workshops, in Asia and Germany, were not particularly successful and H. J. is apprehensive about conducting future courses in other cultures. To increase her confidence and skills, the business has hired a behavioral coach who specializes in cross-cultural coaching. The coach's role was chiefly that of a resource provider. For instance, she provided information and knowledge sources about differences between German and Asian cultures in relation to their preferred learning style, how they viewed success, how they worked in teams and measured the effectiveness of the team, different organizational structures and how people related socially and after hours. The coach and H. J. then developed a series of goals around H. J. making significant changes to the workshop content and furthering her knowledge of cross-cultural organization, leadership and management styles.

COACHING AND ADAPTING TO CULTURE

L. J. spent two years on an international assignment. Since her return, she has found it extremely difficult to settle back into the organization. She especially resents the fact that she no longer has the autonomy she previously enjoyed. L. J. also feels marginalized by her colleagues, who have been slow to accept her back as a member of the team. She misses her friends, the organizational culture and the relaxed lifestyle to which she had become accustomed. A senior colleague, who himself had experienced similar reactions on his return to the company, suggested L. J. consult a coach. Together, the behavioral coach and L. J. explored her values, future career plans and aspirations. L. J. did not wish to leave the company, as her promotion prospects were excellent and she enjoyed the actual work. However, it was unlikely that L. J. would be given another long-term international assignment in the foreseeable future. The coach and L. J. established an action plan, which included requesting short-term international assignments and strategies that would facilitate her "re-entry" into the team. These involved behavioral changes such as refraining from making constant comparisons between the two cultures, meeting with each team member to clarify her role and the team's expectations, and participating in some of the company's social events. L. J. initially used part of the coaching sessions to reminisce and express her frustration and feelings of loss and alienation. Nevertheless, over three months, she gradually focused more on her current situation and the challenges and opportunities she faced.

Sales coaching

Sales coaching is another rapidly expanding niche for behavioral coaches. Research shows that an organization's ability to foster top performers directly affects the bottom line. For example, figures suggest that high performers are as much as 25 per cent to 50 per cent more productive than average performers.

Coaching has been shown to enhance performance significantly. A recent study in a financial services organization that put part of its retail sales force through an intensive coaching program showed a 35 per cent increase in productivity. Moreover, 78 per cent of the sales agents later pursued a new license or other professional designation, and 50 per cent identified new markets. Similarly, a large motor insurance company introduced a sales agent performance management development system, whereby team leaders identified and monitored behavioral strengths and weaknesses in the execution of agents' sales skills. Such information was then used as the basis for individual sales coaching. Behavioral coaching and the introduction of a performance-based reward system resulted in an average increase in weekly sales of up to 50 per cent.

In our first book, *The Complete Guide to Coaching at Work*, we explored sales coaching in relation to negative beliefs and expectations that can affect sales performance, and the coach's role in working with salespeople in the "flow," "panic" and "drone" zones. We also discussed coaching skills for the sales manager. Increasingly, behavioral coaches work with sales managers to enhance their management and coaching competencies. In particular, coaching sessions focus on established competencies such as leadership, which involves developing, communicating and aligning the team to a vision that is in line with the organization's objectives; coaching and developing the team through personal development plans, tapping into their intrinsic motivation and providing ongoing training and development opportunities; and fostering accountability for self and others through constructive feedback, support and challenging, as well as ongoing measurement and evaluation.

Another area in sales coaching that behavioral coaches focus on is emotion-regulation. Selling demands a high level of emotional input, which can cause significant stress. Research shows that salespeople attempt to regulate their emotions at work through downward social comparisons, self-reward, distraction, socializing, venting and psychopharmacological agents. Other strategies include helping others, talking to a friend or mentor and thinking about the future. Behavioral coaches discuss these methods of self-regulation and build the positive ones into action steps.

COACHING FOR IMPROVED SALES

F. W. and associates are behavioral coaches whose niche area is sales coaching. They have been employed by a medium-sized insurance company to conduct a sales coaching program. It is the first time coaching has been implemented at the company, and the stakeholders are enthusiastic but cautious. As a result, it has been agreed that the initial program will begin with one sales team, and, depending on the results, training will be extended to four other teams. The program was conducted over three months, and focused on areas of "psychological preparedness" such as self-awareness, motivation, beliefs and coping with pressure. Methods of self-regulating emotions were given particular emphasis. Each coachee received a 45-minute to one-hour telephone coaching session once a week for three months, with an option to renew the contract for a further three months At the end of three months, there was a 10 per cent increase in sales, improved morale, and better cohesion within the team. Consequently, the program was refined (e.g., with increased attention to identifying and coaching for a coachee's specific business objectives) and extended to the four other teams, which reported an average 40 per cent increase in sales after a six-month program. Some intangible benefits of coaching included greater staff retention and greater sharing of information between sales team members.

SALES COACHING AND PSYCHOLOGICAL READINESS

A medium-sized, specialist computer software company has recently undergone restructuring and is now experiencing a downturn in sales that seems unrelated to its product offering or the general economic climate. The sales team is underperforming amid growing conflict and unhappiness. Two of the team members are new to sales and although their product knowledge is excellent, their performance levels are below par. The sales manager, G. D., who himself is relatively new to the position, has consulted a former colleague who is a sales coach. The coaching budget does not allow for team and individual coaching sessions, so the coach and G. D. have agreed to work together on G. D.'s sales management skills. The coach introduced the sales manager to the performance model discussed above. During the ensuing coaching sessions, the coach and G. D. practiced fundamental coaching skills and developed methods to assess and build action plans around those aspects of "psychological readiness" the team lacked. One of the strategies introduced was regulating emotions. At the end of the eight sessions, G. D. had already met with and established long- and short-term objectives with each team member. He continued to meet with them individually on a weekly basis to develop strategies to achieve the stated goals.

Coaching program managers

Coaching program managers who are trained in behavioral coaching methods and techniques fulfill many roles. Typically, they are involved in coaching programs from their inception. As internal coaches, they often introduce coaching into the workplace and oversee and manage its delivery. They may also be the person designated to manage a coaching program introduced by an external coach.

Regardless of their entry point, one of the major responsibilities of the coaching program manager is to educate individuals in the organization about coaching. This includes the process of coaching, its benefits and the roles and responsibilities of the coach and coachee. Education is conducted through seminars, workshops and presentations to key stakeholders.

Coaching program managers also play an important role in data collection. They insure that questionnaires, surveys and 360-degree or other multirater assessments are distributed and collected. Importantly, a coaching program manager functions as a resource person and provides ongoing support to the coachee in the workplace. The coaching program manager is aware of the coachee's objectives and goals, and, apart from providing support and feedback, observes and reports on the behaviors selected for change.

External coaches attest to the critical importance of aligning a motivated, enthusiastic coaching program manager with their coaching program. They provide valuable insights on the organization's culture and politics, as well as potential sources of resistance to change. Moreover, they can offer a third-party view of a coachee's progress.

Finally, as mentioned earlier in the book, coaching program managers play a crucial role in the maintenance of a coachee's behavioral changes. After formal coaching sessions have ended, the coachee and coaching program manager can continue to work on the coachee's personal development plan, reviewing progress and discussing current challenges to allow for ongoing reinforcement and adjustment. The coaching program manager effectively supports the coachee in the continuing process of self-coaching.

Coaching in health-care settings

The health-care industry is under siege and facing increasing pressures, including inadequate government and private funding, staff retention issues and staff shortages. Some hospital systems are in a state of disrepair, even crisis. As a result, many health-care workers are frustrated and disillusioned. Physicians, registrars, therapists, nurses and administrative staff are looking to improve the quality of their professional and personal lives or to transition to a new, possibly allied, career. Behavioral coaching methodologies are especially effective in these areas.

Behavioral coaching within the health industry has broad applications. For example, trained behavioral coaches may work with individuals using Prochaska's change methodology in areas such as chronic pain, drug and alcohol dependence, cigarette smoking and weight loss. Research shows that cancer patients who receive only one individual coaching session on pain control suffer significantly less pain than those who receive a standardized session involving simply going over a pain education booklet. Individual and team coaching for anger management and team coaching for wives of angry men also produce significant results.

Behavioral coaches work with individual physicians, supervisors and administrative personnel in hospitals and other public and private health organizations. Some of the coaching areas include personal leadership, management skills, managing interpersonal conflicts with and among staff, career development and career transition. Executive coaching services around leadership and management skills in hospitals typically focus on competencies for doctors and other personnel in management and leadership positions. These include resource allocation, strategic planning and meeting the demand for profitability while maintaining medical values and ethics.

In addition to executive coaching, behavioral coaches work with individuals and teams at other levels of an organization, including newly appointed staff and team leaders. Behavioral coaches provide training and establish and oversee peer coaching programs for inexperienced or new nurses. Such programs include a documented personal development plan, and goals and action strategies to enhance coachees' personal and professional growth.

Within the health services, behavioral coaches may specialize in bereavement and death. Some work with individuals and groups through the documented stages of death and dying. As well as providing support, coaches challenge individuals and open up possibilities for new choices, attitudes and actions. Existentialist thought, as well as logotherapy, as discussed in Chapter 2, underpin a coach's behavioral framework when working in these areas.

Team coaching provides a forum for individuals in health-care settings to discuss strategic planning, change initiatives and conflict management. Stress-management and anger management workshops are conducted, frequently with individual follow-up sessions. Conducting follow-up sessions after a training program yields significantly better results.

Behavioral coaches working in the health industry usually have a background in the medical or paramedical field. They are aware of the tremendous pressures and challenges facing many individuals in the profession and are able to tailor coaching sessions accordingly. Coaches also help individual health practitioners to establish and develop a private practice. Many professionals lack business skills, so business planning, marketing practices and customer service are often the initial targets of the coaching sessions.

COACHING AND THE HEALTH PROFESSION

N. D. is a trained physiotherapist who works on a contract basis at several physiotherapy centers in the city. She is tired from the constant traveling and frustrated by the increased productivity demands of the practice managers at two of the centers. She has always wanted to establish her own holistic health center, but lacks management and general business skills. N. D. has hired a business coach who specializes in coaching professionals in small businesses. The coach first worked with N. D. on her seeming ambivalence about launching her own business. The basis for N. D.'s concern was that she did not have a business degree, and, therefore, was likely to fail. N. D. agreed to complete a diploma in small business at a local college. Then, N. D. and the coach drew up a five-year business plan and did a SWOT analysis around the major business objectives. N. D. did not want to work alone, so she and the coach devised criteria, competencies and advertising in order to recruit another person who would work with her on a contract basis with the intention of later forming a partnership. The holistic health model N. D. envisaged included a professional masseuse, a reflexologist and a nutritionist. She and the coach set goals and time frames around achieving this vision. The coach worked with N. D. over a twelve-month period, during which time she formed a partnership and employed a reflexologist and a nutritionist on a part-time, contractual basis.

Most professionals choose private practice as a way of having more autonomy, a better lifestyle, more personal time and less stress. Nevertheless, it is not uncommon for business demands to escalate to the stage where individuals actually have less free time, feel more stressed and pressured and believe the business is taking over their lives. In these situations, coaches assist practitioners to manage their time more effectively and to delegate and make decisions based on conscious choice and life balance.

COACHING HEALTH PRACTITIONERS

L. R. is a successful chiropractor who, together with her husband, has expanded their practice to include three contract chiropractors and a business manager. Although the business is thriving, L. L. is unhappy. She suffers from debilitating headaches, has frequent arguments with her husband and colleagues, and performs below her usual standard. She has employed the services of the coach who worked with her and her husband when they were setting up the business. Although L. L. and her husband are equal partners, he feels she isn't contributing on an equal basis. The husband, according to L. L., is a rather domineering, hard-driven "classic Type A" to whom work comes first. She, on the other hand, wants more personal time and feels overwhelmed. The coach first explored L. L.'s values and life goals, which included professional success, wealth and a healthy, balanced life. It was clear that, under the current circumstances, these were not attainable and that she had to prioritize her values and make a difficult choice. L. L.'s husband made most of the business decisions and she was somewhat intimidated by his superior commercial knowledge and his tendency to belittle her whenever she offered a business opinion.

After completing a decisional balance chart and estimating the changes she would have to make to accommodate a reduced income, L. L. had two possible scenarios she wished to discuss with her husband: to hire another chiropractor so that both their workloads were lessened, or, if this were unacceptable, to alter the 50:50 profit-sharing basis to 60:40 and work less hours. The coach and L. L. worked on a script that L. L. would use to initiate the discussion with her husband and prepared a document outlining the proposed changes. Although her husband initially rejected both propositions, L. L. stood her ground and he eventually settled for the change in profit share. Three months later, L. L. was considerably more satisfied with her life. She had resumed regular social contact with a long-time friend and was pursuing her interest in sculpting. Moreover, she reported that her relationship with her husband had improved significantly.

Chartered public accountants and coaching

Increasingly, chartered public accountants (CPAs), attorneys and other financial advisors are coaching other practitioners and entrepreneurs as an add-on to their traditional services. CPAs, in particular, are recognizing the need to become a trusted advisor to their clients who is able to work on vision, mission and strategic planning. Studies show that clients benefit particularly in the areas of smarter goal setting and achieving a more balanced lifestyle.

CPAs coach their clients in areas that come under the rubric of business coaching. These include increasing productivity, improving leadership style, enhancing management skills, strategic planning, relationship building, networking, enhancing staff relationships and employee satisfaction, delegation and improving life quality. Typically, the coach conducts a 360-degree feedback process that includes employees, clients, peers and sometimes family members. Some of the areas these assessments focus on are quality of work, customer relations, respect in the business community, meeting deadlines and time management skills.

Coaches working in this area are moving away from standard coaching around business plans, goals and action planning to a behavioral coaching model. Both coaches and coachees are recognizing the need to look at blocks to progress, self-limiting beliefs, emotion regulation and targeting and measuring behaviors.

A CHARTERED PUBLIC ACCOUNTANT AND COACHING

J. A. is a CPA who recognized some years ago that her clients wanted more than financial advice from her. She consequently found herself giving advice on strategic planning and setting long- and short-term goals. Repeatedly, she was struck by the fact that her clients failed to reach these goals, usually claiming they had insufficient time to do anything other than manage the business. J. A. trained as a behavioral coach, and, as a result, is now able to offer a wide range of behavioral assessment and change techniques as additional services to her clients. She finds that exploring values, motivation and self-efficacy are critical to understanding her clients' behaviors and what is blocking their progress. In the context of setting goals around strategic planning and business development, J. A. encourages her clients to examine limiting beliefs, decision-making styles, values and priorities, and to institute techniques to change their behaviors. Overall, coaching has proven a valuable add-on service for her growing clientele.

Personal coaching

There are many personal or life coaches in the profession. While some remain generalists, most specialize in order to gain entry into a highly competitive marketplace. Some of the broad categories that life coaching addresses include personal growth and development, coaching for life balance, transition coaching, spiritual coaching, coaching for health and well-being, loss and bereavement coaching, life skills coaching for young people, retirement coaching and coaching for careers and career transition.

PERSONAL TRANSITION COACHING

P. D. is a 48-year-old librarian who has relocated to assume a part-time position in a provincial university. Her father has recently died and her only son is marrying and moving to another country. P. D. complains of loneliness, of not meeting anyone interesting and is feeling generally miserable. On the recommendation of a former colleague, she has decided to consult a life coach. The coach, whose specialty was transition coaching, listened carefully as P. D. told her story. However, after quite intensive questioning and dialogue, it became apparent that P. D. did have opportunities to be more socially involved, but that she declined most invitations. In fact, P. D. was a relatively solitary person who, apart from family and one or two long-term friends, preferred her own company. Her real complaint was not that she didn't have a vast number of friends and acquaintances; what was lacking was a companion or friend with whom she could share her passion for art and opera. Interestingly, it was quite a shock for P. D. to realize that her affiliation needs were relatively low, as her self-concept was that of an extroverted, sociable individual who needed people. Rather than embarking on strategies to broaden P. D.'s social network, then, she and the coach devised strategies to meet her true needs. These included enrolling in a postgraduate course in art and joining a small opera lovers' group, which met monthly and attended the opera season in the city together.

As we have mentioned throughout this book, aspects of the individual's personal life intersect with executive and business coaching. In this forum, personal matters are typically explored only in relation to how they affect the individual's business or professional development and goals. While such topics as balancing life and work and managing stress are of interest in the corporate world and personal coaches present workshops and individual coaching sessions around these topics, coaching that focuses solely on these issues is more the domain of personal coaching. Some of the common lifestyle issues that personal coaches work on with coachees include weight management, healthy living, stress reduction, enhancing the quality of personal relationships, developing personal support networks, establishing priorities and goal setting, maintaining changes and time management.

LIFESTYLE COACHING

T. Z. has employed a personal coach because she feels her life is out of balance and that her general health is suffering as a result. She is not depressed, but is frequently tired and stressed and finds social contact demanding and exhausting. T. Z. completed a life balance wheel and nominated the least satisfactory area of her life as her health. The coach worked with T. Z. to establish goals around improving her health and energy levels. These included walking for twenty minutes a day, attending a gym three times a week, and cooking nutritious meals at home four nights a week. In order to reduce stress levels at work, and thus have more energy and enthusiasm for social occasions, the coach taught T. Z. two meditation techniques that T. Z. agreed to practice for twenty minutes a day. T. Z. also employed behavioral change techniques such as stimulus control and alternative responses to manage a difficult work colleague. The coach explored and challenged two beliefs that appeared to be contributing to T. Z.'s stress. These were, "It's the nature of work to be stressful" and "Everyone I know is stressed, that's what life is about." Once T. Z. was able to refute these beliefs, she began to see how in certain areas of her life she was "self-stressing," and she gained more control over these.

Others areas of behavioral coaching

The application of behavioral coaching, of course, is not limited to the above areas. Behavioral coaches also coach other coaches, including those in the executive, business, personal and sports arenas. Additionally, behavioral coaching is undertaken in the military, the civil service and other public institutions and in non-profit organizations and the legal profession. Christian coaching and spirituality coaching also employ behavioral coaching methods, tools and techniques.

In summary, behavioral coaching methodologies are applied in a growing number of areas, including corporations, small businesses, public and private health and education organizations and the personal development realm. Within this vast arena, behavioral coaches form alliances based on trust and commitment that foster productivity, growth and well-being.

8
Future Challenges

The professionalism of coaching

Coaching is gaining acceptance as an effective method of learning and change. Indeed, many industry sources now state that the global business demand for coaching is almost doubling each year. With a worldwide shortage of *skilled* behavioral professionals and ever-increasing demand, workplace coaching contracts are exceeding supply and salaries are rising. Businesses and organizations recognize the wide range of benefits that a successful coaching program can provide. Nevertheless, issues remain around the "professionalism" of the occupation. Professionalism refers to the process by which an occupational grouping develops and strengthens the extent to which it is characterized by criteria reflecting a mature, crystallized and industry-approved occupational activity (Lyle 2002). Such professionalism includes expertise and knowledge, extended education and an ethics-based code of practice.

Expertise and knowledge

Today, anyone interested in hiring a business, executive or organizational coach must be cautious. Many lay persons, trainers, advisors, consultants, motivational speakers and media personalities refer to themselves as coaches, and it can be difficult to distinguish a true resource among all the hype. There is clearly a need to establish from within the profession standards and criteria against which the marketplace can judge the competencies, training and experience of coaches. These criteria would include specialist training in the use of behavioral change techniques and practices, as well as client management skills. Consumers also have the right to be informed of a coach's methodologies and use of objective data to plan, implement and evaluate the effectiveness of a proposed intervention. Professional coaching requires considerable levels of skill, experience, integrity and judgment. It is not, as we have noted throughout this book, a form of psychotherapy. Nevertheless, as coaching does utilize scientific models for behavioral change, it demands the same level of professional respect, guidelines and care.

Executive and business coaches should be hired only after a review and verification of their education/training and credentials; confirmation of industry experience; investigation of specialist skills; agreement on the format of the coaching needs analysis; agreement on what diagnostic instruments and interventions will be used; consideration of the projected return on investment (ROI) or return on expectation (ROE); and confirmation of how the coaching program will be measured and evaluated. Any professional coach should welcome the opportunity to present her or his specialist training credentials. Those with minimum or no qualifications in the use of validated change techniques and learning tools will be hesitant to provide this information. A coach who has failed to formally develop the appropriate professional skills and experience can inflict confusion, pain or suffering. In turn, this can be legally and financially costly for both the coach and the client.

Coaching involves bringing about profound changes in thinking and behavior. It is not something that can simply be an "add-on" to a consultant's or trainer's existing services. Furthermore, certification as a "professional coach," especially via a "cookie-cutter e-learning" course, does not qualify an individual to undertake a business or executive coaching assignment While these people may have received some basic training in coaching, they still require professional development by highly trained, experienced and accredited educators if they are to be truly effective.

As noted in Chapter 1, many more colleges and universities are conducting coach training courses. In many cases, however, these are delivered by individuals who are not experienced coaching practitioners. Typically, these courses focus on applied psychology but pay little attention to the practical application of the coaching model within business or workplace settings.

The faculty members of any professional coach training school should be:

- university-trained educators and facilitators who preferably network with other coaches around the world so they can establish international "best skill practice standards"
- licensed, experienced behavioral scientists (e.g., psychologists, counselors)
- experienced business and executive coaches who practice what they teach.

Coaching credentials

The requisite knowledge and expertise of coaches is also related to the issue of credentialing. As we noted in *The Coaching at Work Toolkit*, the question of coaching credentials and licensing remains a serious concern for coaches. As yet, there is no agreement on training and academic standards, requisite competencies, a code of ethics or ongoing professional development. While some coaching bodies ostensibly are working together on this issue, such work is typically characterized by competitivencss rather than true collaboration.

The demand for credentialing in coaching has gathered momentum in light of the increasing number of coaches working both full and part time, and the proliferation of coach training schools. Furthermore, internationally, there is growing public accountability for organizations and professionals. Clients, coachees and the general business world have the right to know what they can expect from coaches in terms of credentials and expertise.

To date, there is no association that has been accredited by any government body and certainly none that is truly representative of full-time, professional practicing coaches. The reality is that some of the larger "international" coaching associations were privately founded by commercial training companies for the purpose of externally "legitimizing" their training courses. These types of associations generally have a private business agenda to add large numbers of members to their databases for commercial purposes.

Finally, the coaching industry is still in its formative stage and we suggest that clients and coaches be cautious of private member organizations that claim to be "recognized" and representative of the industry. If prospective coaches wish to network with likeminded professional coaches, they should first research coach training schools' student and teaching profiles. Ideally, a school should have some form of federal or state government association, or, better still, the government as a client.

Ethics

Many professions, such as law, medicine and psychology, have developed parameters that serve as standards of professional conduct and as guiding rules in practice and rcscarch. Coaching has not yet reached this stage of consensus or regulation and there are no clearly defined professional standards. Coaches, therefore, have to self-monitor and self-regulate their professional conduct. As a result of the lack of standardization, coaching ethics are, by necessity, informed by examples of similar professions such as therapy and sports coaching.

The following professional guidelincs, adapted from the American Psychological Association (APA 1992), pertain to all coaches across all coaching areas.

- *Competence* Coaches must carry out their work competently and recognize their limits. This includes offering only those services they are trained in and being certain that their work does not cross into the area of therapy.
- *Integrity* Coaches must strive to be honest and fair toward others, especially in presenting descriptions of qualifications and expertise.
- *Professional and scientific responsibility* Coaches should consult with colleagues and other professionals to prevent unethical conduct and to serve the interests of those who receive their services.
- *Respect the individual's rights to privacy, confidentiality and autonomy* Confidentiality will always be a critical issue in coaching because of

"dual accountability," or the fact that the coachee is not always the client or the person who pays for the sessions.

- *Acknowledge individual and cultural differences* This is particularly important in relation to age, gender, ethnicity, national origin, religion, sexual orientation, language and socioeconomic status.

Some ethical safeguards in coaching

In order to adhere to the above standards and to insure the delivery of ethical, professional services, the following guidelines are suggested for all coaches.

- Coaches should obtain the highest standard of coach education. They require training and experience in identified coaching competencies and practices based on validated methods and techniques. Only in this way can they insure that their clients and coachees receive the most effective, proven coaching interventions.
- As noted, there are now many more coach training courses, and the quality of these varies considerably. For instance, we frequently receive feedback from students about their dissatisfaction with the models, methodologies and processes presented in some of these programs. The courses offered at The Behavioral Coaching Institute were designed specifically to meet the demands of coaches for best practice, behaviorally based, coach training.
- Clearly contract around confidentiality before the commencement of coaching sessions. Make certain that the client and coachee are both aware of what will be reported and to whom. Ideally, both parties should sign off on the terms of confidentiality. All records maintained by the coach should be kept confidential.
- Document the needs and expectations of both the organization and the coachee and provide a forum for open discussions around goals, values and objectives. If there is any conflict or potential conflict, clearly establish how you intend to balance these differences.
- Understand clearly the differences between coaching and therapy. Be able to recognize "red flags" that may indicate a need for therapy, and refer the individual to a clinical psychologist if any of these are seen. Some coaches contract for coachees to notify the coach if they have a psychological problem at the beginning of a program or if one arises during the course of sessions.
- Although it is important to understand one's limits in terms of competency, we are not suggesting that coaches refrain from entering new territories and new industries. Clearly, professional growth and development would be hampered by this. Nevertheless, it is necessary to have a supervisor, coach or mentor when entering new areas of coaching.
- Undertake training and professional development that includes helping skills and psychology-based methods of change. Insure supervision by a qualified educator with some psychological expertise, as this not only contributes to a coach's learning and development but insures that he or she is working within an appropriate level of competency.

- Establish clear guidelines and criteria for the types of clients considered appropriate for telephone coaching. For instance, if a coachee is undergoing a crisis, either personal or professional, face-to-face interaction is mandatory.
- Select validated, best practice coaching processes, tools and techniques that will produce genuine, measurable, sustainable and satisfactory outcomes.
- Maintain records of the data collected and the methods employed. These should be available to coachees and clients. Maintaining records also allows a process to be replicated.
- Determine whether there are any potential negative effects of your coaching services. For example, are you certain an individual's independence is being maintained and that she or he will be equipped to self-coach when you are no longer available?
- Carefully choose the assessment instruments you employ. Apart from issues of reliability, validity and specificity as discussed earlier in this book, coachees must be protected from any potential negative repercussions. For example, assessments can be damaging to coachees' self-esteem, and multirater instruments have the potential to generate friction and distrust among colleagues and team members.
- Choose the most effective and least intrusive and restrictive change techniques. Insure that no psychological harm will come to coachees and that you have informed consent about the various change techniques you will employ.
- Be a model of lifelong learning by updating and enhancing your coaching knowledge, skills and abilities.

Research issues

Research into coaching demands various methods of inquiry, such as controlled outcome studies, surveys, interviews and observation to further the knowledge base. Because coaching is relatively new, the current body of research is limited, although growing. The following are suggested questions for research in coaching:

- What are the most effective behavioral change techniques for different coaching issues?
- How can coaching change techniques be modified to better achieve successful outcomes?
- Is a typology of coaching "areas" possible?
- Are there definable coaching "styles"?
- What are the critical elements of a successful coaching program? (e.g., the relationship between the coach and coachee; goal setting; the number of sessions; the focus of the sessions)
- What are the major organizational factors (including culture) that contribute to a successful coaching program?
- Are there significant differences in coaching outcomes for truly voluntary coachees and for those who are "referred"?

- How does self-efficacy affect group or team performance?

In summary, the growth of professional coaching will contribute to the requisite body of knowledge and to advances in the quality of education and training. In turn, the status and authority of coaches will be enhanced. There will be significant contributions from research and practitioners in terms of theories and models of coaching, coaching skills, coaching competencies, methodologies for change and client management skills. Behavioral coaching is an integral part of this landscape.

Appendixes

Appendix 1

The following items are derived from Dr. Charles Spielberger's State–Trait Anxiety Inventory:

1 restlessness and nervousness
2 tension
3 feeling insecure
4 feeling inadequate
5 worrying over trivial matters
6 lacking self-confidence
7 feeling dissatisfied with self
8 feeling like a failure
9 wishing one could be as happy as others
10 not feeling like a steady person.

Appendix 2

The following items are based on the Center for Epidemiological Studies' (CES) definition of depression:

1 bothered by things that don't usually bother you
2 poor appetite
3 feeling unable to get rid of the blues even with help from others
4 feeling that you are not as good as others
5 trouble concentrating
6 feeling depressed
7 feeling that everything is an effort
8 feeling hopeless about the future
9 thinking your life has been a failure
10 feeling fearful
11 having restless sleep
12 feeling unhappy
13 talking less than usual
14 feeling lonely
15 thinking people are unfriendly
16 not enjoying life
17 having crying spells
18 feeling sad
19 feeling people dislike you
20 not able to get going.

Glossary

accelerated learning A broad term referring to a variety of techniques to enhance the rate of learning. In behavioral coaching, these techniques include providing a positive, intimate and emotionally supportive learning environment; assessing and working with the individual's preferred learning style; reducing barriers to learning; and employing accelerated metacognition or new thinking approaches.

accelerated metacognition Also referred to as the new thinking, it is a style of learning in which individuals must think through an old behavior before learning a new one. Otherwise, pre-existing, incorrect learning interferes with new learning through a process of proactive inhibition.

accreditation This is a system that provides recognition of educational and professional performance standards of external coaching practitioners or in-house coaching programs. A "signature event of accreditation" is an on-site assessment of the educational, professional and program performance standards conducted by an internationally recognized assessor on "world-best practice" coaching standards. The process, involving analysis, peer review and self-study, heightens clients' and prospects' awareness of the practice and educational standards of the coaching provider. For example, accreditation of coaching providers and their programs by Dr. Skiffington is on a three-tier rating basis; see http://www.1to1coachingschool.com/accreditation.htm for private coaching practices and http://www.behavioral-coaching-institute.com/accreditation.html for coaching programs conducted by organizations.

alternative or competing responses Actions that interfere with or are incompatible with other, desired behaviors.

appreciative coaching An approach to coaching, based on the work of David Cooperrider and colleagues, which emphasizes that individuals, executives and organizations do not need to "be fixed." Rather, it focuses on accessing existing strengths and distinctive competencies, reaffirming these and bringing them more into play to move the individual or organization forward.

assessment Measuring behavior and performance and documenting it in such a way that highlights both strengths and areas for growth and development. In behavioral coaching, assessment includes coaching needs analyses, structured interviews, profiles, self-reports, multirater assessments, functional analyses of behavior and ongoing measurement of behavioral change.

attribution The way individuals attempt to account for the causes of behavior. Typically, we make external attributions (e.g., someone's behavior is due to situational factors) or internal attributions (e.g., behavior is the result of personality or values).

authenticity Living an authentic life involves striving to determine life's meaning, seeking purpose in life and living according to one's own chosen values.

behavior Any measurable response of an individual, including anything the individual does, says or feels in response to external or internal events. In behavioral coaching, behavior is a broad term that covers the actions, responses and reactions of an individual, team or organization.

behavioral coaching A structured, process-driven relationship between a trained professional coach and an individual or team that includes assessment, examining values and motivation, setting measurable goals, defining action plans and using validated tools and techniques to develop competencies and remove blocks in order to achieve valuable and sustainable changes in both the professional and personal spheres. The process includes behavioral feedback and monitoring of both the coachee and coach (e.g., for coaches, see http://www.1to1coachingschool.com; for organizations see http://www.behavioral-coaching-institute.com).

behavioral coach—registered A coach trained and certified by a credentialed educator and behavioral scientist in the use and application of psychology-based tools and techniques to achieve sustainable change and/or learning acquisition. Graduates names are listed on an open, on-line register for scrutiny by the general public (e.g., for coaches see http://www.1to1coachingschool.com/graduates_directory.htm; for organizations see http://www.behavioral-coaching-institute.com/Nnetwork.html).

behaviorism The school of thought that emphasizes the study of observable, measurable responses and proposes that behavior can be explained mostly in terms of operant and classical conditioning.

big five personality factors These are extraversion, agreeableness, conscientiousness, neuroticism and openness to experience. Examples of instruments used to assess these personality dimensions include the Hogan Personality Inventory (HPI: Hogan 1985) and the Neo Five Factor Inventory (NEO: Costa, P. & Mccrea, R., 1989).

certification The documentation and validation of a behavioral coach's specialist training in "best skill practice standards" and the use of psychologically based coaching tools and techniques by accredited, university-trained educators and facilitators who are experienced business coaches, executive coaches and licensed, experienced behavioral scientists (e.g., for coaches, see http://www.1to1coachingschool.com; for organizations, see http://www.behavioral-coaching-institute.com).

classical conditioning A learning process, associated with Pavlov, in which a stimulus (e.g., a bell) gains the ability to elicit a particular response (e.g., salivation) through repeated associations with an unconditional stimulus (e.g., food) that already elicits the response. Sometimes referred to as respondent conditioning.

coaching change processes (CCPs) Based on Prochaska's ten processes of change, CCPs are the activities individuals initiate to help modify their thinking, feeling or behavior at the different stages of change. These change processes include numerous behavioral change techniques.

coaching education The coach acts as a teacher and educator to inform prospective clients, coachees and other stakeholders about the process, benefits and mutual obligations of a coaching relationship.

coaching practice A broad term that covers a coach's entire professional activity. It includes the type of business the coach runs (sole practitioner, partnership, etc.), the clientele, niche markets and marketing strategies, assessment instruments, coaching models, tools and techniques and methods of evaluation.

cognitive coaching A method of coaching based on the understanding that metacognition (or being aware of one's own thinking processes) fosters independent learning by providing insights into one's thinking processes. Objectives are to enhance confidence in thinking skills and improve conceptual thinking and decision making.

cognitive dissonance A concept developed by Festinger referring to the state of tension that exists when a person holds inconsistent beliefs or attitudes and is motivated to reduce this dissonance.

cognitive–systemic framework of self-actualizing An attempt (Heylighenl 1992) to situate the works of Maslow within a scientific, cognitive and systemic, rather than a purely humanistic, framework.

congruence A state of being, associated with Carl Rogers's client-centered therapy, in which the individual is integrated, authentic, spontaneous and self-disclosing. It exists on a continuum.

constructivist psychologies These theorize about and investigate how human beings create systems for meaningfully understanding their world and experiences.

control styles The means or styles individuals use to gain control, including positive assertive, positive yielding, negative assertive and negative yielding (The Shapiro Control Inventory: SCI 1994).

coping statements The statements, either negative or positive, individuals make to themselves that emphasize their ability to tolerate unpleasant situations.

defense mechanism An enduring pattern of protective behavior, the purpose of which is to protect the individual against the awareness of something that provokes anxiety. Some defenses are unconscious, while others are conscious. Furthermore, some defenses are limiting, while others are positive.

displacement A defense mechanism whereby unacceptable feelings are transferred to another person, group or organization, even though the feelings were triggered or belong elsewhere.

distraction A technique individuals use to shift their attention from stressful events (either internal or external) to other stimuli.

EMDR An acronym for eye movement desensitization and reprocessing, which integrates many elements of a range of therapeutic approaches with eye movements or other forms of rhythmical stimulation in ways that stimulate the brain's information-processing system. It is often used in the treatment of trauma.

empathy According to Carl Rogers, it involves experiencing an accurate understanding of the client's world as seen from the inside. There are two aspects to empathy: understanding the client, and acknowledging this understanding. One without the other cannot engender a client-centered relationship.

existentialism A twentieth-century philosophy associated with Kierkegaarde and Nietzsche and later "popularized" by Sartre that emphasizes personal responsibility and choice in a world without reason and purpose.

expectancy A cognitive approach to motivation and the management of human behavior. Motivation is seen as a function of three components: expectancy, instrumentality and valence.

extinction A law of learning that states that if a person is not reinforced for a behavior that was previously reinforced, the person is less likely to act the same way when faced with a similar situation. Initially, there is an "extinction burst," meaning that the unwanted behavior actually increases in intensity and frequency before it decreases.

fading A behavioral change technique that involves gradually removing any prompts in the learning situation (coaching sessions) that won't occur in the individual's everyday work or personal life.

functional analysis of behavior A procedure to assess the connections between the target behavior and its antecedents and consequences.

Gestalt therapy Led by Fritz Perls in the 1950s and 1960s, this type of therapy focuses on increasing the individual's self-awareness in the present by drawing on past experiences, memories, emotional states and bodily sensations. It emphasizes taking responsibility for one's choices.

GROW model Developed by Graham Alexander in 1984, the grow model (goals, reality, options, wrap-up) has been employed, although unacknowledged, by several authors on coaching and remains one of the most popular coaching models for life coaches.

help-rejecting complaining A defensive mechanism whereby the individual complains and makes repeated requests for help, but never follows through on any suggestions. This behavior frequently disguises covert feelings of hostility or reproof toward others.

humanism A movement that espouses a belief in the individual's capacity for self-growth, self-determination and autonomy. Human beings are not simply pawns in a game, but can make a difference to the world.

intellectualization A defense mechanism involving the excessive use of abstract thinking or generalizations to control or minimize unpleasant feelings. Some individuals hide their feelings behind jargon or philosophical discussions.

learning A relatively permanent change in a person's behavior due to experience.

life (personal) coaching A structured process of examining values and setting goals and action plans to help individuals remove blocks and achieve measurable changes and benefits in all aspects of their lives.

linguistic coaching An approach to coaching based on a system of conversational analysis and communication developed by Fernando Flores and colleagues. It involves cognitive challenging, which is underpinned by the premise that we cannot communicate effectively if we are unable to distinguish between fact and interpretation.

logotherapy A therapy developed by Victor Frankl that emphasizes the client's recognizing and accepting himself or herself and living in a meaningful and purposeful way.

mediation In accelerated learning it refers to the individual's ability to "stand between" the old and new behaviors and to sort out the differences between them.

modeling The learning process whereby we observe someone in the environment and then think, feel and behave in a similar or imitative manner. Also referred to as vicarious learning, imitation and social learning.

neurolinguistic programming (NLP) The study of the structure of subjective experience. The word "neuro" refers to an understanding of the brain and its functioning. "Linguistic" relates to the communication aspects (both verbal and non-verbal) of our information processing. "Programming" refers to the behavioral and thinking patterns we all go through. There is a relationship between perceptions, thinking and behavior that is neuro-linguistic in nature. NLP consists of a set of models, skills and techniques to organize ideas and actions for improved communication, positive change and personal and professional growth.

observational coaching Sometimes used synonymously with "live coaching," it involves the coach collecting data by directly observing or shadowing the individual as she or he performs certain tasks (phase one). At phase two, data is analyzed in order to clarify the coaching issues and goals. At phase three, strategies and action plans are put in place to achieve the stated goals. Observation is undertaken throughout the entire coaching process.

operant conditioning The learning process associated with B. F. Skinner whereby behavior is changed by the consequences of that behavior. For example, if we are rewarded for a particular behavior we are likely to perform it again, and if we are punished, we are unlikely to perform it again. Also referred to as instrumental conditioning.

organizational behavioral coaching The science (see *behavioral coaching*) of facilitating the performance, learning and development of the individual or team, which in turn will assist the growth of the individual and the organization.

passive-aggression A pattern of aggressive behavior whereby the individual indirectly or unassertively expresses hostility toward others. It sometimes takes the form of over-compliance, obstructionism, pedantry or procrastination.

peer coaching Colleagues coach and support each other in a non-threatening, egalitarian relationship in order to achieve mutual growth and personal and professional development. Teachers in particular benefit from peer coaching to enhance their teaching skills and general professional development.

performance coaching The coachee fully applies the newly acquired skills in the workplace. There is ongoing measurement and feedback on the coachee's execution of the skills.

phenomenology A philosophy originally based on the works of Husserl, but later refined by Sartre and others. It is an attempt to describe our subjective experiences directly and independently of causal explanations.

pinpointing Translating broad or vague descriptions of an individual's behavior into specific, objective and measurable responses.

postmodernism A philosophy associated particularly with Foucault, Derrida and Lyotard, which views knowledge not as objective and fixed, but rather as fluid and the product of social discourse. There is no one truth but a multiplicity of truths. The coaching interaction therefore is not between an expert and non-expert, but is a collaborative and egalitarian shared inquiry.

primal therapy Developed by Arthur Janov and popular in the 1970s, it focuses on the client recognizing and expressing (screaming) his or her emotions toward his or her parents in order to make a connection with the primal birth trauma.

proactive inhibition (PI) The interference with learning that occurs whenever the way we currently perform differs from and conflicts with the new knowledge and skills we are trying to learn.

Prochaska's methodology The change model employed by behavioral coaching, based on the transtheoretical model of change by James Prochaska, John Norcross, Carlo Diclemente and Wayne Velicer. According to their model, there are five stages of change: precontemplation, contemplation, preparation, action and maintenance. Behavioral coaching has adapted this model to include four stages: the reflective stage—phase one, when the individual is not intending to change her or his behavior in the near future, and phase two, when the individual is aware there is an issue to address but has not yet committed or is unsure about moving ahead; the preparation stage, where assessments are made, goals are set and action plans put in place; the action stage, during which behavioral changes are put in place in the workplace; and the maintenance stage, which involves the use of tools and techniques to insure that the new behaviors are sustained and that regression does not occur.

prompting A behavioral change technique that involves the use of a stimulus to remind us to perform a behavior we already know how to do or to help us perform a behavior we don't do often or well.

psychological distance and values Dr. David Upton combined the construct of psychological distance (Micholt 1992) with Argyris's (1982) concept of the gaps between stated and in-use or applied values. Upton developed a complex model of interaction that can chart the distance factor in both stated and in-use values. It is particularly useful in organizational settings to track the distance and possible collusion between the coach, coachee and organization.

rationalization A defense mechanism that helps us deal with anxiety by concealing our true motivations from ourselves, for the most part by making reassuring, or self-serving statements.

rational-emotive therapy (RET) Developed by Albert Ellis, it is a directive form of psychotherapy that focuses on the rational, problem-solving aspects of emotional and behavioral responses. Challenging or disputing irrational beliefs is a key feature of RET.

reaction formation A defense mechanism whereby we think, feel or act in a way that is diametrically opposed to our true, unacceptable feelings. For example, if we have unacceptable feelings of resentment and hostility toward a colleague, we may treat that person with exaggerated respect and affection.

reality therapy Developed by William Glasser, this therapy proposes that we choose our behavior and that we are therefore responsible for what we think, feel and do. The overall aim of reality therapy is to help individuals find more effective methods of meeting their needs for belonging, power, freedom and fun.

reciprocal determinism According to Albert Bandura, behavior is influenced by multiple determinants that exist in the environment as well as within the individual in the form of affect, cognition, and constitutional disposition. These have an interactive effect on each other. External rewards and punishments, as well as internal beliefs and expectancies, all form part of a complex system, and change in one aspect of the system requires change in all others, so that balance and equilibrium can once again be achieved.

reflective coaching This approach to coaching posits that change does not occur by directly influencing behavior, but through working on the individual's "structure of interpretation" (how he or she sees the world). New distinctions and new meanings allow new actions to be taken.

reframing situations A technique that helps us to redefine unpleasant situations or events, thereby making them easier to manage

rehearsal coaching Once a coachee has learned new skills, these are rehearsed in the coaching sessions (e.g., role plays, analogue situations and video rehearsal) and in the workplace prior to full performance.

reinforcement An event that, when presented following a behavior, causes the behavior to increase or decrease in frequency. Positive reinforcement, synonymous with reward, increases the likelihood of the behavior occurring again. Negative reinforcement is the removal of an unpleasant event, such as stress or craving. It also increases the likelihood of the behavior recurring.

ROE Return on expectations involves the coach, client and coachee identifying and agreeing on expectations, including the "critical success factors" that the coaching program will meet.

ROI Return on investment, or putting a monetary value against the benefits of coaching, is a method of evaluating a coaching program. Because of its high time demands and the difficulty of measuring the intangible benefits of coaching, many coaches prefer to conduct a return on expectations (ROE).

schedules of reinforcement The rules that state how many or which responses will be reinforced. Such a schedule determines how effective a reinforcer will be. Continuous reinforcement occurs when a response is rewarded every time it occurs. Intermittent reinforcement occurs when a response is rewarded only some of the time.

self-actualization The final level of development that individuals can reach, according to Abraham Maslow's theory of personality. Some qualities associated with this stage include independence, autonomy, few but deep friendships, a philosophical sense of humor and a resistance to external pressures.

self-coaching The ultimate goal of coaching is for a coachee to be able to self-coach; that is, to be self-managing and self-regulating. As well as insuring that the coachee has learned new methods of problem solving, techniques to manage beliefs and emotions and "hard skills," the coach and coachee establish maintenance strategies so that the coachee does not revert to earlier behaviors and there is ongoing support for the coachee.

self-concept based motivation Developed by Nancy Leonard and colleagues, it explores the individual's motivation in organizations within the context of four levels of self-concept (the perceived self, the ideal self, social identity and self-esteem).

self-determination theory (SDT) A theory developed over the past three decades from research by E. L. Deci and R. M. Ryan, which focuses on the degree to which human behaviors are volitional or self-determined. It introduces a continuum from "controlled behavior" (or taking action because you have to) to autonomous behavior (doing something because it is one's choice). SDT is based on the assumption that people are active organisms with an innate tendency toward psychological growth and development. However, the social context can either support or thwart this tendency.

self-efficacy A construct developed by Albert Bandura that refers to our belief in our capability to organize and carry out the actions necessary to manage prospective situations. It influences our choices, efforts, feelings and persistence.

self-esteem The evaluation that we make, and usually maintain, in regard to ourselves. In behavioral coaching it is explored under the three types proposed by Nancy Leonard and colleagues: chronic self-esteem, task-specific self-esteem and socially influenced self-esteem.

self-instructions Antecedent statements we make to ourselves that describe, direct or guide the behavior we will perform. They can affect our performance positively or negatively.

self-monitoring or self-observation Systematically observing one's own behavior over time, on several occasions in an ongoing manner.

self-regulation The individual's ability to recognize, direct and modulate her or his own thoughts, feelings and behavior. Enhancing a coachee's self-regulation skills is a critical component of behavioral coaching.

shaping A behavioral change technique that leads to the development of a behavior not presently performed by the individual. The coach reinforces or rewards successive approximations of the desired behavior.

skills coaching According to the behavioral coaching model, skills coaching is an essential part of any coaching program rather than a specific type of coaching. All coaching involves coachees acquiring new skills or enhancing current ones.

social learning theory (SLT) An integration of behavioral principles (e.g., operant conditioning) and cognitive factors to understand how we learn and then exhibit behaviors. Developed by Albert Bandura, it includes antecedents and consequences of behavior, modeling, self-efficacy, self-set goals and self-regulation.

Socratic dialogue A method of asking questions to prompt reflection, which in turn will lead to knowledge or the individual's awareness of his or her own ignorance.

stimulus control The term used to indicate that a certain behavior (e.g., yelling) occurs in the presence of certain stimuli (e.g., a football match) and not in others (e.g., in church). Various stimulus control techniques are employed in behavioral coaching (e.g., controlling the antecedents of a behavior).

subjective well-being A construct developed by Diener and colleagues to measure and explore happiness, joy, life and work satisfaction and morale.

transactional analysis (TA) Developed by Eric Berne, TA is a type of psychotherapy that focuses on what people say and do to themselves and to each other. It assumes that we make current decisions based on past premises that may no longer be valid. Our life scripts or personal life plans, which include parental injunctions, are created early in life. Nevertheless, we can transcend our early programming by understanding past decisions and making new choices.

transfer of learning The extent to which the knowledge, skills and abilities acquired in the coaching situation are applied, generalized and maintained over some time in the work or personal environment.

unconditional positive regard According to Carl Rogers' client-centered approach, the therapist (or the coach) cares about the client but this caring is not conditional on how the person behaves. Ideally, it is a non-possessive kind of caring that does not demand personal gratification.

Zen A variant of Buddhism according to which various practical and meditative methods practiced under the guidance of a master will lead to a "sudden awakening" or insight into the nature of reality.

Bibliography

Adler, A. 1964, "The Individual Psychology of Alfred Adler," in H. L. Ansbacher & R. R. Ansbacher (eds.) *The Individual Psychology of Alfred Adler*, Harper & Row (Torchbooks), New York.

American Diagnostic Association, *Diagnostic and Statistical Manual of Mental Disorders* (DSM-IV), 1994, 4th edn, American Psychiatric Association, Washington, DC.

Anderson, H. & Burney, J. P. 1999, "Collaborative inquiry: A post modern approach to organizational consultation," in A. Cooklin (ed.) *Changing Organizations: Clinicians as Agents of Change*, Karnac Books, London.

Argyris, C., 1982, *Reasoning, Learning and Action: Individual and Organisational*, Jossey-Bass, San Francisco.

Argyris, C. & Schon, D. A. 1996, *Organizational Learning 11: Theory, Method and Practice*, Addison-Wesley, New York.

Ashkanasy, N. M., Hartel, C. E. J. & Zerbe, W. J. (eds.) 2000, *Emotions in the Workplace; Research, Theory and Practice*, Quorum Books, Westpoint, Connecticut.

Auerbach, J. E. 2001, *Personal and Executive Coaching: The Complete Guide for Mental Health Professionals*, Executive College Press, Ventura, California.

Bandura, A. 1997, *Self-efficacy*, W. H. Freeman, New York.

Baumeister, R. F. & Boden, J. M. 1944, "Shrinking the Self," in T. M. Brinthaupt & R. P. Lipka (eds.) *Changing the Self: Philosophies, Techniques and Experiences*, State University of New York Press, Albany, NY.

Baxter, P. & Dole, S. 1990, "Working with the Brain, Not Against it: Correction of Systematic Errors in Subtraction," *British Journal of Special Education*, Vol. 17, No. 1 Research Supplement, pp. 19–22.

Block, P. 2000, *Flawless Consulting: A Guide to Getting Your Expertise Used*, 2nd edn, Jossey-Bass Pfeiffer, San Francisco.

Bowditch, J. L. & Buono, A. F. 2001, *A Primer on Organizational Behavior*, 5th edn, John Wiley & Sons, New York.

Braksick, L. W. 2000, *Unlock Behaviour, Unleash Profits: How your Leadership Can Unlock Profitability in Your Organization*, McGraw-Hill, New York.

Branden, N. 1994, *The Six Pillars of Self-Esteem*, Bantam Books, New York.

Branden, N. 1996, *Taking Responsibility: Self-Reliance and the Accountable Life*, Fireside/Simon & Schuster, New York.

Bridges, W. 2000, *The Character of Organizations: Using Personality Type in Organizational Development*, Davies-Black Publishing, Palo Alto, CA.

Brinthaupt, T. M. & Lipka, R. P. (eds.) 1994, *Changing the Self: Philosophies, Techniques, and Experiences*. State University of New York Press, Albany, NY.

Buber, M. 1955, *Between Man and Man*, Beacon Paperbacks, Boston.

Butler, R. J. 1996, *Sports Psychology in Action*, Butterworth-Heinemann, London.

Butler-Bowdon, T. 2001, *50 Self Help Classics: Books to Change Your Life*, Simon & Schuster, Australia.

Champoux, J. E. 2000, *Organizational Behavior: Essential Tenets for a New Millennium*, South-Western College Publishing, Mason, OH.

Chang, R. Y. & Morgan, M. W. 2000, *Performance Scorecards: Measuring the right things in the real world*, Jossey-Bass, San Francisco.

Clark, R. E. & Estes. F. 2000, *Turning Research into Results: A Guide to Selecting the Right Performance Solutions*, CEP Press, Atlanta, Georgia.

Cone, J. D. 2001, *Evaluating Outcomes: Empirical Tools for Effective Practice*, American Psychological Association, Washington, DC.

Cooklin, A. (ed.) 1999, *Changing Organizations: Clinicians as Agents of Change*, Karnac Books, London.

Cooper, R. K. & Sawaf, A. 1997, *Executive EQ: Emotional Intelligence in Leadership & Organizations*, Grosset/Putnam, New York.

Cooperrider, D. 1995, *Introduction to Appreciative Inquiry: Organization Development*, 5th edn, Prentice Hall, New York.

Coopersmith, S. 1967, *The Antecedents of Self-Esteem*. W. H. Freeman, New York.

Cope, M. 2000, *The Seven C's of Consulting*, Financial Times/Prentice Hall, Englewood Cliffs, NJ.

Corey, G. 1991, *Theory and Practice of Counselling and Psychotherapy*, 4th edn, Brooks/Cole, Pacific Grove, CA.

Crain, W. 2000, *Theories of Development: Concepts and Applications*, 4th edn, Prentice Hall, Englewood Cliffs, NJ.

Csikzentmihalyi, M. 1993, *The Evolving Self*, HarperCollins, New York.

Daniels, A. C. 2000, *Bringing out the Best in People: How to Apply the Astonishing Power of Positive Reinforcement*, McGraw-Hill, New York.

Daniels, M. 1988, "The Myth of Self-Actualization," *Journal of Humanistic Psychology*, Vol. 28, No. 1, pp. 7–38.

Davidson, K. P. & Pennebaker, J. W. 2000, "Who Talks? The Social Psychology of Illness Support Groups," *American Psychologist*, Vol. 55, No. 2, pp. 78–82.

Diener, E. 1994, "Assessing Subjective Well-Being; Progress and Opportunities," *Social Indicators Research*, Vol. 31, pp. 103–57.

Diener, E. & Lucas, R. E. 2000, "Subjective Emotional Well-Being," in M. Lewis & J. M. Haviland (eds.) *Handbook of Emotions*, 2nd edn, Guilford, New York, pp. 325–37.

Downs, A. 2002, *Secrets of an Executive Coach: Proven Methods for Helping Leaders Excel Under Pressure*, AMACOM, New York.

Ekman, P. & Davidson, R. 1994, *The Nature of Emotion: Fundamental Questions*, Oxford University Press, New York.

Ellis, A. 1973, *Humanistic Psychotherapy: The Rational-Emotive Approach*, McGraw-Hill, New York.

Ellis, A. & Dryden, W. 1987, *The Practice of Rational-Emotive Therapy*, Springer, New York.

English, F. 1975, "The Three Cornered Contract," *Transactional Analysis Journal*, Vol. 5, pp. 383–4.

Epstein, M. 1995, *Thoughts Without a Thinker: Psychotherapy From a Buddhist Perspective*, Basic Books, New York.

Erikson, E. H. 1963, *Childhood and Society*, 2nd edn, Norton, New York.

Erikson, E. 1982, *The Life Cycle Completed*, Norton, New York.

Evered, R. & Selman, J. 1989, "Coaching and the Art of Management," *Organizational Dynamics*, Vol. 18, pp. 16–32.

Fitzgerald, C. & Garvey Berger, J. (eds.) 2002, *Executive Coaching: Practices and Perspectives*, Davies-Black Publishing, California.

Flaherty, J. 1999, *Coaching: Evoking Excellence in Others*, Butterworth, Woburn, MA.

Foster, S. & Lendl, J. 1996, "Eye Movement Desensitization and Reprocessing: Four case studies of a new tool for executive coaching and restoring employee performance after setbacks," *Consulting Psychology Journal: Practice and Research*, Vol. 48, pp. 155–61.

Frame, J. D. 1994, *The New Project Management: Corporate Reengineering and Other Business Realities*, Jossey-Bass, San Francisco.

Frankl, V. E. 1984, *Man's Search for Meaning*, Simon & Schuster, New York.

Freud, S. 1910, *The Origin and Development of Psychoanalysis*, Henry Regnery (Gateway Editions), New York.

Freud, S. 1949, *An Outline of Psychoanalysis*, Norton, New York.

Frijda, N. 1988, "The Laws of Emotion," *American Psychologist*, Vol. 43, pp. 349–58.

Fromm, E. 1942, *Fear of Freedom*, Routledge, London.

Galt, V. 2002, "The High Cost of Integration: Executive Failure Rate Runs High," http:///www.rhrinternational.com/Globe_&_Mail.htm.

Garvin, D. A. 1993, "Building a Learning Organization," *Harvard Business Review*, Vol. 73, No. 4, pp. 78–91.

Gegner, C. 1997, "Research study on the effectiveness of coaching," http://www.coachexecs.com/researchstudy.html.

Gharajedaghi, J. 1999, *Systems Thinking—Managing Chaos and Complexity: A Platform for Designing Business Architecture*, Butterworth–Heinemann, Oxford.

Gilligan, C. 1993, *In a Different Voice: Psychological Theory and Women's Development*, Harvard University Press, Cambridge, Massachusetts.

Glasser, W. 1965, *Reality Therapy: A New Approach to Psychiatry*, Harper & Row, New York.

Glasser, W. 1981, *Stations of the Mind*, Harper & Row, New York.

Goleman, D. 1995, *Emotional Intelligence*, New York, Bantam Books.

Goleman, D. 2002, "Leadership that Gets Results," *Harvard Business Review*, April, pp. 78–90.

Greenberg, L. S. 2002, *Emotion-Focused Therapy: Coaching Clients to Work Through Their Feelings*, American Psychological Association, Washington, DC.

Grimley, D. & Prochaska, J. O., Velicer, W. F., Blais, L. M. & DiClemente, C. C. 1994, "The Transtheoretical Model of Change," in T. M. Brinthaupt & R. P. Lipka (eds.) *Changing the Self: Philosophies, Techniques and Experiences*, State University of New York Press, Albany, NY.

Hahn, T. N. 1975, *The Miracle of Mindfulness: A Manual on Meditation*, Beacon Press, Boston.

Hall, D. T., Otazo, K. L. & Hollenbeck, G. P. 1999, "Behind Closed Doors: What Really Happens in Executive Coaching," *Organizational Dynamics*, Vol. 27, No. 3, pp. 39–52.

Hamachek, D. 1994, "Changes in the Self from a Developmental/Psychosocial Perspective," in T. M. Brinthaupt & R. P. Lipka (eds.) *Changing the Self: Philosophies, Techniques and Experiences*, State University of New York Press, Albany.

Handy, C. 1993, *Understanding Organizations*, 4th edn, Penguin, Harmondsworth, UK.

Hart, V., Blattner, J. & Leipsic, S. 2001, "Coaching Versus Therapy: A Perspective," *Consulting Psychology Journal: Practice and Research*, Vol. 48, pp. 229–37.

Hersey, P. & Blanchard, K. H. 1993, *Management of Organizational Behavior*, 6th edn, Prentice Hall, Englewood Cliffs, NJ.

Heylighenl, F. 1992, "A Cognitive-Systemic Reconstruction of Maslow's Theory of Self-Actualization," *Behavioral Science*, Vol. 37, pp. 39–58.

Hofstede, G. 1993, "Cultural Constraints in Management Theories," *Academy of Management Executive*, Vol. 1, No. 4, pp. 8–16.

Honey, P. & Mumford, A. 1983, *Using Your Learning Styles*, Peter Honey Publications, Maidenhead, UK.

Hudson, F. 1992, *The Handbook of Coaching: A Comprehensive Source Guide for Managers, Executives, Consultants, and Human Resource Professionals*, Jossey-Bass, San Francisco.

Hummel, J. & Huitt, W. 1994, "What You Measure Is What You Get," *GaASCD Newsletter: The Reporter*, pp. 10–11.

Hunt, J. M. & Weintraub, J. R. 2002, *The Coaching Manager: Developing Top Talent in Business*, Sage Publications, California.

Isen, A. 1999, "Positive Affect," in T. Dagleish & M. Power (eds.) *Handbook of Cognition and Emotion*, Wiley, London, pp. 520–42.

Jackson, P. Z. & McKergow, M. 2002, *The Solutions Focus: The Simple Way to Positive Change*, Nicholas Brealey, London.

Johnson, C. M., Redmon, W. K. & Mawhinney, T. C. (eds.) 2001, *Handbook of Organizational Performance: Behavior Analysis and Management*, The Hawthorne Press, New York.

Jung, C. G. 1962, *Modern Man in Search of a Soul*, Routledge & Kegan Paul, London.

Kalin, N. 2002, "The Neurobiology of Fear," *Scientific American*, Vol. 12, pp. 172–81.

Kampa-Kokesch, S. & Anderson, M. Z. 2001, "Executive Coaching; A Comprehensive Review of the Literature," *Consulting Psychology Journal: Practice and Research*, Vol. 53, No. 4, pp. 205–28.

Kaplan, R. & Norton, D. 1996, *The Balanced Scorecard*, Harvard Business Press, Boston.

Kaye, B. 1977, *Up Is Not the Only Way*, 2nd edn, Davis Black, Palo Alto, CA.

Kazdin, A. E. 2001, *Behaviour Modification in Applied Settings*, Wadsworth, USA.

Keegan, R. & Lahey, L. 2001, *How the Way We Talk Can Change the Way We Work: Seven Languages for Transformation*, Jossey-Bass, San Francisco.

Kegan, R. 1994, *In Over Our Heads: The Demands of Modern Life*, Oxford University Press, Cambridge.

Kerouac, J. 1957, *On the Road*, Penguin, New York.

Kilburg, R. R. 2000, *Executive Coaching: Developing Managerial Wisdom in a World of Chaos*, American Psychological Association, Washington, DC.

Knowles, M. 1980, *The Modern Practice of Adult Education: From Pedagogy to Andragogy*, revised edition, Prentice-Hall, Englewood Cliffs, NJ.

Koestenbaum, P. & Block, P. 2001, *Freedom and Accountability at Work: Applying Philosophic Insights to the Real World*, Jossey-Bass Pfeiffer, San Francisco.

Kottler, J. A. 2001, *Making Changes Last*, Brunner-Routledge, Philadelphia.

Laing, R. D. 1960, *The Divided Self: An Existential Study in Sanity and Madness*, Tavistock, London.

Laing, R. D. 1961, *Self and Others*, Pelican, London.

Langer, E. 1990, *Mindfulness*, Addison-Wesley, New York.

Lasch, C. 1979, *The Culture of Narcissism: American Life in an Age of Diminishing Expectations*, Norton, New York.

LeDoux, J. 2002, "Emotion, Memory and the Brain," *Scientific American*, Vol. 12, No. 1, pp. 62–71.

Leonard, N., Beauvais, L. L. & Scholl, R. W. 1995, *A Self Concept-Based Model of Work Motivation*, paper presented at the annual meeting of the Academy of Management, Vancouver, BC.

Levinson, D. 1977, "The Mid Life Transition," *Psychiatry*, Vol. 40, pp. 99–112.

Levinson, D. 1978, *The Seasons of a Man's Life*, Ballantine, New York.

Lord, R. G., Klimowski, R. J. & Kanfer, R. (eds.) 2002, *Emotions in the Workplace: Understanding the Structure and Role of Emotions in Organizational Behaviour*, Jossey-Bass, San Francisco.

Lyle, J. 2002, *Sports Coaching Concepts: A Framework for Coaches' Behaviour*, Routledge, London.

Magruder Watkins, J. & Mohr, B. J. 2001, *Appreciative Inquiry: Change at the Speed of Imagination*, Jossey-Bass Pfeiffer, San Francisco.

Mahoney, M. J., Norcross, J. C., Prochaska, J. O. & Missar, C. D. 1989, "Psychological Development and Optimal Psychotherapy: Converging Perspectives Among Clinical Psychologists," *Journal of Integrative and Eclectic Psychotherapy*, Vol. 8, pp. 251–63.

Martin, C. 2001, *The Life Coaching Handbook: Everything You Need to be an Effective Life Coach*, Crown House Publishing, Wales.

Martin, G. & Pear, J. 1999, *Behavior Modification: What It Is and How to Do It*, 6th edn, Prentice-Hall, Englewood Cliffs, NJ.

Maslow, A. H. 1954, *Motivation and Personality*, Harper & Row, New York.

Maslow, A. H. 1973, *The Farther Reaches of Human Nature*, Penguin, Harmondsworth, UK.

Mautner, T. (ed.) 2000, *The Penguin Dictionary of Philosophy*, Penguin, London.

Mayer, J. D. & Salovey, P. 1995, "Emotional Intelligence and the Construction and Regulation of Feelings," *Applied and Preventive Psychology*, Vol. 4, pp. 197–208.

McGrath, D. & Edwards, H. 2000, *Difficult Personalities: A Practical Guide to Managing the Hurtful Behaviour of Others (and maybe your own)*, Choice Books, Australia.

Micholt, N., 1992, "Psychological Distance and Group Interventions," *Transactional Analysis Journal*, Vol. 22, pp. 228–33.

Miller, L. K. 1997, *Principles of Everyday Behavior Analysis*, Brooks/Cole, Pacific Grove, CA.

Mortley, R. 1991, *French Philosophers in Conversation*, Routledge, London.

Neenan, M. & Dryden, W. 2002, *Life Coaching: A Cognitive-Behavioural Approach*, Brunner-Routledge, East Sussex, UK.

Nietzsche, F. 1966, *Beyond Good And Evil* (trans. W. Kaufman), Vintage Books, New York.

Nietzsche, F. 1967, *On the Genealogy of Morals* (trans. W. Kaufman & R. J. Hollingdale), Vintage Books, New York.

Olivero, G., Bane, K. D. & Kopleman, R. E. 1997, "Executive Coaching as a transfer of training tools: Effects on productivity in a public agency," *Public Personnel Management*, Vol. 26, No. 4, pp. 461–9.

O'Neill, M. B. 2000, *Executive Coaching With Backbone and Heart: A Systems Approach to Engaging Leaders with their Challenges*, Jossey-Bass, San Francisco.

Peltier, B. 2001, *Psychology of Executive Coaching: Theory and Applications*, Brunner-Routledge, New York.

Perls, F. 1969, *Gestalt Therapy Verbatim*, Real People Press, Lafayette, CA.

Peterson, D. B. & Hicks, M. D. 1999, "Strategic coaching: Five ways to get the most value," *Human Resources Focus*, Vol. 76, No. 2, pp. 7–8.

Peterson, D., Uranowitz, S. & Hicks, M. D. 1997, *Management Coaching at Work: Current Practice in Multinational and Fortune 250 Companies*, Personnel Decisions International Corporation, Minneapolis, MN.

Phillips, J. J. 2000, *The Consultant's Scorecard: Tracking Results and Bottom-Line Impact of Consulting Projects*, McGraw-Hill, New York.

Prochaska, J. O., Norcross, J. C. & Diclemente, C. C. 1994, *Changing for Good*, Avon Books, New York.

Richard, J. T. 1999, "Multimodal Therapy: A Useful Model for the Executive Coach," *Consulting Psychology Journal: Practice and Research*, Vol. 51, pp. 24–30.

Rogers, C. 1951, *Client-Centered Therapy*, Houghton Mifflin, Boston.

Rogers, C. R. 1961, *On Becoming a Person*, Houghton Mifflin, Boston.

Rogers, C. 1980, *A Way of Being*, Houghton Mifflin, Boston.

Rosen, R., Digh, D., Singer, M. & Phillips, C. 2000, *Global Literacies: Lessons on Business Leadership and National Cultures*, Simon & Schuster, New York.

Ryan, R. M. & Deci, E. L. 2000, "Self-determination theory and the facilitation of intrinsic motivation, social development, and well-being," *American Psychologist*, Vol. 55, pp. 68–78.

Salas, E. & Cannon-Bower, J. A. 2001, "The Science of Training: A Decade of Progress," *Annual Review of Psychology*, Vol. 52, pp. 471–99.

Sarafino, E. P. 2001, *Behaviour Modification: Understanding principles of behaviour change*, 2nd edn, Mayfield Publishing, California.

Sartre, J. P. 1956, *Being and Nothingness: An Essay on Phenomenological Ontology*, Philosophical Library, New York.

Sartre, J. P. 1959, *The Age of Reason*, Bantam Books, New York.

Segal, J. 1985, *Phantasy in Everyday Life; A Psychoanalytical Approach to Understanding Ourselves*, Penguin, Harmondsworth, UK.

Seligman, M. E. P. 1993, *What You Can Change and What You Can't*, Fawcett Columbine, New York.

Senge, P. 1999, *The Dance of Change: The Challenges of Sustaining Momentum in Learning Organizations*, Nicholas Brealey, London.

Sennett, R. 1998, *The Corrosion of Character: The Personal Consequences of Work in the New Capitalism*, Norton, New York.

Shapiro, D. H. 1997, *The Human Quest for Control*, Tarcher/Putnam, New York.

Silberman. M. 2001, *The Consultant's Tool Kit: High-Impact Questionnaires, Activities and How-to Guides for Diagnosing and Solving Client Problems*, McGraw-Hill, New York.

Skinner, H. A. 2002, *Promoting Health Through Organizational Change*, Benjamin Cummings, San Francisco.

Solomon, R. C. & Flores, F. 2001, *Building Trust in Business, Politics, Relationships and Life*, Oxford University Press, New York.

Ulrich, D., Zenger, J. & Smallwood, N. 1999, *Results Based Leadership*, Harvard Business School Press, Boston.

Upton, D. 1995, *Psychological Distance, Stated Values and Values in Use: An approach to considering interactions for counseling situations in general*, http://website.lineone.net/~dave.upton/MICHPA2.htm.

Vygotsky, L. 1986, *Thought and Language*, MIT Press, Cambridge, MA.

Waldersee, R. & Luthans, F. 2001, "Social Learning Analysis of Behavioral Management," in C. M. Johnson, W. K. Redmon & T. C. Mawhinney (eds.) *Handbook of Organizational Performance: Behavior Analysis and Management*, The Haworth Press, New York.

Warr, P. B. & Bourne, A. 2000, "Associations between rating content and self-other agreement in multi-source feedback," *European Journal of Work and Organizational Psychology*, Vol. 9, pp. 321–4.

Watson, D. L. & Tharp, R. G. 1993, *Self-Directed Behaviour: Self modification for personal adjustment*, 6th edn, Brooks/Cole, Pacific Grove, CA.

Watts, A. 1958, *The Spirit of Zen: A Way of Life, Work, and Art in the Far East*, Grove Press, New York.

Watts, A. 1963, *The Two hands of God: The Myths of Polarity*, Collier Books, New York.

Weick, K. E. 1999, "Organizational Change and Development," *Annual Review of Psychology*, pp. 76–94.

Weiss, A. 2000, *Getting Started in Consulting*, John Wiley & Sons, New York.

West, L. & Milan, M. 2001, *The Reflecting Glass: Professional Coaching for Leadership Development*, Palgrave, New York.

Winograd, T. & Flores, F. 1987, *Understanding Computers and Cognition: A New Foundation for Design*, Addison Wesley Professional, New York.

Wong, P. T. P. 1998, "Meaning-centred counselling," in P. T. P. Wong & P. S. Fry (eds.) *The Human Quest for Meaning: A Handbook of Psychological Research and Clinical Applications*, Lawrence Erlbaum, Mahwah, NJ.

Zacarro, S. J. 2001, *The Nature of Executive Leadership: A Conceptual and Empirical Analysis of Success*, American Psychological Association, Washington, DC.

Zeus, P. & Skiffington, S. 2000, *The Complete Guide to Coaching At Work*, McGraw-Hill, Sydney.

Zeus, P. & Skiffington, S. 2002, *The Coaching at Work Toolkit: A Complete Guide to Techniques and Practices*, McGraw-Hill, Sydney.

Index